The BYTE Book of
COMPUTER MUSIC

EDITED BY
CHRISTOPHER P. MORGAN

"BOOKS OF INTEREST TO COMPUTER PEOPLE"

A DIVISION OF BYTE PUBLICATIONS, INC.

70 Main St., • Peterborough, N.H. 03458 • (603) 924-7217

The authors of the programs provided with this book have carefully reviewed them to ensure their performance in accordance with the specifications described in the book. The authors, however, make no warranties whatever concerning the programs, and assume no responsibility or liability of any kind for errors in the programs or for the consequences of any such errors. The programs are the sole property of the authors and have been registered with the United States Copyright Office.

Library of Congress Cataloging in Publication Data

The BYTE Book of Computer Music

    1. Computer composition.   2. Music—Data Processing.   I. Morgan, Christopher P.
MT41.B98   789.9   78-27681
ISBN 0-931718-11-2

Printed in the United States of America

TABLE OF CONTENTS

Introduction

Computer music means many things to many people, but to the personal computer experimenter it means creating music with the aid of a small computer system. The first experiments with computer music were conducted in the 1950's at Bell Labs and RCA. The expense of using the huge computers of the day meant that only a handful of people could benefit from the experiments, though.

The microcomputer revolution has changed all that. Armed with inexpensive personal computers, a new generation of music enthusiasts, would-be musicologists and fugue fanciers are sampling the delights of digital music synthesis.

The BYTE Book of Computer Music is designed to help you get the most out of your computer music experiments. The best articles from past issues of BYTE have been combined with new material, all geared to the computer experimenter.

Beginners to the field (as well as veterans) will enjoy Hal Chamberlin's "A Sampling of Techniques for Computer Performance of Music", which discusses the basics of polyphonic synthesis and gives you directions for playing four-part melodies on a KIM computer. Or perhaps you're interested in random composition—if so, read Rich Gold's new "Terrain Reader", a remarkable program that composes music based on land terrain maps.

Other articles range from flights of fancy about the reproductive systems of pianos to a practical $19 music interface circuit. For the more adventuresome reader we offer two new fast Fourier transform programs written in BASIC and 6800 machine language. The fast Fourier transform is a useful tool for analyzing the harmonic content of music.

Also included is Steve Robert's "Polyphony Made Easy"; a handy circuit allows you to enter more than one note at a time into your computer from a musical keyboard.

The list goes on, but we'll let the material speak for itself. We hope this information, collected in one place for the first time, will be a useful addition to your music and computer libraries.

Christopher Morgan
Editor

SCORTOS:
Implementation of a Music Language

Hal Taylor

Photo 1: The modified ADM-III video terminal. The keytops on the ASCII keyboard have been modified to enable the user to easily encode musical compositions. See figure 1.

Perhaps nowhere can technology better serve the creative end of the music arts than through the computer. The computer has a natural affinity for the application to music since it is capable of carrying out processes which create and perform music. It can be programmed to learn any language the composer wishes to use to describe his musical ideas. It can manipulate the symbols of that language to produce transformations of the composer's original ideas. It can enlarge and improve the quality of the composer's creative output by allowing him to work in an interactive mode where he can hear his musical works performed within minutes of their conception.

The computer owes this affinity to its unerring accuracy and high bandwidth, qualities which its human inventors do not possess. The human mind is slow and noisy and requires years of exercise to achieve the coordination necessary to perform complex musical passages. Although the computer may never be able to match the expressive subtleties of a concert soloist, it is in some cases more suitable for the performance of music than a human being.

If a program can be devised to convert musical symbols to the sounds they repre-

sent, then the computer can be of value to the composer as a means of developing composition prototypes, that is, preliminary designs of musical works that he could hear performed before he copied the parts and gave them to the orchestra. An editing capability would also be available to him to alter the music until it produced the desired results. When the computer performed the work to his satisfaction, the original score and the instrumental parts could be published on a computer controlled plotter. With such a system the composer could avoid the drudgery of hand copying parts, and would be encouraged to experiment with new forms that he might otherwise hesitate to give to an orchestra.

The computer can also be useful to the composer as an originator of musical ideas since it can simulate the process by which the human mind creates music. A music composition consists of a series of musical events chosen from a minimum of about 200 different possibilities (consider, just 12 tones and 18 types of notes). Only certain of these combinations are pleasing to the human ear. The composer's job is to discover those combinations which produce aesthetic results. The manner in which he or she does this is personal, intuitive, and cannot by itself form the basis for a workable algorithm. It is possible, however, to infer some of the underlying rules of music by analyzing it. Whether we are composing with our minds or with a computer, we follow a set of rules that determine which pitches will be chosen, in what order they will be arranged, and how long each will last in time.

The set of rules describes the style and structure of the music and can be represented in a computer by a statistical model. A process can be programmed into the computer that uses the model to decide which musical events are suitable for use in the composition. The process is one in which random choices are discarded according to a stochastic model. *[According to Webster's, stochastic processes are processes based on the behavior of random variables. Random variables, in turn, are functions which are the result of statistical experiments in which each outcome has a fixed probability. For example, the number of spots showing if two dice are thrown is a random variable . . .* CM]* In order to produce a musical event, the program generates a random number which it associates with a variable such as pitch or time. The number is then subjected to the constraints of the model. The model is constructed by feeding specimens to an analysis program which are representative of the desired compositional style. The specimens are analyzed according to pitch, time and chord structure, and a probability matrix of n dimensions is generated, where n is the degree of order desired and represents the extent to which the analysis was carried out. As n increases, progressively more order is imposed upon the process, since more information is available to describe the

desired composition and less is left up to chance.

Zeroth order stochastic control is no control at all. Random choices are used to build the composition without testing them against the model producing unlistenable music in most cases. In *first* order control, the transitions between pitches and rhythms are governed by the probability distribution of those transitions as they occurred in all the analyzed samples. Music produced in this manner still sounds amorphous, but will have fewer pitches that sound alien.

It is not until we impose higher order control that a melody as we know it will take shape with its symmetrical phrases and regular intervals. In *second* order control, the selection of an event depends upon the event that preceded it; in *third* order control the previous two notes, and so on. For example, if the previous note chosen was a B-flat and the random number generator has just produced a C, the program refers to that location in the probability matrix which gives the probability of a C following a B-flat. If there is no probability of this happening, the C is rejected. If the probability is 1.00 then a C always follows a B-flat in this style of music, and the program will reject random numbers that are not Cs.

Of course the source of the information within the model need not be music specimens, as in this example, but may originate from mathematical functions, poetry or any one of a hundred other sources. It is this capability which makes the computer so intriguing as a composer's tool.

The Score to Sound System

The Score to Sound System (SCORTOS) was developed to provide the composer with

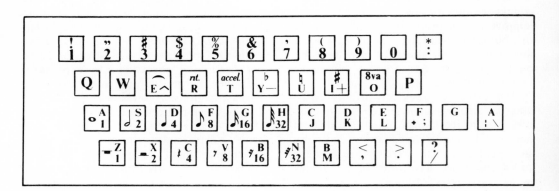

Figure 1: A standard alphanumeric keyboard modified for the SCORTOS language. SCORTOS is a language dedicated solely to the processing of musical information. The keyboard is a standard ASCII unit which has been relabeled with music symbols. The user enters a musical composition by striking the keys which correspond to the symbols in the music score of the composition (see also photo 1).

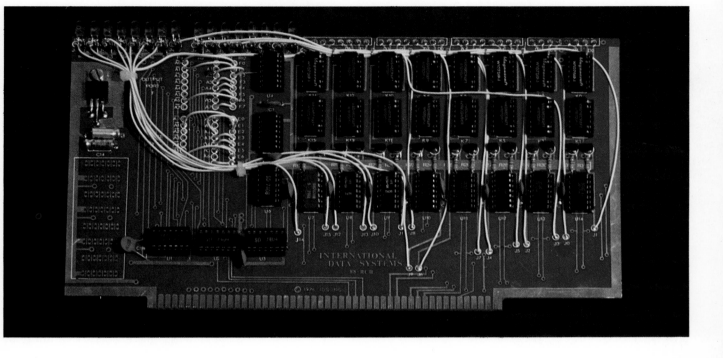

an inexpensive means of conducting computer implemented music research and composition prototype development. The system has the capability to perform conventional music scores by allowing music symbols to be entered through a terminal keyboard by an operator. Music of computer generated specifications can be performed through user program calls to a set of subroutines that interface the user program to the SCORTOS system software.

Music is produced by the computer driving relays that are wired in parallel to the keyboard switches of electronic music instruments — organs, synthesizers, etc. This allows a simple and inexpensive interface between the composer's studio instruments and the computer. The limitation of this approach is in its inability to provide the computer with access to the timbre controls of the synthesizer, an encumbrance which may be tolerable to experimenters primarily interested in the musical variables of tonality and syntax. Also, there is a rich assortment of preset timbres available in commercial keyboard instruments, among them, the Orchestron which generates actual orchestral and choral sounds from a prerecorded optical disk.

The system consists of an Altair 8800 computer with 32 K bytes of memory, an ADM-III video terminal, a mass storage device (either cassette or floppy disk), one or more International Data Systems 88-RCB relay control boards and any electronic keyboard instruments the user wishes to connect to the 88-RCBs.

The ADM-III has a standard ASCII keyboard whose keytops have been relabeled with music symbols (see figure 1 and photo 1). The composer enters the composition into the computer by striking the key corresponding to each musical symbol as it appears in the score. This creates a music text file. The source text is passed to a language processor which maps each musical event represented in the source text into a physical IO address plus a timing value, and writes this to a binary output file. The result is a list of records each of which defines which key of which instrument will be turned on and for how long. The binary output of the language processor is read by a driver program which uses the IO addresses and timing values in each record to determine what data is to be loaded into the data registers of the 88-RCBs, and at what time it is to be loaded. The keyboard instrument responds by playing the piece just as if someone were playing on its keyboard. In fact, the system can be thought of as an organist with 16 very flexible fingers, because it is capable of performing 16 separate parts simultaneously.

Keyboard Instrument to Computer Interface

The 88-RCB is the interface between the computer and the electronic keyboard instruments. It was designed expressly for the SCORTOS system project, but is also useful for other low current switching applications. The board has two 8 bit data registers which are "write only" accessible to the central processing unit (CPU) through

Photo 2: A close-up view of the component side of the 88-RCB 16 channel relay interface board which can drive a musical keyboard with signals from the computer.

3

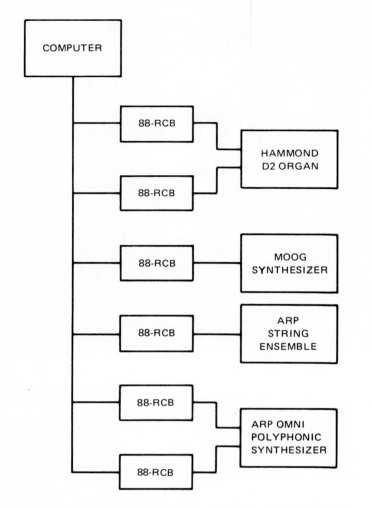

COMPUTER

88-RCB

88-RCB

HAMMOND D2 ORGAN

88-RCB

MOOG SYNTHESIZER

88-RCB

ARP STRING ENSEMBLE

88-RCB

88-RCB

ARP OMNI POLYPHONIC SYNTHESIZER

Figure 2: A medium scale SCORTOS configuration. The 88-RCB units are relay boards which can be driven by the computer to operate organs, synthesizers or other similar instruments. Each board consists of two 8 bit data registers which can be loaded from the central processing unit. Each of these bits in turn drives a transistor which energizes a relay. One 88-RCB board can control 16 keys, or 1 1/4 octaves of a musical keyboard. The system can address (and therefore control) up to 256 keys.

two output ports which are individually strappable to any address in the 8080 IO channel. The data register latches the contents of the CPU's A register when an OUT instruction has been executed to that register's output port address. The outputs of each bit of the data registers drive a transistor which in turn drives a board mounted DIP relay.

The complement outputs of the data register latches are used to drive light emitting diodes (LEDs) which can be mounted on the board or on a front panel to monitor the status of each relay. The relays are wired in parallel to the keyboard switches of the electronic music instruments which electrically isolate the peripherals from the computer and ensure plug-to-plug compatibility among most keyboard instruments.

Each 88-RCB controls 16 keys, or 1 1/4 octaves of keyboard. To ensure an adequate tonal range, two 88-RCBs may be configured on any instrument (see figure 2).

The maximum number of keys the system can address is 256. In arriving at a figure of maximum connectivity, it was necessary to balance programming considerations against what was thought to be an adequate number of system-controllable sound producing peripherals. 256 keys are equal to about 20 octaves of keyboard (three full piano keyboards) which may be distributed among ten sound-producing peripherals, giving each instrument a 2 octave range. This maximum configuration seems adequate to provide for the largest studio application.

A simple method of representing keyboard address was chosen to minimize the execution time of the DRIVER program. One byte is used to represent the keyboard address (pitch), and one byte contains the length of time the event will last (rhythm). Since a music piece consists of so many events, the size of the data record is critical. It affects the total performance of the system by limiting the length of any performance to the number of event records that will fit in available memory. For this reason, it is not practical to increase the size of the event data record to accommodate a connectivity greater than 256.

The Alphanumeric Representation of Music

The conventional music score format is not the most perfect method for entering music into computers. The music symbols must be somehow transformed into a code the computer understands. In the conventional method, the operator enters data from a music score into an alphanumeric keyboard. This method has two disadvantages: it often requires multiple alphanumeric symbols to define one musical event (one character for pitch, one character for rhythm, one character for dynamics). The second disadvantage is that the choice of alphanumeric symbols must relate in some way to the quality of the musical symbols they represent, which in the past has meant that the symbols were scattered about the keyboard with no regard to their qualitative value. As a result, the data entry process was a hunt and peck procedure which may have been too discouraging for all but the most enthusiastic.

The human to computer interface should provide maximum ease in data entry and data editing. There are four ways to accomplish this:

● Choose a set of alphanumeric symbols to represent the set of musical symbols that will enable music passages to be

Music Symbol	Description	SCORTOS Code	Music Symbol	Description	SCORTOS Code
o	whole note	X1	↓	quarter rest	4
♩	half note	X2	↗	eighth rest	8
♩	quarter note	X4	↗	sixteenth rest	16
♪	eighth note	X8	↗	thirty-second rest	32
♪	sixteenth note	X16	‖:	left hand repeat	[
♪	thirty-second note	X32	:‖	right hand repeat	]
▬	whole rest	1	≡	bar	/
▬	half rest	2	♫ (3)	triplets	3(XnXnXn)

Music Symbol	Description	SCORTOS Code
C	Pitch representations	C
D		D
E		E
F		F
G		G
A		A
B		B
♯	sharp	+
♮	natural	N
♭	flat	—
♩♩	slur	∧
	dot	.

Table 1: The alphanumeric music coding convention used by the SCORTOS system. The X symbol preceding each numeric SCORTOS code symbol indicates that the numeric symbol must be preceded by a pitch representation before it can be recognized as a note. For example, C2 would be a half note with pitch C.

best recognized in alphanumeric form.
- Eliminate all redundancies in the music score.
- Position the alphanumeric symbols on the keyboard logically in the order of their musical value and group them by type.
- Generate bar markings and bar numbers automatically during data entry.

Table 1 shows the alphanumeric symbols used to represent conventional music notation in the Score to Sound System. Note that each alphanumeric symbol alludes to the quality of the music symbol it represents. A musical event can be defined by one or two symbols, depending upon whether the event is a rest or a note. A numeric symbol which is not preceded by a letter character is recognized as a rest. Notes always occur as a pair of symbols, that is, a letter character followed by a numeric symbol. Figure 3 illustrates a portion of an actual orchestral score along with its corresponding SCORTOS code.

Since the characters generated by the SCORTOS keyboard hardware do not correspond to those desired to represent the music symbols, the data entry software echoes back the desired character with the terminal in full duplex mode.

System Software

The SCORTOS System Software consists of a group of programs written in 8080 assembler language which carry out the four major functions of the system:

- entry and manipulation of the symbolic music text.
- conversion of the text to binary data.
- conversion of events initiated by user programs to binary data.
- conversion of the binary data to music.

The interaction of these programs with each other is shown in figure 4.
The monitor allows the user to control the system's major functions. It recognizes

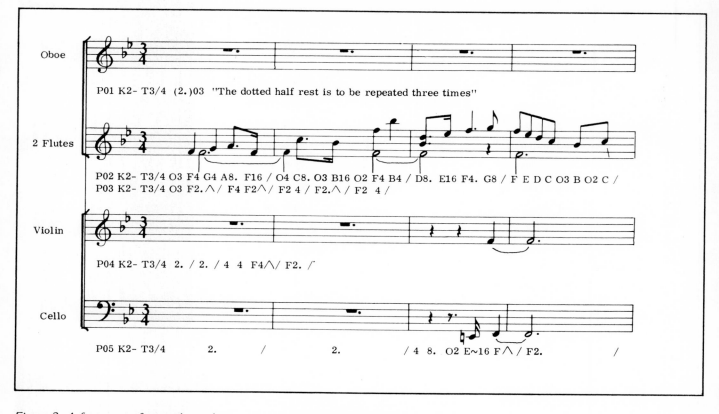

Figure 3: A fragment of an orchestral score annotated in SCORTOS code (see listing 1).

three command verbs with one or more arguments per verb. Each verb calls a system module, and its arguments specify the data file which is to be operated upon by that module. Table 3 is a list of command verbs recognized by the monitor.

The editor allows the user to enter music text through the terminal keyboard and provides a means by which it may be easily manipulated.

As text is entered through the keyboard, the editor's data entry processor keeps a running count of the bar number and automatically informs the user when he has come to the end of a bar by displaying a slash and the next bar number on the terminal. This provides a checksum for each bar and a milestone to keep the operator informed of his position in the score. Listing 1 shows a sample of the dialog between the operator and the editor as the operator enters the score fragment in figure 3. The italicized type is supplied by the editor, the bold type by the operator.

Conventional string oriented text editors are inconvenient for use with music text since music is prone to have too many occurrences of any given string. Allowing the user to access the text by part number and bar number is more suitable since he refers to a written score in the same way. Various commands are available within the editor

which allow a user to list selected bars and make insertions and deletions in the music text at selected bar boundaries.

The converter is the system's music language processor. It scans the text of the music text file and translates the logical entities of rhythm and pitch to the physical values of time and keyboard address. For each event described in the file the converter outputs a 2 byte record which contains the duration of that event in standard system timing units, and the location of the event on the system controlled music keyboards.

Table 2 is a list of control characters recognized by the converter. In keeping with the design goal of eliminating redundancies in the music score, an equate (=) statement was developed. Using equate, repeated groups of notes need only be typed in once and equated to a symbol. Thereafter they may be brought into the music source text by typing the symbol to which they have been equated.

The driver interface subroutines allow the user to communicate with the DRIVER by providing him access to the binary output file. Through their use, a sequence of musical events may be generated from within the computer by a user written program. For example, the researcher may have made an analysis of a particular composer's style (following the procedure de-

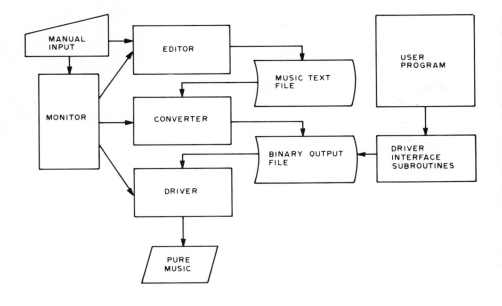

Figure 4: The flow of information through the SCORTOS software. The monitor controls the system's major functions. The editor allows the user to enter music through the computer's keyboard (see figure 1) and to modify it as desired. Listing 1 describes this in more detail. The converter scans the text of the music text file and converts the values for rhythm and pitch into physical values of time and keyboard address. The driver interface subroutines allow the computer to play music that it has composed based on stochastic or random elements contained in the user's programs.

scribed earlier in this article) and may wish to write a program in BASIC which creates a composition based upon the properties of that style. The sequence of events that constitute the composition would be produced by calls to the driver interface subroutines.

The EVENT subroutine is the principal interface subroutine. Its calling sequence is:

```
CALL EVENT
DS    ARG1
DS    ARG2
DS    ARG3
DS    ARG4
```

where:

ARG1 = part number.
ARG2 = duration of event.
ARG3 = address of keyboard switch.
ARG4 = slur code (0= no slur, 1= slur this event to next event).

The DRIVER is a software representation of the inner workings of a player piano where the binary output file, subroutine CLOCK, and the DRIVER's main code are the respective analogs of the piano roll, sprocket drive and mechanical read head. All of the control features of its mechanical counterpart are available within the program, including start performance, pause, and stop performance, and some which are unique to a software simulation, such as discrete tempo control and part selection.

The DRIVER causes music to be performed by initiating and terminating musical events according to the information contained in the binary output file. The program keeps a timer for each part that is participating in the performance. When an event is initiated, the address data in the event's data record is output to the appro-

priate 88-RCB data register. This causes sound to emanate from the instrument to which the 88-RCB is connected. The timer is set to zero, then incremented 20 times per second and compared at each incrementation to the event duration field of the event's data record. When these two quantities are equal, the event is terminated by a logical exclusive OR of that event's keyboard address data with the 88-RCB data register. The DRIVER then proceeds to the next event record and repeats the process.

Timing is provided internally by subroutine CLOCK which contains a timing loop and which also interprets control commands from the terminal. When a call is made to CLOCK, the caller will not receive control back until a specified interval of time has passed. In this way it can be used as a time source. The time interval provided by CLOCK is used as the basic unit of time in the system. An interval of 1/20 of a second is sufficient to provide the resolution necessary to perform the most complex musical passages.

The internal generation of timing is less expensive and permits the tempo of the performance to be easily varied on line. By

Table 2: Control characters used by the SCORTOS language processor.

Control Character	Meaning
Pnn	musical part number declaration, where nn=a number from 00 to 16
Knc	key signature declaration, where n is a number and c is a "+" or a "−"
Tn/n	time signature declaration; ie: "T4/4" means 4/4 time
Onn	positions the CDEFGAB scale on the terminal keyboard to octave nn of the external instrument's keyboard
( )nn	repeat text within parens nn times
< > = C	equate all text within brackets to symbol C
Q+n	transpose all subsequent text up n steps
Q−n	transpose all subsequent text down n steps
" "	all text within quotes is treated as commentary
CTRL A	marks the end of the MUSIC TEXT FILE

Command	Meaning	
*E ab	Call the EDITOR and load the source text file identified by the characters ab	*Table 3: A list of command verbs recognized by the system monitor. Each verb calls a system module, and its arguments specify the data file which is to be operated on by that module.*
*C ab,cd	Load the file identified by the two character code ab and use it as input to the CONVERTER. Write the output of the CONVERTER to file cd	
*P cd	Load the file identified by the characters cd. Call the DRIVER and perform the music described by the data in file cd	

```
EDITOR
COMMAND?              N
FILE CODE?           S5
ENTER PART NO.              P01
   0001          "SYMPHONY NO 5 (PROKOFIEV)*****OBOE" K2- T3/4 (2.)03
   0005          P02
   0001          " 1st FLUTE " K2-T3/4 O3 F4 G4 A8. F16 /
   0002          O4 C8. O3 B16 O4 F4 B4 /
   0003          D8. E16 F4. G8 /
   0004          F8 E8 D8 C8 O3 B8 O2 C8 /
   0005          P03
   0001          " 2ND FLUTE " K2- T3/4 . . . . . . etc.
```

Listing 1: A sample of the dialog between the operator and the system editor as the operator enters the score fragment in figure 3. The italicized type is supplied by the editor.

striking the keys labeled "rit" or "accel" on the terminal keyboard, the operator can retard or accelerate the tempo of the performance by 2.5% for each stroke of the key.

The use of processor cycles to generate timing puts a great strain on the DRIVER. It must complete its work so quickly that the listener is not aware of any delay between music parts that are supposed to be occurring simultaneously. Musicians can time a musical event to within 10 ms of its desired occurrence. This imposes on the DRIVER the specification that, for worst case conditions, it must initiate an event for all 16 parts within the same period of time. For this reason great care was taken in the design of the program to ensure that its execution time is held to the minimum.

Conclusion

The functional possibilities addressed by the SCORTOS system are, of course rudimentary. In its present state it provides a foundation on which additional application programs can be built, notably a music language which treats the performer of the music as a computer and not a human. Other possibilities include a set-complex processor to analyze music and statistically model its characteristics, and a plotter interface that will draw musical scores on a plotter. Some of these programs already exist and need only be converted from FORTRAN to BASIC.

I am presently developing a macro capability that allows the user to equate a rhythm sequence to a symbol, and then associate different pitches with each note in the rhythm sequence by means of an argument list in a macro declaration.

The implications of this macro capability go further than just providing a way to eliminate redundancy. The composer often deals in "primitives" which are at a higher level than those allowed by his conventional music language. That is, the composer often thinks in terms of whole musical phrases and note groupings rather than individual notes of which he is compelled to construct those phrases and groupings. In using this higher level language, the composer is able to construct his compositions of larger building blocks and may easily vary the tonal parameters within those building blocks to achieve various aesthetic effects.

The purpose of the SCORTOS system project is to foster computer implemented composition among individuals and institutions whose financial and talent resources have prevented them from undertaking such projects in the past. Over the years various projects of this nature have been conducted at the larger educational centers of the country. The adoption of these projects by individuals and poorer institutions has not been widespread due to the large hardware costs involved, or lack of programming experience within the music departments. I hope that more modestly endowed music institutions will respond to a turnkey installation costing less than $10,000, and that we may shortly see the computer joining the synthesizer and tape recorder as standard equipment in every electronic music studio.■

A Two Computer Music System

Jeffrey H Lederer
Tom Dwyer
Margot Critchfield

The music system described here started out a few years ago as a project in the Soloworks Lab. The idea was to put together a "manipulable" system that allowed students to work with the powerful mathematical idea of *synthesis*. We felt that mathematics and science students should be able to experience firsthand what could be done by superimposing components that worked together to synthesize some bigger concept.

Real, full-blown professional music seemed like an ideal metaphor for working with this "superimposition" principle. It's easy for a student to see that a musical performance is really a multitude of small, discrete events working in perfect synchronism. But it's even easier to sense that the resultant whole is greater than the sum of its parts. In fact, the "whole" can be a human experience of quite thrilling proportions.

The system that evolved has met this goal very well. Students of varied backgrounds are able (and motivated) to work patiently with complex scores, making the final performance a proof of the power of the principle of superimposition.

But a funny thing happened on the way to this goal. The total system began to look more and more like a "micro" computer science curriculum. The documentation that evolved began to contain much of the jargon that permeates computing, but this seemed to be easier to take when interpreted in terms of the friendlier worlds of music and art.

In writing this condensed description of the system, we therefore decided to leave the jargon in. Our purpose is to not only describe the music system but to suggest that interesting new approaches to teaching computer science might be developed along similar lines. There is equally good promise for teaching computer science subject matter in terms of visual art. Abstract games are another fruitful area. It's probably no coincidence that all these examples illustrate the kind of computing most people would call "fun." There's undoubtedly a deep educational lesson lurking here, but that's another subject.

Photo 1: The authors' overall system with graphics terminal on the left and the disk drive and two computers on top of the organ console. The wooden pipes at top right are the flute rank; the metal pipes are a viola rank. The stop tablets for selecting ranks and harmonics can be seen just above the top keyboard.

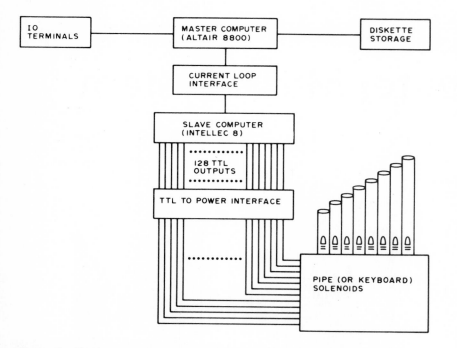

Figure 1: Hardware components of the authors' computerized organ music system. This design requires one TTL output line for each pipe to be controlled.

Why a Pipe Organ?

The system described here is general enough to apply to a variety of musical instruments. It was implemented with a small pipe organ because this illustrates the general kind of performance ensemble used by composers who write orchestral works. A pipe organ has several sets of pipes called *ranks*, each set having a distinctive tonal characteristic called timbre. The ranks are selected by pressing switches called *stop tablets*, so that an organist is able to control an entire "orchestra" of sounds by using different stop settings. Further, since most pipe organs have several keyboards (often including one for the feet), the ranks can be played independently. Thus both chorded (several notes played simultaneously) and contrapuntal (independent melody lines played simultaneously) music can be played on one or more keyboards.

The organ is also the original "synthetic music" instrument. This is because a performer can add harmonics to fundamental tones by pressing suitable stop tablets. When the stop tablet marked "8 foot flute" is pressed, one gets flutelike sounds, in the normal register (where A=440 Hz). (The phrase "8 foot" comes from the fact that the largest pipe in the rank is eight feet high.) But when the stop marked "4 foot flute" is pressed, everything sounds an octave higher. If *both* stops are activated, we then have a sound rich in second harmonics. Tradi-

tional organs have stops labeled "8 foot," "4 foot," "2 2/3 foot," "2 foot," etc. However, the stop settings in the computer system described here are software generated, so any harmonic can be specified (of course there are only a finite number of pipes available for playing these harmonics).

Overview of the System

The Music System uses two microcomputers (an Altair 8800b system and an Intellec 8/MOD 80), a small pipe organ, and a Magnavox plasma display graphics terminal. Figure 1 shows how these components are interconnected.

In addition to the hardware, there are three software packages. The first is a graphics music editor that allows a composer to "draw" his score on a graphics display terminal. The editor converts the graphic representation of the score into a MUSIC language program. The program may also be created and edited using a standard text editor, in which case an alphanumeric terminal can be used. Either type of editor is run on the master system. The MUSIC language programs can be saved on a diskette as files.

Before a MUSIC language program can be played, it must be "compiled." Our compiler is a program that accepts MUSIC language programs as input, and outputs an annotated listing of the MUSIC language program along with error messages and an "object" program. The object program consists of instructions which are easily interpreted by the slave computer. The compiler runs on the master computer.

The object program is "played" using both computers. First, the object program is transferred from the master to the slave computer. The slave computer executes the object program in order to drive the pipe organ. A pair of programs (one on each computer) controls the transfer of the object program and its execution. Figure 2 shows the relationship between software components.

System Hardware

The slave microcomputer is an Intellec 8/MOD 80 with 8 K bytes of programmable memory, 2 K bytes of read only memory containing a system monitor program, 256 bytes of programmable read only memory that contains the second performance program, 16 latching output ports, and a serial bidirectional IO port. Each latching port is eight bits wide, with each bit dedicated to controlling a pipe valve of the organ. Thus, 16 × 8 = 128 pipes can be controlled. The interface between

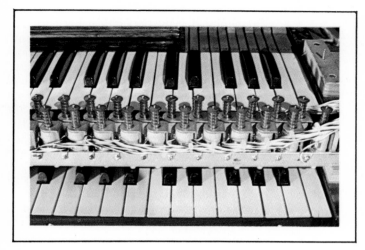

Photo 2: A set of solenoids used to automatically play the keys. Since this setup plays the keys directly, it could be easily adapted to any standard keyboard instrument including harpsichord and piano.

each pipe and its controlling port is a Darlington switching transistor connected as shown in figure 3.

The master computer is an Altair 8800b with 60 K bytes of memory, two diskette drives and two serial ports. One serial port is used as the console line and is connected to a Magnavox plasma graphics terminal. This terminal has a plasma display with 512 by 512 dots. A character generator is used to display 32 lines of 64 characters; the characters can be either a set of standard ASCII characters or a user loaded set (musical symbols in our case). The terminal has a vector generator and dot addressability. Sections of the screen can be selectively erased and written. The graphics terminal is optional, and there is no reason why other lower cost graphics displays couldn't be used if appropriate changes in software were made. The Intecolor 8001 might be particularly appropriate since different colors could be used to distinguish voices in polyphonic music.

The second serial line connects the Altair to the Intellec over a 2400 bps current loop. A special interface had to be built to isolate the two active current loops. The schematic is shown in figure 4.

MUSIC Language

MUSIC is a high level music notation language that uses the standard 64 character ASCII character set. A MUSIC language program consists of one or more statements; each statement is a single line in length (see figure 5 and listing 1).

There are three types of statements in this language: command, data, and comment statements. Comment statements, which begin with two asterisks, may be placed anywhere in the program; they are ignored by the compiler.

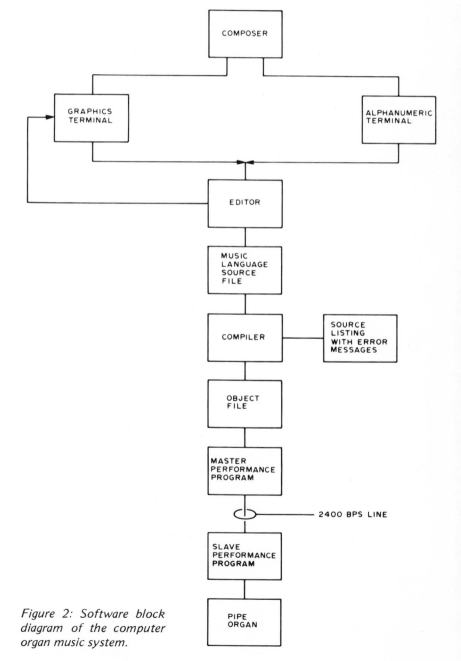

Figure 2: Software block diagram of the computer organ music system.

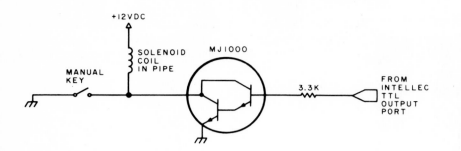

Figure 3: Interface between an organ pipe solenoid and a computer output bit. One such circuit is needed for each pipe to be controlled in this design. The solenoid in each pipe opens a valve that admits air to the pipe.

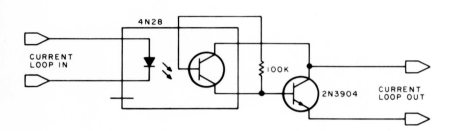

Figure 4: Interface used to isolate the two 2400 bps active current loops which send information back and forth between the master and slave computers.

The command statements consist of a single asterisk followed by the command mnemonic and the command's parameters. The commands in this language are divided into three categories: delimiter commands, repeat commands, and context commands.

The delimiter commands separate measures (BAR), parts of measures (CHANGE), and mark the end of the last measure of the program (END). The parameters of the first two commands, when used, set a temporary time signature for a measure.

The repeat commands control the repetition of sections of the score. The limits of a repeated section are bracketed by HEAD and TAIL commands. When necessary, each separate ending of a repeated section starts with an ENDING command, and sections of a score between SIGN commands can be skipped the second time through a repeated section. Repeated sections can be nested within each other.

The context commands are used to change the condition under which the notes of the program are compiled. These commands set the key signature (KEY), time signature (TIME) and metronome setting with or without accelerandos and ritards (TEMPO). A special context command (STOPS) controls the number of voices allowed in each measure and the stop (timbre) settings for each voice.

The notes for a MUSIC language program are placed in the data statements. Each data statement consists of one or more events; each event is separated from the previous event by a semicolon. An event is a note, chord, glissando, tremolo or rest. The notes can be played with different articulations (staccato, legato, or normal). [See the glossary at the end of this article.] Each data statement contains the events to be performed by one voice during a single measure or fraction of a measure.

A normal measure of music consists of a starting BAR command followed by zero or more context commands and one data statement for each active voice. When a context change occurs inside a measure, the form of that measure is slightly different. In this case the measure starts with a BAR command, zero or more context commands and one data statement for each voice. These data statements contain those events that occur before the context change. Following the data statements is a CHANGE command, one or more context commands and one data statement for each voice. These latter data statements contain the events that occur after the context change. Repeat commands may be intermixed with the context commands of a measure.

The voices in each measure are performed concurrently. Each voice is assigned a group of stop settings. Each stop setting takes a note, displaces it a set amount of tones, and assigns that new pitch to a given rank of pipes. Multiple stop settings for a voice will generate multiple pitches for each note in an event. These pitches are played simultaneously. The number of voices and their stop settings are controlled by the STOPS command.

This all sounds pretty complicated, but new users quickly get proficient with the language. Having all the features of musical notation available has proven to be well worth the extra complexity.

The Music Editor

An editor is a program that allows a user to easily create and modify files (which of course may be programs). The Music Editor is a program that allows composers to graphically create and modify MUSIC language programs. The Music Editor is written in Altair Extended BASIC 4.0 and runs on the Altair 8800b system using a Magnavox plasma display terminal.

At the simplest level, the editor allows the user to type in and alter statements like any text editor. It also permits the user to copy or move blocks of statements. The editor verifies the syntax of each statement entered.

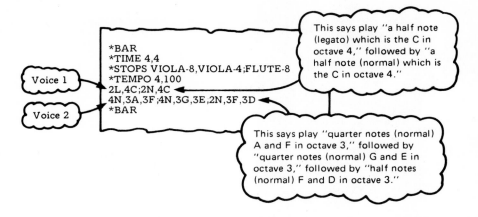

Listing 1: The musical example of figure 5 written in the MUSIC language. "Normal" means that there is to be a slight pause between notes. "Legato" indicates a smooth transition with no gaps.

At a higher level, the editor can be used to graphically display and edit data statements. When entering this level, the editor draws the staves. If an existing data statement is to be altered, the notes of this data statement are drawn; otherwise the staves will be empty, awaiting the input of a new data statement. The user edits a data statement by moving a cursor about the staves and entering commands. Special macro-like commands permit the user to create and copy chords, delete events and insert new ones. Upon leaving this higher level, a data statement in MUSIC is derived from the graphic display of the staves and inserted into a scratch file. Photo 3 shows what a graphics editing session looks like to the user.

Object Language

The MUSIC language is compiled into code for a "make-believe" machine, one with a simple set of instructions. Thus we can say that the object language is in pseudo-machine code. Each object language instruction is two 8 bit bytes in length. The first byte in each instruction is interpreted as an operation code (op code); the second byte is used as a data parameter. There are three classes of object language instructions: set port, wait, and repeat.

Op codes with values of 0 to 253 are interpreted as set port instructions. For example, 27-3 means turn on the right-most two bits in port 27 (since 3=00000011 in binary). These instructions cause the data byte to be deposited in the port number given by the op code itself (each latching port has a unique address). The bit pattern of the data byte specifies which pipe valves attached to that port are to be opened and which ones are to be closed. The pipe

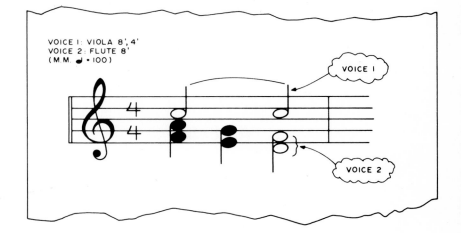

Figure 5: An example of how musical notation is represented in the MUSIC language.

valves will remain in that state until they are reset by another set port instruction.

Repeat instructions (op code value of 254) are trapped by the master system. The master processor handles repeats by retransmitting parts of the object program to the slave processor as specified by the data byte of the repeat instruction.

The wait instruction has an op code value of 255. The second byte of the instruction is interpreted as a nonnegative integer. This byte's value fixes a delay period computed in 10 ms units. For example, 255-60 means wait 600 ms.

An object program consists of a series of "frames." Each frame contains zero or

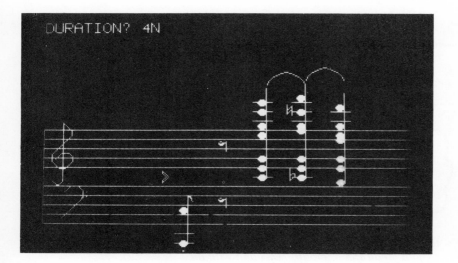

DURATION? 4N

Photo 3: The authors' Magnavox plasma display terminal during an editing session. Notes and chords can be created or modified by moving a cursor to the desired position. Entire musical phrases can be copied if desired. Chords or whole measures that repeat need be entered only once.

Listing 2a: An example of how the program in listing 1 is compiled in MUSIC. The first step is error checking, followed by the production of intermediate code for each voice.

Voice 1

48	The note 4C is 48 half tones up from C$_0$
−3000	A legato half note gets a timing of 3000 units
48	This is the second C
−2400	Timing for a normal half note
−600	Pause after a normal half note

Voice 2

45	This is 3A
41	This is 3F
−1200	Timing for a normal quarter note
−300	Pause
43	This is 3G
40	This is 3E
−1200	Timing for a normal quarter note
−300	Pause
41	This is 3F
38	This is 3D
−2400	Timing for a normal half note
−600	Pause

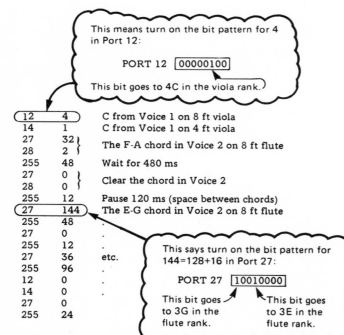

Listing 2b: Here the compiler combines the voices in listing 2a to produce the final object code.

more set port instructions and is terminated by a wait instruction. A frame is executed by the slave computer by first executing all set port instructions in a frame almost simultaneously. The set port instructions cause some pipes to be turned on and others to be turned off. If a particular port is not addressed by any set port instruction during a frame, this port's pipes remain in their current state. This new pipe state lasts for the duration given by the frame's wait instruction. At the end of this duration, the next frame's execution begins. Thus each frame causes a combination of pipes to be played for a set length of time. An example of an object program is given in listings 2a and 2b.

The execution of the object program is controlled by two performance programs that couple the master and the slave computers together. There are two reasons why we decided to use a pair of computers to handle the performance of the music: one, the correct latching output ports were already available on the Intellec, and, two, the slave could handle all the real time demands while the master handled the retrieval and loading of "pages" of the score from the diskette. (A page is defined as 256 bytes of object code.)

The slave microcomputer's memory acts as a circular buffer. The master initiates an object program execution by sending a header message to the slave. The master then waits for a Block Request (BR) message. At the receipt of each BR message, another page (256 bytes) of the object program is sent to the slave.

After receiving the header message, the slave sends enough BR messages to fill its memory with object code. After receiving enough pages or an end of program instruction, the slave starts executing the object program. After finishing one page of object code, the slave sends out a BR message. The next page sent is placed in the space released by the previous page that was executed. The execution of the object program and the refilling of the buffer proceed concurrently.

After sending the entire object program, the master processor ignores all further Block Request messages. When the slave executes the end of program instruction (which is a WAIT instruction with duration zero), it sends a completion message back to the master processor. The master processor can then inform the user that the slave is ready to accept another program.

This performance system software consists of two programs. The "slave" program is written in Intel 8080 assembly language. Its machine code representation is stored on read only memory in the slave microcomputer. The "master" performance program is written in Extended BASIC 4.0 for the Altair 8800b computer.

The Compiler

The compiler accepts a MUSIC language program and outputs an annotated listing file. If no errors are detected, an object program is then generated and saved on a diskette as a file. Thus the compiler's work can be divided into two phases: error checking and code generation.

The error checking consists of two types of operations: syntax verifying and context checking. A syntax verifier examines each statement to insure that it conforms to the rules of the language. For context commands it checks for correct number and types of arguments and correct placement of this statement in the measure. The repeat command's arguments and placement are checked and the nesting of these statements is verified. Data statement arguments are checked for syntax correctness.

In addition to syntax, the context correctness of data statements is checked. The number of data statements in a measure must equal the number of voices currently active as declared by the last STOPS command encountered in the program. The duration of each data statement must equal the measure duration as declared in the currently active time signature. This checking is a real help to the composer since it handles all the petty details.

The code generation phase of the compiler is divided into four operations: generating repeat instructions, handling context commands, processing data statements, and coordinating measures.

Each repeat command causes one object code repeat instruction to be generated. Repeat instructions cause all the data

between HEAD and TAIL commands to be used twice.

The context commands serve a function similar to declaration statements in conventional computer languages. Their main function is to alter the values of the global arrays and variables that determine the note address and note timing calculations. A note address is a number that relates a note to a pipe, while a timing determines how many milliseconds the associated notes are to be held.

The data statement handler processes the data statements to determine the notes to be played for a particular measure. Each voice has its own First-In-First-Out (FIFO) queue for storing information about the events of the current measure. As each event in a voice's data statement is processed, its FIFO queue is filled from the top down. First the notes of the event, then the duration of the event, and finally the duration of the pause between this event and the next one are placed on the queue. At this stage, note values are stored as integer numbers representing a number of semitones above a base pitch, without regard to stop settings. The durations are computed in basic time units regardless of the current tempo setting. The durations are stored as negative numbers in order to distinguish them from note values. Figure 6 shows the general format of a queue for one voice. It represents a sequence of four chords with a rest between the last two.

In this example there is no pause duration between events 2 and 3, indicating that event 2 is played legato with event 3. Event 4 has no note values, therefore it is a rest. Glissandos and tremolos are treated like event macros. They are translated into a series of events by the data statement parser before they are processed onto the queue.

After each voice in a measure has been parsed, the voice coordination routine generates the object code using the following algorithm:

1. The duration counter for each active voice is set to 0.
2. The duration counter for each voice is examined. Those voices with a zeroed duration counter have their top sequence removed from their queue for processing. (A sequence is all the information from the top of the queue down to and including the first duration of pause found.) The sequence's duration is stored in the voice's duration counter.
3. The voice's bit map is cleared. (The bit map is an array of bits where one bit is used to represent the state of one organ pipe.) As each note value of a voice's sequence is processed, it is expanded into as many note addresses as the number of stop settings

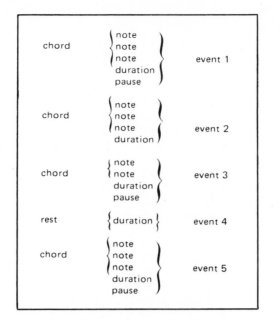

Figure 6: The general format of a queue for one voice used in the MUSIC language.

defined for that voice. Each note address generated causes a particular bit in the voice's bit map to be set to 1.

4. All the voice bit maps are ORed into a master bit map.

5. The master bit map is compared to the previous master bit map.

6. Those output ports whose bit pattern has changed generate set port instructions with the port's new bit pattern as the data byte of that instruction.

7. To generate the wait instruction, the duration counter for each voice is examined and the minimum duration is found. This minimum duration is subtracted from each voice's duration counter.

8. The minimum duration is multiplied by the tempo variable to yield the actual timing of the object code frame produced. If a frame is within an accelerando or ritard passage, the timing is altered to reflect the gradual change in tempo, the tempo variable is updated, and the duration remaining in the tempo changing passage is decremented. The final actual timing is used to produce a WAIT object code instruction.

9. The current master bit map is labeled as the previous master bit map.

10. The routine now goes back to step 2 if all the queues are not empty; otherwise the next measure in the MUSIC language program is processed.

The queues should empty simultaneously since each voice's data statement should have a duration equal to the one set by the time signature. (This is checked during

phase 1 of the compiler.)

The above algorithm was designed to compile multivoice music efficiently. An important feature of this algorithm is that it allows more than one voice to share the same rank of pipes. In addition, it permits the user to generate from each note specified many pitches through the stop setting mechanism. Since the stop settings are performed through software, a user can transpose each note of a voice any number of tones and into any rank of pipes. Listings 2a and 2b show how the above algorithm works for the simple two voice example given in figure 5.

Future Plans

While the system described here is not meant to compete with large dedicated music research systems, it nevertheless has several advantages over a number of other computer controlled music systems. Currently, we have two ranks of pipes with 64 pipes in each rank. However, additional ranks of pipes could easily be added to the system. Each 64 pipe rank requires only eight more latching output ports. The theoretical limit for an Intel 8080 based system is over 2000 pipes. Mircocomputers that use memory mapped IO could conceivably control hundreds of thousands of pipes.

The system can be extended to other musical instruments. By using solenoids, any keyboard instrument can be controlled through the output ports. Alternatively, the solenoids might be placed inside the instrument, driving something like the jacks in a harpsichord directly. To play the harpsichord along with the organ would just require the addition of a harpsichord stop to the MUSIC language.

Electronic synthesizer music is not incorporated in our system because of the high cost of the special hardware needed, but at least three low cost analog output boards designed for Altair (S-100) bus microcomputers have recently been announced. It seems reasonable to expect that the MUSIC language could be applied to these new pieces of hardware.

The voice concept has some application to "synthetic" music composition because it allows the user to create new timbres by specifying nonstandard overtone ranks (eg: a 3.1416 foot flute). By assigning dummy stop settings to certain voices, the composer can also isolate the effect of these harmonics during a test performance.

We are planning to eliminate the need to compile and save object programs. An assembly language version of the compiler is being written that will interpret MUSIC language programs in real time. This will be done by sending the bit pattern computed in step 6 of the measure coordinating routine to the designated output port and use the time value generated in step 8 to set an interval timer. This new software system will allow a user to interact with a performance. We also hope to build a subsystem to capture keyboard performance and translate it into a MUSIC language program.

Aside from musical application, the programs written for this system can be used as a realistic basis for explaining many important concepts of computer science in a context that removes much of the mystery surrounding computing. In many ways, this could be the most useful contribution of the music system, suggesting as it does that the teaching of complex ideas has much to gain from a liaison with the creative arts. ■

A Glossary of Some Musical Terms

Accelerando: A direction telling the musician to make the music gradually faster (increase tempo).

Bar: Vertical line on the musical staff separating the measures of music. Sometimes used as a synonym for a measure.

Glissando: A rapid sliding up or down the musical scale.

Key Signature: The sharps or flats placed after a musical clef to indicate the key.

Legato: A direction telling the musician to play in a smooth and connected manner.

Ritard: A direction telling the musician to make the music gradually slower (decrease tempo).

Semitone: The interval between two tones in the chromatic (well tempered) scale (ie: the distance between A♭ and A is a semitone).

Staccato: In a broken or clipped manner.

Tremolo: Effect produced by the rapid repetition of a note.

Jef Raskin

The

Microcomputer

and the

Pipe Organ

Photo 1: Pipe organ console shown in the home of the author's colleague, Jim Brennan, who did the custom installation work. The console was obtained from a church in Pasadena CA.

One night I got a call from a man who had been wandering through the personal computer stores in the area. He was looking for a computer to operate his huge pipe organ. Inevitably, he was given my phone number, since I had been going around to the same stores telling everyone that I was working on a controller for my pipe organ.

There are several gimmicky reasons for wanting to attach a computer to an organ. My reason is that the combination can provide the performer with a more flexible, easier to play instrument. And then there are all those gimmicks. As it turns out, using a microcomputer can be less expensive than conventional console wiring. Before we get into the subject too deeply, the "organization" of the king of instruments should be made clear.

The performer sits at the *console*. The performer's hands rest on one or more keyboards called *manuals*. There are usually from two to four manuals. The feet play on a set of keys placed beneath the bench called the *pedals*. On most organs since the late 1800s, the console is separate from the rest of the instrument and is connected to it by means of electrical cables. As with the computer, the console is the "command center" of the instrument. In addition to the keyboards there are a number of other controls on the console that will be discussed later.

Blockflotes and Zimbels

The sounding portion of the organ consists of many pipes. Each pipe sounds one note. There are typically many different pipes for a given note, each of which has a different sound quality or *timbre*. A set of pipes, all of similar timbre, one for each key on a manual, is called a *rank*. Each rank has a name, many of which are hallowed by centuries of use. Some, like *diapason* (dia pay zen) or *bourdon* describe sounds that are characteristic of organs and nothing else. Others, such as *trompette* or *blockflote* are reminiscent of trumpets and wooden flutes, respectively. Obviously one rank is a minimum for an organ. (Renaissance *portative* organs had one rank.) A small organ usually has three or four ranks, controlled from two manuals. The one being installed in my house has 26 ranks. A large organ will have 70 or more. The organ owned by my friend mentioned above has 140 ranks. That is very large, and only a few cathedrals have more.

Each rank has 61 pipes, as there are 61 notes on a manual. Thus for a pipe organ of a 100 ranks there are 6,100 pipes. Each rank is turned off or on by a knob or switch labelled with the rank's name. These knobs are called *stops*. (The terms stop and rank are sometimes used interchangeably, but in this discussion rank will refer to a set of pipes, and stop to the controlling knob.)

A large organ often has four manuals (named great, swell, choir and echo or positiv) each having 61 keys, a 32 note pedalboard, 100 or so stop knobs, and a few dozen assorted controls. Thus there are about 500 controls that the organist must manipulate: a complicated instrument, indeed.

Photo 2: A view of three ranks of organ pipes in the living room, including a Rauschepfeife, left, Holtzregal, center, and Zimbel bass on the right. Each rank has its own particular tonal color.

Key Decisions

And now we come to the microcomputer. It must keep constant watch on 500 switches and control some 6,000 relays, one for each pipe. It must never miss a switch closure or release, and must operate the correct pipes (sometimes dozens simultaneously) within 1/20 of a second. Is this within the capabilities of an 8080? As it happens, it is. But not without a bit of tricky IO design and some swift algorithms.

For completeness, it should be mentioned that some ranks are not exactly 61 notes. "Unified" ranks often have 75 pipes, and some special ranks have fewer than 61. But fortunately these exceptions are easily handled. The problem is simplified in some organs (a little) by sets of ranks grouped into "straight" *chests*. Instead of each pipe having its own electrically operated valve (a "unit" chest), each rank in the chest has a valve. Then all notes of the same name (such as all Cs or all F#s) have one valve. This loses some generality, but requires fewer valves and electrical connections. For M ranks of N notes each, a "straight" chest requires M+N valves. A "unit" chest has MxN valves.

Organs also traditionally have *couplers*, which operate either within a keyboard or between keyboards. An intermanual coupler has the effect of operating a note on one manual when you press the corresponding note on another. (On some old organs both keys actually move when you press one of them. This may have given rise to "phantom of the opera" stories.) A coupler that works

within a keyboard plays a note typically one octave higher or lower than the key you are playing, but on the same keyboard. Intervals other than an octave are also available on some organs.

An organ is also separated into *divisions*. These have the same names as the manuals: typically, great, swell, choir, echo and positiv. The pipes played by the pedals form another division: the pedal division. Each rank belongs to exactly one division. In the traditional organ, a manual can play pipes only in its division. You can couple manuals together, but it is impossible to play a rank in the swell division from the great manual without playing *all* stops that are pulled in the swell division from the great manual. This separation into divisions has no musical benefits, but is done merely to simplify the construction of the switching in the console. By means of a microcomputer, divisions can be eliminated. The organist can then independently assign any rank to any keyboard. This is the first of a number of nongimmick improvements that can be appreciated by any organist.

The switching in the traditional organ is done by the most incredible collection of electrical, mechanical and pneumatic switches imaginable. That it works at all, being made mostly of slats of wood and strips of leather with silver wires for contacts, seems miraculous. It is not surprising, then, that freedom in interconnection has been restricted in the past.

The wiring from the console to the pipes over distances from ten to over 100 feet reminds one of a cross between the innards of a computer before the mother board was invented and a telephone company switching office. A major advantage of the computerized organ is the elimination of most of this wiring. In a very large organ, the cost of the computer system may be *less* than the cost of the cabling alone.

When an organist plays a piece, it has a characteristic sound quality produced by a judiciously selected set of stops being activated. A particular collection of stops is called a *registration*. It is usually desirable to be able to store such combinations. There are a number of buttons called *pistons* which recall combinations of stops. Logically enough these collections of stops are called *combinations* or *presets*. There are often a few fixed presets, and a number of pistons are provided whose registration the organist can change at will. Another advantage of the computer controlled organ is that many more presets are available. 4 K bytes of memory can store hundreds of different presets, more than on any conventional organ. This amount of memory costs less than one preset done mechanically! And it's a lot easier to install.

Consider what happens when a single key is pressed. First, any keys that are coupled to it are also activated on its keyboard as well as on other keyboards. For each of those resultant keys, as well as the original key, the applicable stops must be looked up. If there are two couplers and four stops activated for each of the three keyboards involved, no less than 12 pipes must sound. When playing a full chord with many couplers and stops engaged, it is not uncommon for 500 pipes to be operated simultaneously.

Getting Organized

A number of schemes were concocted for driving the pipes and reading the keys. One scheme, which has been used on smaller organs for computer control, was to have each key send out a unique code. Each pipe recognizes its own address. The computer would receive key codes as well as stop and coupler codes, and compute the appropriate pipe addresses. A decoder at each pipe, as well as a diode matrix or other encoder for the console, would be required. Since on a large organ there are over 2^{12} pipes, even a 12 bit code would not be long enough. This would mean assembling two 8 bit words for each pipe. Putting out over 500 of these in 1/30 of a second (considering the number of steps required in the program) would have been impossible. Further, the cost for decoders at each pipe is prohibitive. This ruled out going to a 16 bit computer, since it wouldn't help the decoder

problem, and a larger word size seemed to hold few advantages in any other way.

Cost alone ruled out the brute force approach of using a very fast computer. Another way to get high data rates from a microcomputer would be to use direct memory access (DMA) circuitry. With this scheme one DMA device scans the keyboard continuously and enters key depression and release information into memory. The main processor (at its own rate) scans the keyboard image in memory and constructs a list of pipes to be played or quieted. Another DMA scans the list of pipes and controls the pipes accordingly. In essence, three computers would share the same memory and would run asynchronously, each going as fast as conditions allowed. This seemed feasible, and is necessary for larger organs. But for smaller organs the DMA is not needed, as will be seen.

Part of the solution lay in hardware. At one extreme of decoding (as explained above), each pipe has its own decoder. It would be more efficient for each group of, say, eight pipes to have a decoder which detects its code and then accepts the next byte as controlling eight pipes in *parallel*. The 8 bit control byte 10001001 would mean that the notes C, E and G are to be played, while leaving C#, D, D#, F and F# silent. This would reduce the number of decoders by a factor of 8, and then operates eight pipes at a time. This was fast enough in the IO department, but the time required to assemble the control bytes by masking or rotation was too great. A microcomputer handles bytes with great efficiency, but manipulating individual bits takes significantly more time. A number of algorithms were considered, but it was apparent that they were not suitable.

At the other extreme from a decoder for each pipe is the idea of having no decoders whatever. This idea was put forward early in the design effort, but was discarded as ridiculous. In the end it became clear that the idea was not only feasible, but fast and cheap to implement in hardware. It also made the software much easier to design. It works like this: A very long serial-in/parallel-out shift register is made. It will have at least one output for each pipe. Using available 8 bit shift registers, the 140 rank organ's 2000 electrically operated valves require about 250 shift registers. (The 7000 pipes require only 2000 controlling lines since most of them are on straight chests.) In effect we build a 2000+ bit shift register, a long "tube" through which 1s and 0s flow in single file. When all the 1s and 0s (standing for pipes sounding or silent) reach their correct positions, a command (strobe) is sent operating *all the pipes at once*. If the process is to take 1/60 of a second, the shift register has to move 2000 bits in that time. But this is a rate of 120,000 bits per second (120 kHz) which is within the capabilities of the shift register and the computer but a bit beyond an unaided 8080. Remember that these calculations are for a mammoth size organ. Most organs are significantly smaller and the problems are correspondingly easier.

A similar approach is used for the keyboards. There exists a 33 input parallel to serial converter made for electronic organs. Just two of these integrated circuits would suffice to encode an entire manual. The 500 controls could be transmitted serially to the computer in 1/200 of a second at 100 kHz. The interface would require fewer than 20 "critters." Again, this is for a huge organ.

Photo 3: Another view of the organ showing the swell chest and echo chest.

My own home organ would require only ten integrated circuit chips for its console.

The hardware for a large organ can now be summarized. A 500 bit parallel to serial converter for input, a 2000 bit serial to parallel converter for output, one input port and one output port are required. Each pipe also needs a power transistor to handle the 0.5 A at 14 V required by the valves (this is a typical figure). Some of the larger pipes might require two stages or a Darlington power transistor, but there is no real difficulty in the design. Another side benefit accrues at this point: Many pipe organs use electro-pneumatic valves for each large pipe. This is because an all electric valve opens too suddenly. To solve the problem, the traditional builders designed the electrical valve to let air into a small bellows which, in turn, operates the valve that lets air into the pipe. A pair of resistor-capacitor (RC) networks and a diode in the base circuit of the power amplifier for each pipe can give the desired slow attack and release usually obtained by the much more expensive and problematical pneumatic system. This can amount to savings of over $1000 in a large organ. It should be mentioned that some organ manufacturers have been successful in making satisfactory all electric valves with appropriate attack and decay curves. They would not require the RC networks.

Software design was as gradual as the hardware design. There were two breakthroughs necessary before it was clear that the 8080 could work quickly enough. (When this design was being done, by the way, the Z-80 and other faster processors were not yet in production.) But the constraints of the 8080 and the very large organ forced a much tighter and more clever design than would have been developed if we had had more powerful computers and a smaller organ. Given the newer computers, of course, larger and more complex pieces of equipment can be controlled. Many industrial plants have fewer than 200 sensors and 2000 elements that need to be operated in real time. A microcomputer using the techniques outlined here could handle them.

The program begins by sweeping in the console settings. To save time only *one bit per word* is used. This wastes 7/8ths of 500 words, but memory is cheap. The same trick can be used in output, eliminating the necessity to pack bits into bytes. Thus over one byte per key and one byte per pipe will be sacrificed to gain speed. That amounts to $40 at most in memory costs. It buys us speed and simplicity, and it is worth it. While it now seems obvious that this is a useful way to proceed, it somehow took four months to find the solution. This is probably because we are so reluctant to

Photo 4: The main organ chamber with portions of an organ taken from a Sacramento church.

waste memory. A pipe organ costs from $20,000 to whatever you care to spend (a million dollars is not unusual). The computer costs are lost in the small change.

For a small organ, the DMA is not even needed, and the input and output loops are very simple:

1. Point to a memory location.
2. Do an input (or output).
3. Move the contents of the accumulator to that location.
4. Increment the location.
5. Check for done. If not done, do an input (or output), etc.

The loop can be done on an 8080A at 66 kHz. Thus, an entire 20 rank organ can be updated in less than 0.02 second. The DMA would do the same algorithm, but at 1 MHz, and would overlap processing. The 8080 with a 2 MHz clock is just fast enough. An 8085 or Z-80 processor would be more than fast enough. Again, remember that for a typical home or small church organ, the plain old 8080 would have the necessary speed and that we are discussing a worst case design.

Even with IO solved, there still remains the problem of deciding which pipes are to go on and which to go off. At first this was a stumbling block in terms of the time it would take to do the computations. On each console scan, it seemed, a table of couplers would have to be made up, as well as a table of stops. A key depression, through the

couplers, results in a number of "virtual" key depressions. Since some virtual keys, being higher or lower on the keyboard than the original key, will go off the end of a keyboard, they must be deleted from the virtual key list. The remaining keys then have to be processed through the stop list to determine which pipes are to be played. Since the IO routines take a total of about 0.04 seconds already, the processing itself must take no more than 0.013 seconds. Just the checking for out of range virtual keys would take more time than we can spare.

The easiest solution to the coupler spill-over problem is to include a few extra places in the shift register on both ends of each rank. This allows all the ranks to have the same shift register length whatever the actual number of pipes. The first advantage is that out of range virtual key depressions need not be checked for, since they fall into unused sections of the shift register. As with the wasted memory, the cost of the unused shift registers is small. The second advantage is that the electronics for every rank, of whatever kind, can be mass-produced. This makes it less expensive to build, as well as making the software easier to write (aside from merely being faster).

Except to satisfy traditional organists, there is no reason to have intermanual couplers on a computer controlled pipe organ. The original reason for including intermanual couplers was to minimize the

Photo 5: A rank of chimes pipes.

anical valves can react. The higher pitched pipes respond quickly, incidentally, and the low pipes sometimes take nearly a second to begin playing. Organists learn to compensate by playing low notes somewhat early. Without introducing a constant across-the-board delay, it does not seem possible to have the computer compensate for the effect, but it is a place where some experimentation might be interesting. Experienced organists, of course, might look askance at such an innovation, but they needn't be told about *all* of our ideas.

To summarize: A cycle of the computer organ system starts by pulling in the state of the console. The second part of the cycle (yet to be described) calculates the pipes that should be playing, given the state of the console. The third portion of the cycle sends the pipe commands along the shift register. This process is repeated at least once every 1/30 of a second.

A coupler (of whatever kind) is merely a displacement. It is easily calculated because all keyboards and ranks are the same nominal length. Likewise, engaging a stop is also a displacement of a distance equal to the difference between the bottom of the manual's image in memory and the bottom of the rank's image in memory. Thus, these displacements or offsets can be simply added to yield the offset for a combined coupler-stop setting.

An example, with a simplified organ, will demonstrate how the algorithm operates. Say there is one manual with ten keys numbered one through ten. They are read into memory locations (all numbers will be in base 10 for this discussion) 1001 through 1010. The ranks each have ten pipes, and there are two of them. The first rank is stored in locations 2001 through 2030. The second rank is stored in locations 3001 through 3030. Remember that the area set aside for each rank is larger than the actual space necessary (here three times as large). There are two stop switches, stored in locations 4001 and 4002. There are two couplers. They are stored in 4003 and 4004. The first couples up five pipes high, the second down three pipes low.

When the low order bit in 4001 is on (or high), the program adds 2010 to the key address to get the pipe address. When the other stop is on, 3010 is added. If the first coupler is on, an *additional* 5 is added, and the second coupler subtracts 3 (or adds a negative 3; it is all the same thing). The addition is done only once. Say the first stop and the second coupler were operated; then, given a key on at location 1005, to get the proper location to turn the pipe on, one merely adds (2010-3) or 2007 to the key location (1005+2007)=3012. This is

limitations imposed by the separation of the pipes into divisions. The computer, by being able to assign any rank to any manual (or to the pedals), eliminates the need for these couplers. They might well be eliminated in my own organ.

Another choice to be made is whether to recalculate all the pipes to be played, or just to modify the previous state on each cycle. It was decided to recalculate from scratch each time to eliminate the possibility of cumulative error. It also means that key bounce is automatically taken care of. In the slight time between updates, an organ pipe cannot even begin to sound. A spurious signal for one cycle is effectively ignored. Continuous pipe-on instructions emitted over a period of approximately 0.1 second or more are required before the slow mech-

indeed the correct pipe.

The microcomputer gives the user another option. When a stop and a coupler are operated, one gets both the note given by the stop and the extra note given by the coupler. With a computer it would be possible to give just the note given by the coupler acting on that stop. Since each stop can have a whole panoply of couplers attached to it, the number of buttons would soon become unworkable. For complete flexibility, the organist would have to be provided with a keyboard and display. One would play the organ by setting up many required presets with whatever degree of flexibility required, and then the easily hit tabs would not activate stops, but would bring in the organist's choice of registrations.

In the example above, choosing both stops and couplers would necessitate the addition of six numbers to each key location to obtain the pipe location. In the actual implementation, the program would, for each manual, do the following:

1. Scan the list of stops, and make a table of addends.
2. Scan the couplers, and add them to each stop, extending the list of addends.
3. Add the addends to the locations of the manual that contain a 1 (meaning a key depression).
4. Turn on the low order bit in the indicated word in the pipe image.

Intermanual couplings look just like any other kind of coupling. Say that one manual is stored in 1001 through 1010, and another manual at 1201 through 1210. Coupling the first manual to the second merely means adding 200 to the locations of the first manual. Just which intermanual couplers will be allowed must be carefully specified. If anything is allowed, we may get the following cat chasing its tail effect: Manual 1 is coupled to manual 2 at the same pitch. Manual 2 is coupled to manual 1, but one key higher (a semitone or *half step* higher in musical terminology). Press C on manual 1. C gets played on manual 2. This forces C# on manual 1. But this makes C# play on manual 2. Every key is thus being played. As implied above, though, intermanual couplings are necessary only on organs where the pipes are separated into divisions. In the computer controlled pipe organ they can and should be eliminated. Everything they can do, and more, can be done by freely assigning ranks to keyboards

as desired. I am not sure that all organists will be convinced by this.

Future Fugues

The organ console of the future, as it appears in the light of the computer mediated organ, looks like this: The manuals and pedals are built to the usual AGO (American Guild of Organists) standards. These standards are excellent, and permit an organist to travel from one instrument to another with a minimum of relearning. Instead of the usual arrangement of stops, there are as many rows of stops as there are keyboards. When a stop is to be assigned to a given keyboard, the button in the row representing that keyboard, and in the column representing that stop, is pressed. Any particular registration may be captured by pressing the "capture" button and, while holding it, operating the chosen preset button. The stop buttons should, as on conventional organs, move (or light up) to show what choices have been made. This is not far from conventional practice.

The possibilities in a console screen, with alphanumeric readout, are endless, and would require another article to explore. Similarly, the gimmicks, from very useful ones that record (on a disk or cassette) the performance in terms of keystrokes, to silly ones (for example, connecting the doorbell to the computer, so that the organ plays "Jesu, Joy of Man's Desiring" when a visitor presses the door button) would again take up too much space here.

Summary

The reasons for using a computer in a pipe organ are these:

1. Simplification of the wiring of the organ.
2. Greater reliability than conventional switching.
3. Lowered expense in medium and large instruments.
4. Much greater control of the instrument by the performer.
5. New freedoms in choosing registrations.

Nothing, it would seem, is lost by going to a microcomputer, and one could keep advantages 1, 2 and 3 above while keeping the appearance and operation of the pipe organ unchanged, in case any organists choose not to use advantages 4 and 5.■

Acknowledgements

Certainly at least half of the ideas expressed in this paper are due to my friend and colleague, Doug Wyatt. All of the ideas were developed in collaboration with him. Thanks are also due to Jim Brennan, who owns the incredibly large organ so often mentioned in and photographed with this article, and whose cooperation and inspiration have been essential to the project.

Tune In With Some Chips

Ted Sierad

Are you fascinated with the idea of computerized music, but find the mechanics of producing such effects too complex? I've come up with a simple technique which is the subject of this article, and which is well within the capabilities of the novice computer experimenter. With less than a dozen inexpensive integrated circuits, a few resistors, capacitors and a small prototyping board you can be well on the way to creating interesting music with your Altair, IMSAI or similar computer. My design creates a programmable music tone generator peripheral which has outputs that sound somewhat reminiscent of a clarinet when it is programmed by simple or complex software used to sequence notes in time. The first attempts I made at music generation required complicated programs and many integrated circuits. But as I gained more familiarity with the problem, the project reduced into a relatively simple solution as illustrated here.

The Hardware

The diagram of the melody box hardware is illustrated in figure 1. This hardware is the key to generation of tones from the computer. Software to be described later is responsible for sequencing the notes in time, thus creating a melody. The basic principle of operation of this melody box peripheral is

use of a latched binary code in eight bits to select one of several adjustable resistors which will be switched into an oscillator circuit as the timing resistor. In the particular circuit shown in figure 1, I used a pair of 7475 latch circuits to hold the code sent from an 8080's IO instruction; then I decoded the 8 bit pattern with a pair of 7441 circuits which I happened to have on hand in my workshop. The 7441s separately decode two 4 bit codes into selection of one of ten open collector output lines. These output lines are low if the line is selected, and effectively disconnected if not selected. The software used to drive the IO port should be set up to select only one active line by giving out a "null code" such as binary 1111 in one half of the 8 bit word, while selecting a given tone in the other half of the 8 bit word. This guarantees that only one line is in the low state out of a possible 20 lines. The line which is in the low logical state will then affect the frequency of the oscillator implemented by the 555 timer integrated circuit, IC7 of figure 1. The pitch of the note selected is determined by the tuning of the potentiometer associated with a given binary code by the decoders.

The low logic level output of the decoder is similar to a ground or zero voltage. Since all the other lines are effectively floating as open collector outputs, a definite low state on the one line inserts the resistor selected

Figure 1: Schematic of the melody box. This circuit works by changing the timing elements of a 555 oscillator integrated circuit to set the pitch. One resistor sets the pitch of each note of the scale. To turn off the oscillator, the circuit detects a special case which turns off the power to the oscillator by raising its ground pin to the high logic level.

Resistor Number	Potentiometer Value	Approximate Setting
R3	100 k	40 k
R4	100 k	48 k
R5	100 k	56 k
R6	100 k	64 k
R7	100 k	68 k
R8	100 k	76 k
R9	100 k	80 k
R10	100 k	86 k
R11	200 k	90 k
R12	100 k	43 k
R13	100 k	56 k
R14	100 k	67 k
R15	100 k	76 k
R16	100 k	86 k
R17	200 k	95 k
R18	200 k	108 k
R19	200 k	135 k
R20	200 k	152 k

Integrated Circuit Power Wiring

Number	Type	+5 V	GND
IC1	7475	5	12
IC2	7475	5	12
IC3	7441	5	12
IC4	7441	5	12
IC5	7404	14	7
IC6	7402	14	7
IC7	555	8	5

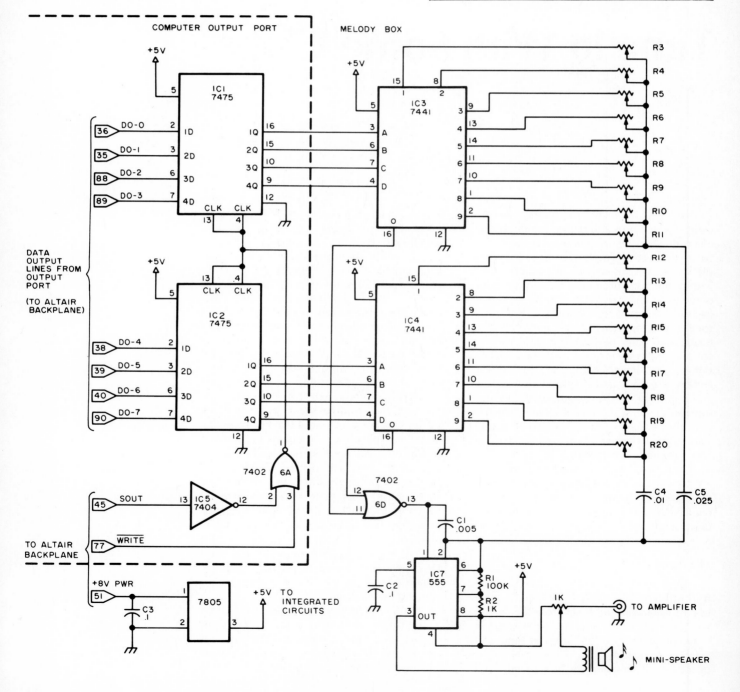

28

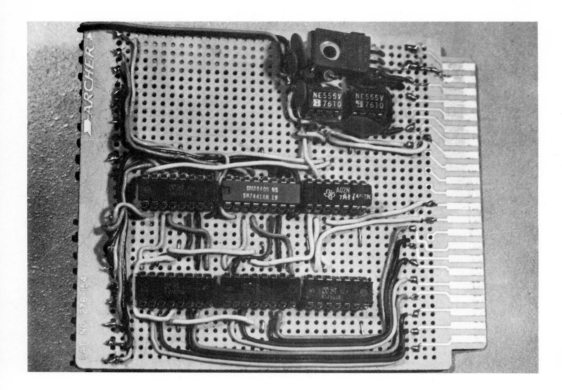

Photo 1: The melody box as constructed, using a Radio Shack prototyping board.

into the 555's timing circuit. The circuit is tuned by running a scale and adjusting the pitches by ear, or even by using a frequency meter.

But what about having no sound at all? Rests are important to music, and there must be some way to turn off the sound. Simply selecting none of the resistors is the first thought which comes to mind, but this does not work very well at all, as you'll find out if you try it. What I did was to put in the NOR gate logic of IC6d to detect when both halves of the 8 bit output word are 0, as indicated by selection of the 0 output line of each decoder. When this happens, the output of the NOR gate is high. Since I use this NOR gate as the power and signal ground of the 555 oscillator, I have effectively removed power from the 555 and turned it off when the double 0 state is output to the port. This may not be optimal engineering, but it certainly works.

My hardware stopped at the point of generating the tones, but for a full range of musical effects, you would certainly want to add some digital controlled filters and amplifiers to this basic pitch generation facility. Some filtration can be accomplished, of course, by manipulation of the tone controls of your high fidelity amplifier.

Further Simplifications of Hardware

The circuit of figure 1 is how I built the melody box; but after building it, it occurred to me that several further simplifica-

tions could be made. For example, the latches and IO port decoding logic outlined by the dotted lines could easily be replaced by an existing IO port on a computer, such as those provided by the peripheral interface adapters (PIA) of typical IO port boards. The 7441 is not the only open collector decoder chip available, and if you want to make 32 or 64 notes, use of two or four 74159 circuits with a 5 or 6 bit binary code would be possible. The only major disadvantage I find with this circuit is that it has to be tuned individual note by individual note.

Construction

The melody box was built on a Radio Shack IC experimental breadboard, #276-154 (Archer), which plugs into their #276-1551 card connector socket. This type of board has a foil pattern on one side. The integrated circuits or sockets are inserted from the nonfoil side and pins are then soldered to pads designed to take the DIP package pins as well as several connecting wires or components. See photo 1 for a look at my version. I used Molex pins to fabricate sockets for the integrated circuits, although solder tail sockets or no sockets at all could be used depending on your preferences and sources of supply. Wiring is done from the nonfoil side, with stripped ends of the wires going through the board to the appropriate pads. I used multiple colors for the wires in order to make tracing of the circuit easy. The space between the solder

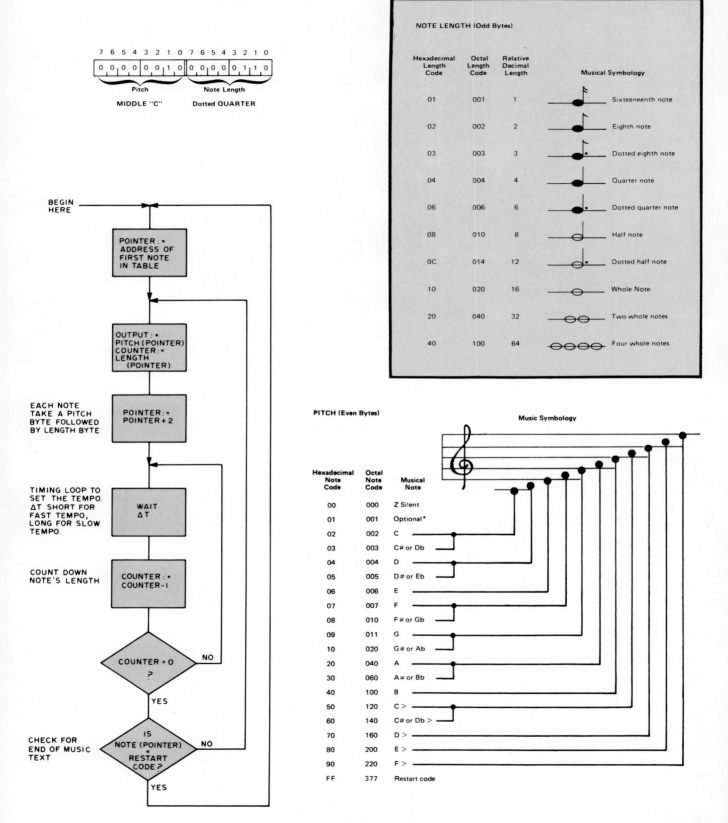

Figure 2: Programming model for the melody box. The note pitch and length codes listed are interpreted by the program shown as a flowchart here. Each note is completely specified by a pitch code and a length code contained in two bytes of memory as shown by the example.

Figure 3: The melody box notes are tuned by running this chromatic scale text through the program of figure 2. While listening to the scale, adjust each note's potentiometer until the sound is a correct musical interval.

A Set of Chromatic Scale Data for Tuning the Melody Box

Octal		Hexadecimal		
Relative Address	Note and Length Code	Relative Address	Note and Length Code	
000	001 002	00	01 02	
002	002 002	02	02 02	
004	003 002	04	03 02	
006	004 002	06	04 02	
010	005 002	08	05 02	
012	006 002	0A	06 02	
014	007 002	0C	07 02	
016	010 002	0E	08 02	
020	011 002	10	09 02	
022	020 002	12	10 02	
024	040 002	14	20 02	
026	060 002	16	30 02	
030	100 002	18	40 02	
032	120 002	1A	50 02	
034	140 002	1C	60 02	
036	160 002	1E	70 02	
040	200 002	20	80 02	
042	220 002	22	90 02	
044	000 040	24	00 40	
046	377 xxx	26	FF xx	repeat code

TABLE LOCATIONS →

OCTAL	000 002 004 006 010 012 —— 014 016 020 022 024 —— 026 030 032 034 036 040 —— 042 044 046 050 ——
HEXADECIMAL	00 02 04 06 08 0A —— 0C 0E 10 12 14 —— 16 18 1A 1C 1E 20 —— 22 24 26 30 ——

Figure 4: A test string, shown in machine code form and in traditional musical representation, sans time signature, using note lengths as defined in figure 2.

A Familiar Tune

Octal		Hexadecimal		
Relative Address	Note and Length Code	Relative Address	Note and Length Code	
000	002 004	00	02 04	
002	002 004	02	02 04	
004	006 004	04	06 04	
006	011 004	06	09 04	
010	120 014	08	50 0C	
012	040 024	0A	20 14	
014	040 004	0C	20 04	
016	007 004	0E	07 04	
020	011 004	10	09 04	
022	040 004	12	20 04	
024	011 040	14	09 20	
026	002 004	16	02 04	
030	002 004	18	02 04	
032	006 004	1A	06 04	
034	011 004	1C	09 04	
036	011 014	1E	09 0C	
040	004 024	20	04 14	
042	006 004	22	06 04	
044	007 004	24	07 04	
046	006 004	26	06 04	
050	004 004	28	04 04	
052	002 030	2A	02 18	
054	000 001	2C	00 01	
056	377 xxx	2E	FF xx	stop

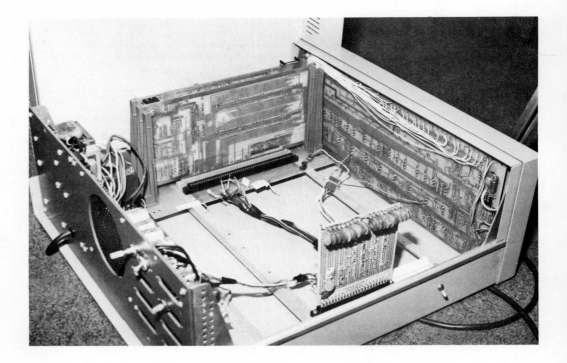

Photo 2: Installation of the melody box inside an Altair 8800 is accomplished by wiring various wires from the backplane of the computer. The power switch and volume control were mounted on the back panel of the computer, so that the melody box could be turned off.

pads and bus lines of the card is relatively small, so care must be used to prevent solder bridges from forming. I recommend a low wattage iron with a pencil tip. 25 to 30 W will work well.

The 20 variable resistors used can typically be found at prices from $.20 to $.49 depending on how good you are at shopping around. I mounted the actual melody box inside my Altair 8800, as shown in photo 2. The circuit connections to the Altair bus were made as shown in figure 1. When mounting the circuit inside the computer cabinet, care should be taken to prevent damage to existing boards of the computer. I found that covering the boards with a layer of paper was a good precautionary measure to prevent any splatter of solder. In order to make the Altair connections, you must remove the mainframe backplane board (the one with all the edge connectors) so that you can solder to the underside.

Software for the Melody Box

The melody box requires instructions to tell it what to do. In an organ, piano or other instrument, a special purpose keyboard gives instructions about what note to play and for how long. Making the melody box play a tune consists of writing a program to generate a time sequence of instructions.

A programming model for the melody box is summarized in figure 2. The data required for each note is the pitch of the note, and the length of the note. In the program I wrote for my Altair, I used one 8

bit byte to represent the pitch, followed by a second 8 bit byte with an integer count giving the length. A table of the pitch codes, referenced to a music stave, and a table of length codes with equivalent note symbols are shown as part of figure 2. The flowchart in figure 2 shows an algorithm which is easy to implement on any small computer. In my own system, I enter these codes with the front panel toggle switches and the "deposit" function.

Once you have coded up the details of a program which will execute the flowchart of figure 2, the first step is to tune the melody box. In figure 3 I've shown the musical representation of an ascending chromatic scale, as well as the corresponding table of byte values (in octal and hexadecimal) for the 2 byte note pitch and length codes required to play this scale. An arbitrarily long rest follows the end of data before the repeat. Tuning is accomplished by ear (assuming you know what a scale sounds like) while playing this chromatic scale with the program. The potentiometers of the circuit in figure 1 should be adjusted until the scale sounds "right."

As a second example, figure 4 shows a familiar tune, both in music notation and as a table of values for the music program to utilize. In the music notation, the table locations are written below in hexadecimal and octal to show how the two representations correspond. The limits on what tunes you can play are only dependent upon how much imagination you have and how big your Altair's memory is.■

A $19 Music Interface

(And Some Music Theory for Computer Nuts)

Bill Struve

"It's all Relative." So it is in physics as it was in music. About 600 BC Pythagoras discovered that strings under equal tension sounded harmonious if their lengths were in ratios of small whole numbers like 2/1, 3/2, 4/3, 5/3, etc. Many experiments throughout the world since that time have told us that in music, it is the ratios of the frequencies of the notes that count, not the absolute frequencies. It has only been in recent times that there has been international agreement that A above middle C is 440 Hz. Musicians call the "distance" between two notes an *interval*. Musical intervals are actually the ratios of the frequencies of two notes, and are so important in music that many of the ratios, or intervals, have names. For example, 2/1 is called the *octave*, 3/2 is called a *perfect fifth*, 4/3 is called a *perfect fourth*, 5/3 is called the *major sixth*, etc. These names make sense to musicians because they represent the distance between two notes on the musical scale like *do re mi fa sol la ti do*, which might be numbered 1 through 8, respectively. An octave is *do* to *do*, a perfect fifth is *do* to *sol*, a perfect fourth is *do* to *fa*, a major sixth is *do* to *la*, etc. The *pure diatonic* scale was constructed to maximize harmony between notes. This scale has been called the natural scale, and is one of the two most widely used scales in Western music. Many unaccompanied singing groups sing on this scale because it sounds right to them, even though they may not be able to tell you the difference between pure diatonic and tempered diatonic scales. Later you'll see how easy it is for a computer to generate notes on this scale.

Pianos, electronic organs, and synthesizers are all tuned to a slightly different scale, the *equally tempered diatonic* scale. J S Bach (1685-1750) played keyboard instruments and composed music which required changing key signatures (which we'll define by example later in this discussion), during the performance. But changing key signatures on an instrument tuned to the pure diatonic scale usually required retuning the instrument as you'll see in a moment. Bach found his way out of this dilemma by slightly mistuning his instruments, a technique which had recently been developed in Europe. This tempering was done so that all key signatures were equally out of tune, or equally tempered. When this is done, the ratio of frequencies of any two adjacent notes turns out to be the twelfth root of two (the value 1.0594631 noted mathematically as $\sqrt[12]{2}$ or calculated in FORTRAN-like languages as 2**(1.0/12)). He chose this ratio because there are twelve half steps per octave and the octave is a ratio of 2/1. Only the octave is kept purely harmonic in this scale: The perfect fifth is 0.11 percent low, the perfect fourth is 0.11 percent high, the major sixth is 0.91 percent high, etc. Since the most discriminating ear can only perceive differences in frequency when they are more than 0.2 percent, the most harmonious intervals (the octave, the fifth and fourth) are indistinguishable between the two scales. But what Bach and the world gained by giving up a little harmonic perfection was a quantum jump in the versatility of fixed tuned instruments (and an added quantum jump in the time and skill required to properly tune one).

Harmonious Computers

Microcomputers can give us both perfection and versatility. Since division by small whole numbers is trivial with digital electronics, it is at first sight more practical to use the pure diatonic scale when digitally generating music, just as it has been more practical to use the equally tempered diatonic scale for music performed on classical keyboard instruments. Changing key signatures in computer generated music is no problem, since the entire instrument may be "retuned" in a few microseconds.

The greatest advantage of the microcomputer is the ease with which anyone can produce music. Years of time consuming practice are not required. Application of computers to music may change music from an activity primarily dominated by motor skills to one dominated by the intellect. Composers no longer have to be skilled at playing an instrument in order to work out their compositions.

Do, re, mi, fa, sol, la, ti, do! North American, English, and Italian children all learn how to sing the scale. Most of them also learn other representations of the same musical scale like: C D E F G A B C, and:

Rarely if ever are any of these youngsters exposed to: 264 Hz, 297 Hz, 330 Hz, 352 Hz, 396 Hz, 440 Hz, 495 Hz, 528 Hz, or to: 1/1, 9/8, 5/4, 4/3, 3/2, 5/3, 15/8, 2/1. These two sets of numbers are also representations of *do, re, mi, fa, sol, la, ti, do* in the pure diatonic scale. Equally valid (especially for the piano) representations of this simple *do* to *do* musical scale are; 261.6 Hz, 293.7 Hz, 329.6 Hz, 349.2 Hz, 392.0 Hz, 440 Hz, 493.9 Hz, 523.3 Hz, which are related to each other by powers of the twelfth root of 2: $2^{0/12}(=1.000)$, $2^{2/12}(=1.1225)$, $2^{4/12}$, $2^{5/12}$, $2^{7/12}$, $2^{9/12}$, $2^{11/12}$, $2^{12/12}$ $(=2.000)$. As you may have guessed by now, these last two sets of numbers are the frequencies and frequency ratios of the equally tempered scale of *do* to *do* played on a piano.

So far, so good, but if you are as fast as I am at absorbing this material, by now it should be as clear as mud! Organization of facts into a pattern often does wonders for the intellect, so let us organize all this information into one table (table 1) and call it the "Key of C Major" so that musicians will think we are talking about music instead of computers.

You should notice a couple of things about table 1. First, at the bottom line you'll see that I've added a new concept: the musician's idea of *step size*. The steps come in two sizes, whole and half. Remembering that everything is relative, we can talk about step size in terms of the ratio of the frequencies of the pitches, or notes. In the pure scale, a half step up in pitch is an increase of 16/15 in frequency and a whole step up is an increase of 9/8 or 10/9. In the tempered scale all half steps up are an increase in frequency by the twelfth root of two $(2^{1/2})$, and all whole steps up in pitch increase the frequency by the sixth root of two $(2^{1/6})$ which is two half steps:

$$2^{1/12} \times 2^{1/12} = 2^{2/12} = 2^{1/6}$$

Secondly, you should note that the difference between the pure and tempered notes is imperceptible for four of the eight notes. You may be wondering why 440/440 = +.91 percent instead of 0 percent and why 261.6/264 = 0 percent instead of -.91 percent. To answer this, look at the "Frequency Ratio to C" lines and recall that everything is relative so: C(tempered)/C(pure) = 1/1, or 0 percent and A(tempered)/A(pure) = $2^{3/4}/(5/3)$ = 1.6818/1.6667, or +.91 percent.

To make this last point clear let's make a *do* to *do* scale from A = 220 Hz to A = 440 Hz, table 2. I could have made C(tempered) = C(pure), but that would violate an international agreement about A = 440 Hz! Besides, this way I can tell you about a scale in the minor mode. We'll impress the musicians looking over our shoulders by calling table 2 "Key of A Minor."

The two major differences between these two keys are the beginning note and the sequence of whole (W) and half (H) steps up the scale. Both the starting place and the sequence are specified in the name of the key. The key of C major begins with C and proceeds in the *major mode* sequence of steps, WWHWWWH. The key of A minor starts with A and proceeds in the *minor mode* sequence, WHWWHWW.

Look at the frequencies of the notes called D and G in these two keys. For tempered tuning, each of these notes keeps the same frequency although the key changes from C major to A minor. For pure tuning, however, each of these notes must be lowered by 1.25 percent when changing from C major to A minor. A singer or violinist does this during a performance, but can you imagine a pianist or organist stopping in the middle of a performance to retune two notes in each octave? Bach's

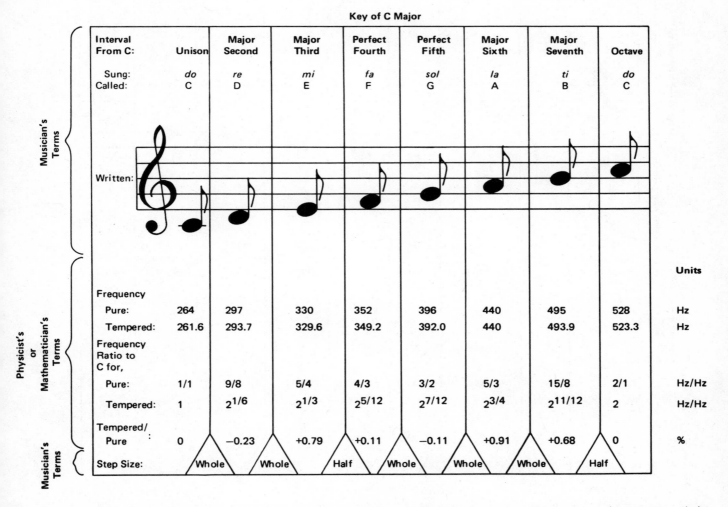

Key of C Major

Interval From C:	Unison	Major Second	Major Third	Perfect Fourth	Perfect Fifth	Major Sixth	Major Seventh	Octave	Units
Sung:	do	re	mi	fa	sol	la	ti	do	
Called:	C	D	E	F	G	A	B	C	
Frequency									
Pure:	264	297	330	352	396	440	495	528	Hz
Tempered:	261.6	293.7	329.6	349.2	392.0	440	493.9	523.3	Hz
Frequency Ratio to C for,									
Pure:	1/1	9/8	5/4	4/3	3/2	5/3	15/8	2/1	Hz/Hz
Tempered:	1	$2^{1/6}$	$2^{1/3}$	$2^{5/12}$	$2^{7/12}$	$2^{3/4}$	$2^{11/12}$	2	Hz/Hz
Tempered/ Pure :	0	−0.23	+0.79	+0.11	−0.11	+0.91	+0.68	0	%
Step Size:		Whole	Whole	Half	Whole	Whole	Whole	Half	

Musician's Terms

Physicist's or Mathematician's Terms

Musician's Terms

Table 1: The key of C major. There is a direct equivalence between a musician's terminology for musical concepts and the physicist's or mathematician's precise measures of the idea. One of the attractions of music is this low level precision involved in the creation of high level emotional sensations.

Key of A Minor

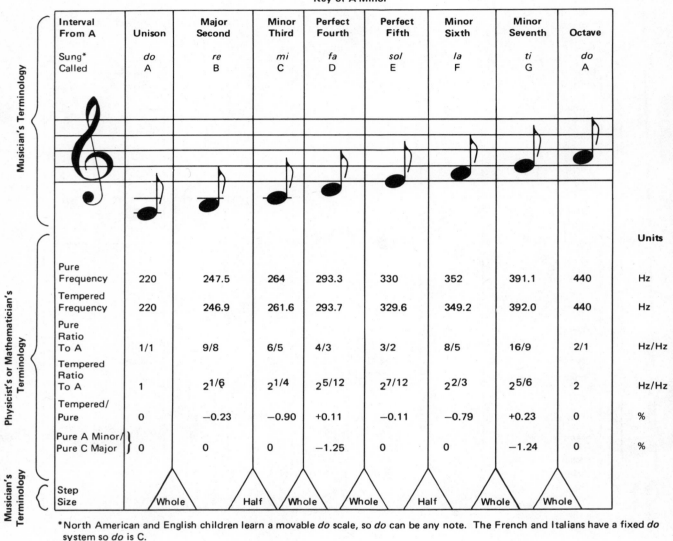

Interval From A	Unison	Major Second	Minor Third	Perfect Fourth	Perfect Fifth	Minor Sixth	Minor Seventh	Octave	Units
Sung*	do	re	mi	fa	sol	la	ti	do	
Called	A	B	C	D	E	F	G	A	
Pure Frequency	220	247.5	264	293.3	330	352	391.1	440	Hz
Tempered Frequency	220	246.9	261.6	293.7	329.6	349.2	392.0	440	Hz
Pure Ratio To A	1/1	9/8	6/5	4/3	3/2	8/5	16/9	2/1	Hz/Hz
Tempered Ratio To A	1	$2^{1/6}$	$2^{1/4}$	$2^{5/12}$	$2^{7/12}$	$2^{2/3}$	$2^{5/6}$	2	Hz/Hz
Tempered/Pure	0	−0.23	−0.90	+0.11	−0.11	−0.79	+0.23	0	%
Pure A Minor/Pure C Major	0	0	0	−1.25	0	0	−1.24	0	%
Step Size	Whole	Half	Whole	Whole	Half	Whole	Whole		

Musician's Terminology / Physicist's or Mathematician's Terminology / Musician's Terminology

*North American and English children learn a movable *do* scale, so *do* can be any note. The French and Italians have a fixed *do* system so *do* is C.

Table 2: The key of A minor. As in table 1, we note the same information, but start the scale on A instead of C. This changes the order of half and whole steps (bottom line) from a major mode sequence to a minor mode sequence; an extra line has been added to show the frequency ratios of the minor key with respect to the major key. Note: Since this example is a minor scale, the terms me, le, and te are used to refer to the minor third, minor sixth, and minor seventh respectively. Another way to label this scale is to assign the name la to the low A. The scale then becomes la, ti, do, re, me, fa, sol, la.

equally tempered tuning survives all such key shifts quite well. The most sensitive intervals (octave, fourth, fifth) are still imperceptibly different from the pure scale, and the other intervals get no worse. You should notice one more thing when you are comparing these two tables. There are two kinds of thirds, sixths, and sevenths. As you may have guessed, there are also two kinds of seconds, major and minor. There is also an interval called the *tritone*, so there can be twelve equal half steps per octave.

So if we list all of the intervals, we find 13 to get 12 half steps per octave. Since these thirteen intervals form what is known as the *chromatic scale*, we'll call this list "Intervals of the Chromatic Scale" and write it down in table 3.

You can learn at least five things by inspecting table 3.

First, the ♭ sign is used to denote a half step down from a note and is called a *flat*. The sign for a half step up is # and is called a *sharp*.

Second, you should now be able to write the notes used in the scales of all major and minor keys. For example, the key of C minor begins with C and proceeds WHWWHWW, so it would be: C, D, E♭, F, G, A♭, B♭, C. The *key signature* is the shorthand used by musicians to specify the key at the beginning of each line of music:

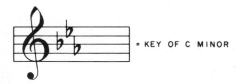 = KEY OF C MINOR

This tells the person playing the music that all of the Es, As, and Bs should be played one half step flat.

Third, the major and minor modes sound different because different intervals are used for the third, sixth, and seventh.

Fourth, the two most dissonant intervals, the minor second and the tritone, are not used in any major or minor key, but are needed for some key changes.

Fifth, and perhaps most important for implementation on a "dinky" computer and for experimentation, is that the only prime numbers used in the pure pitch ratios are 2, 3, and 5. Also, 5 only appears to the first power and 3 only to the first and second powers. You will see later how easy it is to implement the pure diatonic scale with inexpensive integrated circuits external to the computer, so the computer is not tied up by generating the pitches itself. In contrast, the powers of the twelfth root of two may be obtained from the moderately ex-

pensive "top octave" integrated circuit, or calculated (but not accurately) in real time by the dinky itself. In the latter case there will be little computer power left for calculating the melody or harmony.

From Music to Mathematics and Back Again

Webster defines *inversion* of a musical interval as: "A simple interval with its upper tone transposed an octave downwards. . . Inverted primes become octaves; seconds become sevenths; thirds, sixths, etc."

A mathematical inversion Webster defines as: "A change in the order of terms of a proportion. . ." So what if a fifth is just an inverted fourth? Simplification, that's what! If we divide the chromatic scale right in the middle at the tritone, the bottom half is just the inverse of the upper half. This means that you only need to learn and think about half as much. This is not only true musically and mathematically, but your own ears will also easily recognize the similarities between an interval and its inverse.

Try the following experiment on any piano or organ that's in tune. Pick out any black or white key and call it 1 for reference. This home note is called the *tonic* and should be located near the center of the keyboard for reasons I'll explain in a moment. Now find note 6 by counting up six keys including 1 and all black and white keys. Now play both 1 and 6 together; that's how a perfect fourth sounds. Try it again with 1 and 8 this time; that's how a perfect fifth sounds. Now go back and forth between 1 and 8 and then 1 and 6 to get a

	Interval	C Major	A Minor	Pure Ratio	Tempered Ratio
1	Unison	C–C	A–A	1/1	$2^{0/12}$
2	Minor Second	C–D♭	A–B♭	16/15	$2^{1/12}$
3	Major Second	C–D	A–B	9/8	$2^{2/12}$
4	Minor Third	C–E♭	A–C	6/5	$2^{3/12}$
5	Major Third	C–E	A–D♭	5/4	$2^{4/12}$
6	Perfect Fourth	C–F	A–D	4/3	$2^{5/12}$
7	Tritone	C–G♭	A–E♭	(64/45 or 45/32)	$2^{6/12}$
8	Perfect Fifth	C–G	A–E	3/2	$2^{7/12}$
9	Minor Sixth	C–A♭	A–F	8/5	$2^{8/12}$
10	Major Sixth	C–A	A–G♭	5/3	$2^{9/12}$
11	Minor Seventh	C–B♭	A–G	16/9	$2^{10/12}$
12	Major Seventh	C–B	A–A♭	15/8	$2^{11/12}$
13	Octave	C–C	A–A'	2/1	$2^{12/12}$

Table 3: Intervals of the chromatic scale.

feel for the fifth and its inverse. Next try the same thing with 2 and 7 then 2 and 9. These two intervals are also the fourth and its inverse, the fifth, but you have *transposed* them up by half a step. Now try a minor third and its inverse, the major sixth. First play 1 and 4 together and then 1 and 10 together.

You should notice that the minor third and major sixth don't sound quite as sweet or harmonious as the fourth and fifth did. Now try transposing up a half step to 2 and 5 then another half step to 3 and 6, and so on up the keyboard. Do the same with the fourth, first 2 and 7, then 3 and 8 and so on up the scale. Notice how the fourth and minor third sound similar regardless of the tonic or home key chosen, and how they are clearly different from each other even if played in different octaves; in music as in physics everything is relative to the observer.

You may even want to make a list for yourself of the intervals which sound alike. You can also note which intervals are most harmonious and which are most dissonant, or rough. I'll even bet your list looks like mine! If you think I've biased you, have your friends or family make lists. I'll bet they all are in agreement. Table 4 contains my list, which I've called "Music to Mathematics to Music" for reasons you'll see in a moment.

Now isn't that a remarkable historical achievement: what musicians have been calling an inverse is also an inverse of the frequencies of pitches according to the mathematical definition of inverse. Although I'm neither mathematician nor musician, I have read a number of books on both subjects, including some on the psychophysics of music, and I have never seen this simple and simplifying correspondence of musical and mathematical inverses mentioned. Perhaps it was information lost with the burning of Pythagoras and his temple 2500 years

ago. A close look at my list of most harmonious to most dissonant reveals that as the top and bottom of the fractions get larger, the harmony decreases and the dissonance increases, (with the exception of the minor second; but let's forget about this exception for the moment).

The order in this list is no accident; neither is it a learned cultural bias! It is as if we had a brain with a center which continually seeks for simplicity, harmony and order. The *harmonic series*: 1, 2, 3, 4, 5, 6, . . . , is found extensively in man's theories about nature. Is this because it is a property of nature, or is it because man's brain can understand things better if they are in such a series? Such a question is interesting, but can only be raised and not answered in an article about music for computer nuts. Music, like speech, is unique to man and is totally abstract. By abstract, I mean that for the most part, no attempt to copy nature is made.

Music is solely a product of man's brain, or ear-brain combination. Here is where we find harmonic series galore. A musical *chord* such as the *major triad* is three notes played together, the frequencies of the notes being related to each other as elements of a harmonic series are related. In the key of C major, the major triad is C, E, and G which have pitch ratios of 4, 5, and 6 (ie: 4/4, 5/4 and 6/4). Often to make the chord sound fuller, a musician will add the C an octave lower, and the C an octave higher. This also fills out the harmonic series some more: 2, , 4, 5, 6, , and 8. How about the missing 1, 3, 7, 9, etc? You can try 1 and 3 for yourself; they are simply the C an octave lower still, and the fifth up from the next C, and they fit in beautifully.

Unfortunately, you won't be able to try 7 on a piano; it would be 7/4, which is 1.8 percent lower than B♭, a minor seventh from the C of the triad. Fortunately, if you

Interval	Ratio	Inverse	Octave Shift	Musical Inverse
Unison	1/1	1/1	2/1	Octave
Fourth	4/3	3/4	3/2	Fifth
Major Third	5/4	4/5	8/5	Minor Sixth
Minor Third	6/5	5/6	5/3	Major Sixth
Major Second	9/8	8/9	16/9	Minor Seventh
Minor Second*	16/15	15/16	15/8	Major Seventh
Tritone	64/45	45/64	45/32	Tritone

*The minor second is more dissonant to me than the tritone, but the tritone seems more dissonant to me than the major seventh, so the minor second doesn't fit in this list very well.

Table 4: Music to mathematics to music. The intervals useful in music are listed in order from the most harmonious to the most dissonant. Most people are in good agreement about the order of evaluation of the relative degrees of harmoniousness in the first five intervals listed.

build the pure diatonic scale interface described below, you will be able to hear for yourself how well 7 fits into the series. Also you will be able to hear 11, and 13, and to hear how, and under what conditions they fit.

The ear-brain wants so much to hear harmonic series that it will even fill in missing pitches. The "missing fundamental," or the lowest note of a harmonic series, has been studied by many doing acoustics research. If your ear is presented with a series of tones whose frequencies are in the ratios of whole numbers such as 2, 3, 4, 5, 6, or 3, 5, 7, 9, your brain tells you that you actually hear the pitch corresponding to 1 (the fundamental) also!

Now let's get back to the dissonance of the minor second and why you needed to stay in the middle of the piano keyboard to do the experiments with intervals. If two pitches are very close together, the ear cannot tell them apart, and they are heard as a single smooth pitch. If the pitches are far enough apart, two smooth and distinct notes are heard. If the distance between the pitches is in the *critical band*, the two notes are heard as two more or less rough notes. This roughness is maximum at 1/4 of the critical band. It turns out that the minor second is 1/4 of the critical band over the middle of the piano range, and this is why it

sounds so dissonant. The width of the critical band is roughly equal to:

$$100 \text{ Hz} + 50 \text{ Hz} \times f$$

where f is the frequency of the note in kHz. You can calculate that, as you go to lower notes on the piano, roughness, or dissonance, will be heard in the minor and then major thirds, and still lower will be heard even in the fourth and fifth, until at the lowest octave the only consonant interval will be the octave itself. Thus, if you want the music you compose to sound harmonious, you should have the pitches related to each other in the harmonic series, and pitches played at the same time should be more than 1/2 of the critical band apart. Analysis of music composed by Bach and Dvorak shows that their chords obey these two simple rules.

To compose interesting music, you'll need a few more rules. Most music has two features, constancy and variety. It is as if the brain center which looked for order, simplicity, and harmony was easily bored, so once it found a pattern, it would soon be looking for another. Our musical needs vary. Sometimes we want very simple tunes so we can unwind, and at other times we need complex melodies to keep our interest. Once you have made a tune with a computer, it will be possible, in principle,

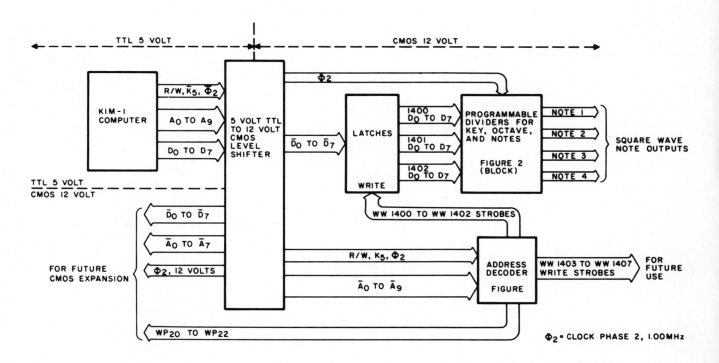

Figure 1: Block diagram of the musical tone generator interface. All logic (see figures 3 and 4) of the tone generator itself is 12 V CMOS, with level conversion from the TTL 5 V levels at the computer output.

for you to have the computer make all sorts of variations of your tune to keep it interesting.

Now let's switch gears from music to computer oriented electronics and find out how to build a diatonic computer music interface. The interface costs less than $19 to build, including 24 integrated circuits, LEDs, resistors, four diodes, and a universal type printed circuit board. It will put out four notes simultaneously, and will play in almost nine octaves (17.36 Hz to 7812.5 Hz). The highest and lowest octaves have 12 and 13 different notes, and the middle seven octaves have 33 notes each, giving a total of 256 unique notes. It uses three bytes of memory space.

The interface can be functionally divided (see figure 1) into four parts:

- A set of programmable frequency dividers.
- A three byte latch.

- An address decoder.
- A level shifter to change the 5 V signals from the computer to 12 V signals for the CMOS circuits so they can operate fast enough to follow the 500 ns write pulse put out by the computer.

The block diagram shows that I've chosen hexadecimal addresses 1400 to 1402 to drive the interface. This is a convenient memory location for me because I have a KIM-1 with 12 K of memory and these locations are not used for anything else. You'll notice that I've also decoded write pulses for hexadecimal addresses 1403 to 1407 and page selects of addresses 20XX to 22XX for future expansion of the interface. Also, eight address lines, eight data lines, a clock line, and the write pulses for addresses 20XX to 22XX, all at 12 V, are brought out to the edge connector for use with other CMOS interfaces.

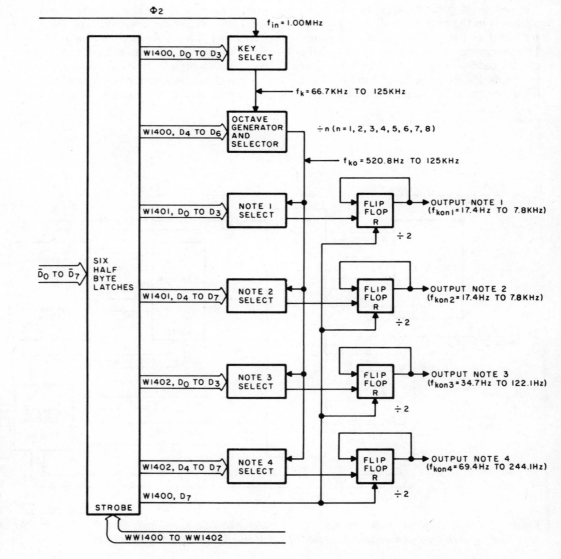

Figure 2: Detail block diagram of the tone generator, which uses the 1 MHz clock of the KIM-1 as its frequency standard. The outputs at right are square wave signals which can be sent to further filtering and signal processing before mixing down to one or two stereo channels.

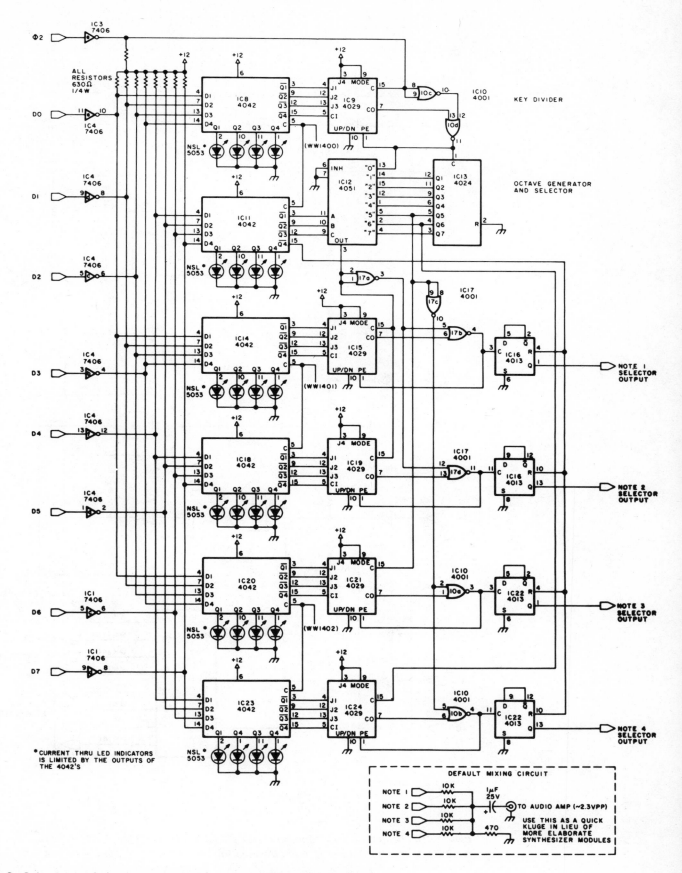

Figure 3: Schematic of the tone generator's key, octave and note selection logic. A default mixing circuit is shown to allow connection of all four outputs directly to one audio amplifier for testing.

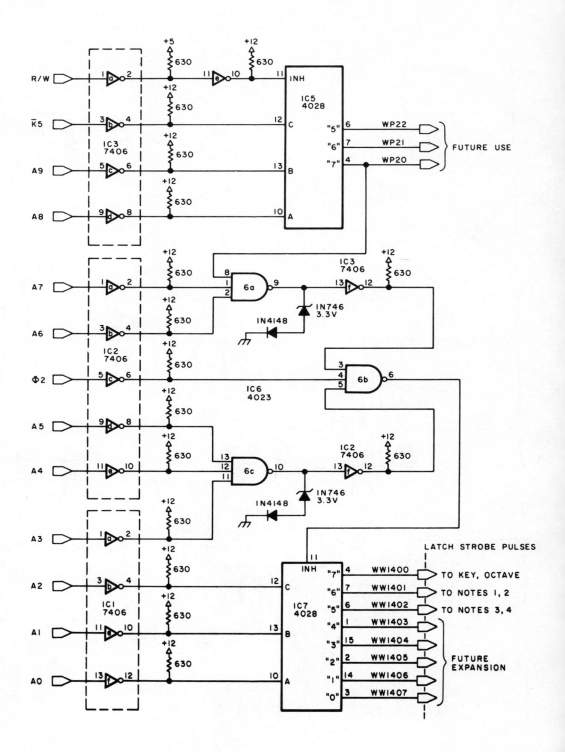

Figure 4: Schematic of the tone generator's KIM-1 address space decoding (top), a diagram of the edge connector (far right), and power wiring table for figures 3 and 4 (right).

The six programmable dividers are the heart of the interface (see the detail block diagram of figure 2 and circuit diagram of figure 3). Five of these are 4029 presettable, bidirectional, binary or decade counters set up to count down in binary mode. In this mode the carry out (CO) line goes low whenever the counter counts down to 0. The CO signal is inverted and returned to the preset enable (PE) input which sets the counter to the value of the binary number on input pins J_4 to J_1. Each positive transition of the clock (C) input causes the counter to count down by one as long as the clock inhibit (CI) is low. Because J_4 (pin 3 on IC9, IC15, IC19, IC21, and IC24) is always high, the counters may be set to divide by 8, 9, 10, 11, 12, 13, 14, or 15, depending on the binary number on inputs J_3 to J_1. This number is stored in 4042 latches by writing the data into D_3 to D_1 of the latch as if it were a memory location. For example, if a binary three (011) were on J_3 to J_1, 8+3, or 11 would be loaded into the counter when PE went high, and the C input would have 11 positive transitions before CO would go low, forcing PE high momentarily, and again

loading the counter with 11. Thus the frequency of PE pulses would be 1/11 of the frequency of positive transitions at C. A flip flop at the output of the note dividers converts the PE impulses into square waves with a 50 percent duty cycle. Each of the Q_4 latch outputs turns off a divider and thus turns off the sound of one or more note outputs. Bits 4 and 8 of hexadecimal location 1400 turn off all the sound, whereas bits 4 and 8 of address 1401 and 1402 turn off notes 1 thru 4, respectively. The reason for all this turn off is that music has a lot more silence in it than is generally recognized. To make notes sound distinct, rather than all run together, the sound must be shut off for periods of 10 to 50 ms (for example).

The key selector divides the computer's 1 MHz clock by a number from 15 to 8 to produce frequency f_K of 66.7 kHz to 125 kHz as shown in the second block diagram. A binary divider, IC13, produces seven more octaves (factors of two in frequency) from f_K, and the 1 of 8 selector, IC12, selects one of the octaves, f_{KO} (520.8 Hz to 125 kHz), based on bits 6 to 4 stored at

Power Wiring Table

Number	Type	+5 V	GND	+12 V
IC1	7406	14	7	—
IC2	7406	14	7	—
IC3	7406	14	7	—
IC4	7406	14	7	—
IC5	4028	—	8	16
IC6	4023	—	7	14
IC7	4028	—	8	16
IC8	4042	—	8	16
IC9	4029	—	8	16
IC10	4001	—	7	14
IC11	4042	—	8	16
IC12	4051	—	8	16
IC13	4024	—	7	14
IC14	4042	—	8	16
IC15	4029	—	8	16
IC16	4013	—	7	14
IC17	4001	—	7	14
IC18	4042	—	8	16
IC19	4029	—	8	16
IC20	4042	—	8	16
IC21	4029	—	8	16
IC22	4013	—	7	14
IC23	4042	—	8	16
IC24	4029	—	8	16

Edge Connector Wiring Diagram

5 V inputs			12 V outputs
+5 V	1	A	ground
12 V output ϕ_2	2	B	write page 20
$\overline{\phi_2}$	3	C	write page 21
R/W	4	D	write page 22
$\overline{K_5}$	5	E	$\overline{D_0}$
D_0	6	F	$\overline{D_1}$
D_1	7	H	$\overline{D_2}$
D_2	8	J	$\overline{D_3}$
D_3	9	K	$\overline{D_4}$
D_4	10	L	$\overline{D_5}$
D_5	11	M	$\overline{D_6}$
D_6	12	N	$\overline{D_7}$
D_7	13	P	$\overline{A_0}$
A_0	14	R	$\overline{A_1}$
A_1	15	S	$\overline{A_2}$
A_2	16	T	$\overline{A_3}$
A_3	17	U	$\overline{A_4}$
A_4	18	V	$\overline{A_5}$
A_5	19	W	$\overline{A_6}$
A_6	20	X	$\overline{A_7}$
A_7	21	Y	A_9 5 V input
A_8	22	Z	+12 V

address 1400, to send to the dividers, IC15 and IC19, for notes 1 and 2. Notes 2 and 3 are only in the low octaves 5 and 6 so up to three octaves may be played at once. I chose these to be in the lower octaves because I use them for rhythm and accompaniment. You may want to add other octave selectors for more control, or add manual switches to have notes 4 and 3 in any octave.

The data from the computer is strobed into the latches by write pulses generated by the address decoder, IC5 to IC7 (figure 4). $\overline{K_5}$ from KIM-1 is low whenever the sixth 1024 block of memory is addressed. K_5 is combined in IC5 with $\overline{A_9}$, $\overline{A_8}$, and R/W to produce pulses when addresses 20XX to 22XX are written into. The pulse indicating addresses 20XX (2000 to 20FF) are being written into is combined with $\overline{A_7}$ to $\overline{A_3}$ and ϕ_2 to produce a negative pulse during phase two of the computer clock when locations 1400 to 1407 are being written into. This short pulse is combined with $\overline{A_2}$ to $\overline{A_0}$ in IC7 to produce strobe pulses for the latches during the 500 ns when the data is stable on the data bus. Generating a tune is done by storing (with a timed sequence) the appropriate data into locations 1400 to 1402 as you would any other memory location. The 5 to 12 V level shifter is simply a high voltage, open collector hex inverter, 7406. In retrospect, diodes D_1 to D_4 are pro-

Nearby Musical Note		Effective Integer N	Key	Note		R Actual Ratio 256/N	Pitch Assuming 1 MHz/(16 N)	W Nearest Well Tempered Ratio	(R−W)/R
B	*	256	8	8		1.0000	244.14	1.0000	0.0000
		252	9	14		1.0159	248.02	1.0000	0.0156
C	*	242	11	11		1.0579	258.26	1.0595	0.0015
	■	240	8	15	(10, 12)	1.0667	260.42	1.0595	0.0068
		234	9	13		1.0940	267.09	1.1225	0.0260
C#	*	225	15	15		1.1378	277.78	1.1225	0.0135
		224	8	14		1.1429	279.02	1.1225	0.0178
		220	10	11		1.1636	284.09	1.1892	0.0220
D	■*	216	9	12		1.1852	289.35	1.1892	0.0034
		210	14	15		1.2190	297.62	1.1892	0.0245
		208	8	13		1.2308	300.48	1.2599	0.0237
D#	*	200	10	10		1.2800	312.50	1.2599	0.0157
		198	9	11		1.2929	315.66	1.2599	0.0255
		196	14	14		1.3061	318.88	1.3348	0.0220
		195	13	15		1.3128	320.51	1.3348	0.0170
E	■*	192	8	12		1.3333	325.52	1.3348	0.0011
F	*	182	13	14		1.4066	343.41	1.4142	0.0054
	■	180	9	10	(12, 15)	1.4222	347.22	1.4142	0.0056
		176	8	11		1.4545	355.11	1.4142	0.0277
F#	*	169	13	13		1.5148	369.82	1.4983	0.0110
		168	12	14		1.5238	372.02	1.4983	0.0167
		165	11	15		1.5515	378.79	1.5874	0.0231
G	*	162	9	9		1.5802	385.80	1.5874	0.0045
	■	160	8	10		1.6000	390.63	1.5874	0.0079
		156	12	13		1.6410	400.64	1.6818	0.0248
G#	*	154	11	14		1.6623	405.84	1.6818	0.0117
		150	10	15		1.7067	416.67	1.6818	0.0146
A	■*	144	8	9	(12, 15)	1.7778	434.03	1.7818	0.0026
		143	11	13		1.7902	437.06	1.7818	0.0047
		140	10	14		1.8286	446.43	1.7818	0.0256
A#	■*	135	9	15		1.8963	462.96	1.8876	0.0045
		132	11	12		1.9394	473.48	1.8876	0.0266
		130	10	13		1.9692	480.77	2.0000	0.0156
B	*	128	8	8	(next octave)	2.0000	488.28	2.0000	0.0000

■ Diatonic major scale notes "best fit" to A = 440 standard.
* Best fit of diatonic major scale to equally tempered scale based on B = 244.14.

Table 5: Table of possible intervals. The circuit of figures 1 to 4 produces the following set of possible frequencies assuming a 1 MHz central processor clock. In this table, outputs have been grouped near the equivalent well tempered scale ratio and frequencies. The asterisk (*) indicates best fit for a logarithmic well tempered scale series starting at a ratio of 1.0000, calculated using a program on a pocket calculator. Notations in parentheses show effective integers derived by shifting to the next octave. Note that with this calculation, use of "best" fit finds the note A in this octave at 434 Hz, 0.7% flat with respect to the standard A of 440 Hz. Table 6 picks a set from this table which is closest to the standard pitches but not optimal with respect to equal temperment.

bably not needed since IC6 probably can't supply enough current to damage IC3, even though the input voltage maximum to IC3 is specified as 5.5 V. The four extra outputs on the quad latches are used with 24 LEDs to give you a bonus light show, and are useful in figuring out what data is being sent to the interface from the computer. The LEDs are lit with 0s instead of 1s at the J inputs, so that the more lights, the lower the divisor and the higher the note. If you want the lights to read the same as the J inputs, reverse them and tie the anodes to +12 V.

The middle seven octaves of the interface each have 33 unique combinations of the key and note dividers. I've made a list of frequencies in one such octave. You'll notice right away that there is no way to get a perfect fifth if you use 244.14 Hz as the home or "tonic" note. This is because to go up in frequency by 3/2s, you need to already be dividing by a number that has 3 in it such as 9, 12, or 15. So if you want to change to a note that is a fifth from the tonic, 248.02 Hz, 260.42 Hz, 267.09 Hz etc can be used as the tonic, but 244.14 Hz, 258.26 Hz, 279.02 Hz can't be. Although this may seem restricting, remember that the octave here has almost three times as many notes as an octave on a piano. For the tritone interval(s), you will find that 10/7 and 7/5 are indistinguishable from 64/45 and 45/32, and are easier to use.

Now to get started using the interface, let's write a program to play the *do* to *do* scale in both major and minor modes. To keep it simple, we'll let note 1 play and keep the others silent. To silence notes 2 to 4, we need to store a 1 in bit 7 of location 1401 and in bits 4 and 7 of location 1402. To hear anything, we also need a 0 in bits 4 and 7 of location 1400 and to hear note 1, a 0 in bit 4 of 1401. One set of data to accomplish this is:

Address	Data
1400	xy
1401	Fz
1402	FF

where x, y, and z are numbers less than 8 and the Fs are any number more than 7 (eg: hexadecimal E).

If you look at the major and minor mode sequences in table 1, "Key of C Major," or in table 2, "Key of A Minor," you'll find that the major scale tonic must contain two 3s and a 5 in the divisor so you can multiply by 9 and 15, and the minor scale tonic must contain two 3s.

The so called "rate multipliers" also do their multiplication by dividing by a smaller number. To make this idea clear to you I've

written out the ratios, divisors, output frequencies, and the data to be written into locations 1400 and 1401 (don't forget to write FF into 1402). For example, if hexadecimal 34 and hexadecimal F7 are written into 1400 and 1401, the 1.00 MHz clock will be divided by (8x12x15x2) to give an output frequency of 347.222 Hz.

To play the major scale, your memory should look like this:

Address	Data
SCALE+0	34
SCALE+1	F7
SCALE+2	40
SCALE+3	F2
	etc

The major and minor diatonic scales and the twelve note chromatic scale are not the only scales that are pleasing to the human ear. With this interface you should be able to create new and pleasing musical scales, and compose music which has never been heard before. You can explore the sounds of intervals with frequency ratios of 7/4, 9/5, 9/7, and 7/6 which are not found in Western music. You should also be able to invent some new and interesting chords since you will have more of the harmonic series available to you. Just watch out for the critical band by keeping your notes more than 50 Hz apart plus 25 Hz for each kHz. ■

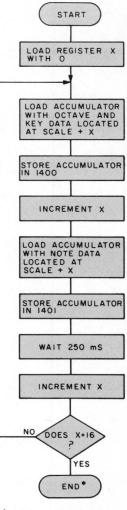

Figure 5: Flowchart of a simple program to cycle through a series of note codes found in a table indexed by register X, with 16 entries.

		Ratio	Divisor Octave	Key	Note	Data 1400	1401	^{f}KON1
Major Scale	Tonic	1/1	8	12	15	34	F7	347.2
	Second	9/8	16	8	10	40	F2	390.6
	Third	5/4	8	12	12	34	F4	434.0
	Fourth	4/3	8	9	15	31	F7	463.0
	Fifth	3/2	8	12	10	34	F2	520.8
	Sixth	5/3	8	12	9	34	F1	578.7
	Seventh	15/8	8	12	8	34	F0	651.0
	Octave	2/1	4	12	15	24	F7	694.4
Minor Scale	Tonic	1/1	8	12	12	34	F4	434.0
	Second	9/8	16	8	8	40	F0	488.3
	Third	6/5	8	12	10	34	F2	520.8
	Fourth	4/3	8	12	9	34	F1	578.7
	Fifth	3/2	8	12	8	34	F0	651.0
	Sixth	8/5	4	12	15	24	F7	694.4
	Seventh	16/9	8	9	9	31	F1	771.6
	Octave	2/1	4	12	12	24	F4	868.1

Table 6: A selection of codes taken from the integers of table 5 and applied to the hardware of figures 1 to 4, to create a major scale (tonic F relative to A = 440) and minor scale (tonic A, relative to A = 440).

A Sampling of Techniques For

Computer Performance of Music

Hal Chamberlin

Computer music is probably one of the most talked about serious applications for home computers. By serious I mean an application that has a degree of complexity and open-endedness which can totally preoccupy experimenters and funded institutions for years. Computer performance of music is a discipline so vast that the final, "best" technique for its implementation or even a good definition of such a technique may never be discovered.

At the same time, computer music is an easy field to break into. With only minimal effort and expenditure a very impressive (to the uninitiated) music performance demonstration may be put together. With a little more work a system may be assembled which is of great value to other family members, particularly children just starting to learn music theory. Such a system could, for example, eliminate manual dexterity as a factor in a child's musical development. Finally, on the highest level, it is no longer very difficult to break into truly original research in serious performance of music by computer. The advances in digital and linear integrated circuits have made putting together the hardware system for supporting such research largely a matter of clever system design rather than brute financial strength. Programming, tempered with musical knowledge, is the real key to obtaining significant results. Thus, in the future, hobbyists working with their own systems will be making important contributions toward advancement of the computer music art.

While the scope of one article cannot

fully cover such an extensive topic, it should serve to acquaint the reader with the more popular techniques, their implementation, strengths, weaknesses, and ultimate potential.

Generally, all computer music performance techniques can be classified into two generic groups. The first includes schemes in which the computer generates the sound directly. The second covers systems where the computer acts as a controller for external sound generation apparatus such as an electronic organ or sound synthesizer.

Early Techniques

Just as soon as standard commercial computers such as the IBM 709 and, later, the 1401 made their appearance, programmers started to do frivolous things with them after hours, such as playing games and music. Since elementary monotonic (one note at a time) music is just a series of tones with different frequencies and durations, and since a computer can be a very precise timing device, it did not take long for these early tinkerers to figure out how to get the machine to play such music. The fundamental concept used was that of a *timed loop.*

A timed loop is a series of machine language instructions which are carefully chosen for their execution time as well as function, and which are organized into a loop. Some of the instructions implement a counter that controls the number of passes through the loop before exiting.

Let's examine some fundamental

47

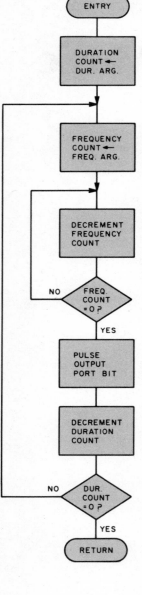

timed loop relationships. If the sum total execution time of the instructions in the loop is M microseconds then we have a loop *frequency* of

$$\left(\frac{10^6}{M}\right) \text{ Hertz (cycles per second).}$$

If the initial value of the decrementing counter that controls the number of loop passes is N, then the total execution time before exit from the loop is (MxN) microseconds. Thus what we really have is a "tone" with a *frequency* of

$$\left(\frac{10^6}{M}\right) \text{Hertz}$$

and a *duration* of

$$\frac{MxN}{10^6} \text{ seconds.}$$

Using different loops with more or fewer instructions will give us different Ms and thus different notes. Using different Ns when entering these loops gives different durations for the notes, and so we have satisfied the definition of elementary monotonic music.

Of course at this point the computer is merely humming to itself. Several techniques, some of them quite strange, have evolved to make the humming audible to mortals.

One such method that doesn't even require a connection to the computer is to use an AM portable radio tuned to a quiet spot on the broadcast band and held close to the computer. Viola! *[Sic]* The humming rings forth in loud, relatively clear notes. As a matter of fact, music programs using this form of output were very popular in the "early days" when most small system computers had only 256 bytes of memory and no IO peripherals except the front panel.

What is actually happening is that the internal logic circuitry with its fast rise time pulses is spewing harmonics that extend up into the broadcast band region of the radio spectrum. Since some logic gates will undoubtedly switch only once per loop iteration, the harmonics of the switching will be separated in frequency by the switching or loop frequency. Those high frequency harmonics that fall within the

passband of the radio are treated as a "carrier" and a bunch of equally spaced nearly equal amplitude sidebands. The radio's detector generates an output frequency equal to the common differences of all these sidebands, which is the loop frequency and its harmonics. The timbre of the resulting tones is altered somewhat by the choice of instructions in the loop, but basically has a flat audio spectrum like that of a narrow pulse waveform. Noise and distortion arise from other logic circuitry in the computer which switches erratically with respect to the timed loops. One practical difficulty with this method is there is no clearly identifiable way to get the computer to "shut up" for rests or space between identical notes.

The Hammer-Klavier

Other early methods used some kind of output peripheral to make sound. In a demonstration of an IBM 1401 over a decade ago this was literally true: the computer played a line printer! It seems that the hookup between a 1401 central processing unit and the 1403 printer was such that software had control of the printer hammer timing. Each time a hammer was fired a pulse of sound was emitted upon impact with the paper. Using a timed loop program with a print hammer fire instruction imbedded in the loop gave a raspy but accurately pitched buzz. *[It also tended to cause IBM customer engineers great trepidation . . .CH]* This same scheme should also be possible on some of the small, completely software controlled dot matrix printers that are now coming on the market.

A sane approach, however, is to connect a speaker to an output port bit through an amplifier. Instructions would then be placed inside the timed loops to toggle the bit and thus produce a clean, noise-free rectangular wave.

Timed Loop Example

Let's look at an example of a timed loop music playing program, not so much for its musical value (which is negligible), but for some insight into what is involved, and also to introduce some terms. The MOS Technology 6502 microprocessor will be used for these examples. These programs are designed to run on a KIM-1 system, and should run on most other 6502-based systems with very minor modifications. Motorola 6800 users should be able to easily convert the programs into 6800 machine language. 8080 users will benefit most because successful conversion indicates a thorough understanding of the concepts involved.

Figure 1: A basic tone generation subroutine. There are two nested loops in this routine: the first, or inner loop controls the frequency (or pitch) of the note to be generated, while the second, outer loop controls the duration of the note. A train of square waves is generated at the output port bit which is used to drive the circuit in figure 2 to produce an audible tone.

The heart of the program is the tone generation subroutine which will be named TONE. Ideally, such a routine would accept as input two arguments: one related to the pitch of the note and the other controlling the duration. With such a subroutine available, playing a piece of music amounts to simply fetching the arguments from a "song" table in memory and calling the routine for each note to be played.

As mentioned previously, we could have a separate, carefully timed loop for each different tone frequency needed. TONE would then call the proper one based on the pitch parameter. Indeed this approach is very accurate (to within 1 μs on the 6502) but a great deal of memory is consumed for the 30 or so notes typically required. It also lacks flexibility. (This will be discussed later.) A better approach is to embed a second, *waiting* loop to control the execution time of one pass through the outer loop, and thus the tone's frequency. Figure 1 is a flowchart illustrating this. When using this scheme, the frequency argument directly determines the number of times through the inner, waiting loop and the duration parameter directly determines the number of times through the outer, tone generation loop.

Now, how are the argument values determined to get the frequencies and durations desired? First the execution time of the nested loops must be determined. In the KIM-1 with a 1 MHz clock and a 6502 the tightest inner waiting loop that can be written is 5 μs, assuming that the inner loop count (frequency argument) is 256 or less and that it is held in a register. The total time spent in the loop is $[(5 \times M)-1]$ microseconds, where M is the frequency argument and the -1 is due to the shorter execution time of an unsuccessful branch. (The observant reader will note that the execution time of some 6502 instructions is altered if they cross a memory "page boundary"; thus, an assumption of no page crossing is made.) But there is still the time required for a pass through the outer loop to output a pulse and decrement the duration counter. This is termed "loop overhead." For an example, let's say that the loop overhead is 25 μs. As a result, the total outer loop time is

$[(5 \times M)-1+25]$, or $[(5 \times M)+24]$ microseconds which is the period of the audio waveform output. In order to determine the M required for a particular note, a table of note frequencies (see table 1) is consulted. Then the equation,

$$M= \frac{\left(\frac{10^6}{F} -24 \right)}{5}$$

where F is the desired frequency, is solved for the nearest integer value of M. Lower frequency notes are preferred so that the percentage error incurred due to rounding M is minimized. The duration argument is actually a count of the number of audio tone cycles which are to be generated for the note, and thus its value is dependent on the tone frequency as well as the duration. Its value can be determined from the relation N=DxF, where N is the duration argument, D is the duration in seconds, and F is the note frequency in Hertz.

As a complete example, let's assume that an eighth note G# an octave above middle C is to be played, and that the piece is in 4/4 time with a metronome marking of 80 beats per minute. Since an eighth note in this case is one half of a beat, the duration will be

$$\frac{0.5 \times 60}{80},$$

or 0.375 seconds. The note table shows that

Note	Frequency (Hz)
Middle C	261.62
C#	277.18
D	293.66
D#	311.13
E	329.63
F	349.23
F#	369.99
G	391.99
G#	415.30
A	440.00
A#	466.16
B	493.88

Table 1: Equally tempered scale note frequencies in Hertz. In order to determine frequencies of notes in the higher octaves, multiply by 2 for each octave above this one. For lower octaves, divide by 2 for each lower octave.

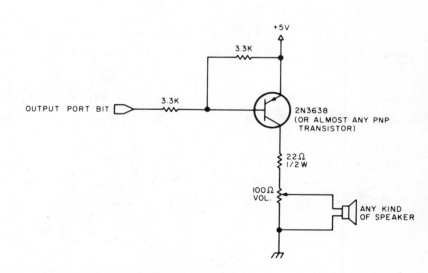

Figure 2: A speaker driver circuit designed to accept square or rectangular waves and produce audible tones through a loudspeaker. In this particular application the circuit is driven from an output port bit of a KIM-1 microcomputer, although the circuit can accept any TTL compatible output port bit. When the input to the circuit is a logical 0 level, the transistor turns on and drives the speaker. When the input is a logical 1, the transistor turns off and current to the speaker is interrupted.

Wave Duty Cycle	Harmonics									
	Fund	2	3	4	5	6	7	8	9	10
1/2	1.00	0	0.333	0	0.200	0	0.143	0	0.111	0
1/3	1.00	0.500	0	0.250	0.200	0	0.143	0.125	0	0.100
1/4	1.00	0.707	0.333	0	0.162	0.236	0.143	0	0.111	0.141
1/5	1.00	0.841	0.561	0.259	0	0.173	0.240	0.210	0.116	0
1/6	1.00	0.867	0.667	0.433	0.200	0	0.143	0.217	0.222	0.173

Table 2: Harmonic amplitudes of rectangular waves. Note that, unlike square waves, asymmetrical rectangular waves contain even numbered harmonics. This simple technique of varying the duty cycle of such waves can have an appreciable effect on the timbre of the resulting sound.

the frequency of G# an octave above middle C is 830.6 Hz, which yields a frequency argument of 236. The duration argument is 311. So if TONE is called with these parameters, a nice G# eighth note will be produced.

Now let's go a step further and look at a practical "music peripheral" and TONE subroutine. Figure 2 shows a circuit for driving a speaker from any kind of TTL compatible output port bit, including those found in the 6530 "combo chips" used in the KIM-1. When the output port bit is a logic 0 level, the transistor turns on and drives a current

determined by the volume control setting through the speaker. When the bit is a logic 1, the current is interrupted. Larger speakers or even a high fidelity speaker system will give a richer timbre to the lower pitched tones. The AUX input to a sound system may also be used instead of the transistor circuit. Using a patch cord, connect the shield to the common terminal of the power supply and the center conductor to the output port bit through a 10 K to 100 K isolation resistor.

Listing 1 shows an assembled listing of a practical timed loop tone generation subroutine for the 6502 microprocessor. Several refinements beyond the flowcharted example have been made to improve tone quality and flexibility. The inner waiting loop has been split into two loops. The first loop determines the length of time that the output rectangular waveform is to be a logic 1 and the second loop determines the 0 time. If both loops receive the same frequency argument (which they do as written) and the loop time of both loops is the same, then a symmetrical square wave output is produced. However, if one or more "do nothing" instructions is inserted into one of the two loops, the output waveform will become nonsymmetrical. The significance of this is that the rectangular waveform's duty cycle affects its harmonic spectrum, and thus its timbre. In particular, there is a large audible difference between a 50%-50% duty cycle (square wave) and a 25%-75% duty cycle. Table 2 lists the harmonic structure of some possible rectangular waves. As a result, some control over the timbre can be exercised if a separate TONE subroutine is written for each "voice" desired. Unfortunately, if this is done the frequency arguments will have to be recomputed since the outer loop time will then be altered.

Real music also possesses *dynamics*,

```
            ;       TONE SUBROUTINE FOR 6502
            ;       ENTER WITH FREQUENCY PARAMETER IN ACCUMULATOR
            ;       DURATION PARAMETER STORED AT LOCATION DUR (LOW PART) AND
            ;       DUR+1 (HIGH PART) WHICH IS ASSUMED TO BE IN PAGE ZERO
            ;       ROUTINE USES A, X, AND DESTROYS DUR
            ;       LOOP TIME = 10*(FREQ PARAMETER)+44 MICROSECONDS

1700        MPORT   =       X'1700          ; ADDRESS OF OUTPUT PORT WITH SPEAKER
00E0        DUR     =       X'E0            ; ARBITRARY PAGE 0 ADDRESS OF DURATION PARM

0100 A2FF   TONE:   LDX     #X'FF           ; SEND ALL 1'S TO THE OUTPUT PORT
0102 8E0017         STX     MPORT
0105 AA             TAX                     ; TRANSFER FREQ PARAMETER TO INDEX X
0106 CA     WHIGH:  DEX                     ; WAIT LOOP FOR WAVEFORM HIGH TIME
0107 D0FD           BNE     WHIGH           ; TIME IN THIS LOOP = 5*FREQ PARAMETER
0109 F000           BEQ     .+2             ; WAIT 15 STATES TO MATCH TIME USED TO
010B F000           BEQ     .+2             ; DECREMENT AND CHECK DURATION COUNT AFTER
010D F000           BEQ     .+2             ; WAVEFORM LOW TIME
010F F000           BEQ     .+2
0111 F000           BEQ     .+2
0113 A200           LDX     #0              ; SEND ALL 0'S TO THE OUTPUT PORT
0115 8E0017         STX     MPORT
0118 AA             TAX                     ; TRANSFER FREQ PARAMETER TO INDEX X
0119 CA     WLOW:   DEX                     ; WAIT LOOP FOR WAVEFORM LOW TIME
011A D0FD           BNE     WLOW            ; TIME IN THIS LOOP = 5*FREQ PARAMETER
011C C6E0           DEC     DUR             ; DECREMENT LOW PART OF DURATION COUNT
011E D005           BNE     TIMWAS          ; BRANCH IF NOT RUN OUT
0120 C6E1           DEC     DUR+1           ; DECREMENT HIGH PART OF DURATION COUNT
0122 D0DC           BNE     TONE            ; GO DO ANOTHER CYCLE OF THE TONE IF NOT 0
0124 60             RTS                     ; RETURN WHEN DURATION COUNT RUNS OUT
0125 F000   TIMWAS: BEQ     .+2             ; WASTE 7 CYCLES TO EQUAL TIME THAT WOULD
0127 F000           BEQ     .+2             ; HAVE BEEN SPENT IF HIGH PART OF DUR WAS
0129 D0D5           BNE     TONE            ; DECREMENTED AND GO DO ANOTHER CYCLE
```

Listing 1: An assembled listing of a practical timed loop tone generation subroutine for the 6502 microprocessor. This routine is an elaboration of the flowchart shown in figure 1 which allows the user to generate nonsymmetrical rectangular waves. Experimenting with the wave's duty cycle affects the harmonic content of the resulting tone and creates many interesting aural effects.

which are the changes in overall volume during a performance. Furthermore, the *amplitude envelope* of a tone is an important contributor to its overall subjective timbre. The latter term refers to rapid changes in volume during a single note. This is the case with a piano note, which builds up rapidly at the beginning and slowly trails off thereafter. Of course the setup described thus far has no control over either of these parameters: the volume level is constant, and the envelope of each note is rectangular with sudden onset and termination.

By graduating to a more sophisticated music peripheral, control of dynamics and amplitude envelopes can be achieved with a timed loop music program. The secret is to use a *digital to analog* converter connected to all eight bits of the output port. A digital to analog converter (DAC) does just what its name implies: it accepts a binary number from the output port as input and generates a corresponding DC voltage as its output. The circuit in figure 3, which can be used with any TTL compatible output port, gives an output voltage

$$V = \left(\frac{1}{255}\right) \times 5$$

where I is the binary number input between 0 and 255. When working with this kind of DAC, it is convenient to regard the binary number, I, as a fraction between 0 and 1 rather than an integer. The benefit of this will become apparent later when calculations will be performed to arrive at the value of I. The output of the DAC must be used with a sound system or the amplifier circuit in figure 8, not the simple transistor speaker driver circuit in figure 2.

As written, the TONE subroutine (see listing 1) alternately sends 0 and 255 to the output port with the music peripheral. With a DAC connected to that port, voltages of 0 and 5 V will be produced for the low and high portions of the rectangular wave. If instead 0 and 127 were output, the DAC would produce only 0 and 2.5 V giving a rectangular wave with about half the amplitude. This in turn produces a less loud tone, and so control over dynamics is possible by altering the byte stored at hexadecimal 101.

Arbitrary amplitude envelopes are also made possible by continuously exercising control over the amplitude during a note. Simple envelope shapes such as a linear attack and decay can be computed in line while the note is being sounded. A more general method is to build a table in memory describing the shape. Such a table can be quickly referenced during note playing. Great care must be taken, however,

to insure that loop timing is kept stable when the additional instructions necessary to implement amplitude envelopes are added.

More Complex Techniques

Even if all of the improvements mentioned above were fully implemented, the elementary timed loop approach falls far

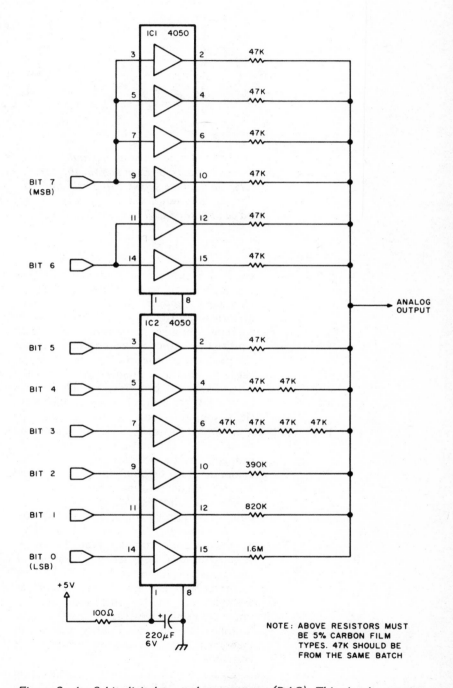

Figure 3: An 8 bit digital to analog converter (DAC). This circuit accepts an 8 bit binary number from the output port and generates a corresponding DC voltage as its output. The output voltage from this circuit is equal to ((1/255) (5)) V, where 1 is the decimal equivalent of the 8 bit input which can take on any value from 0 to 225.

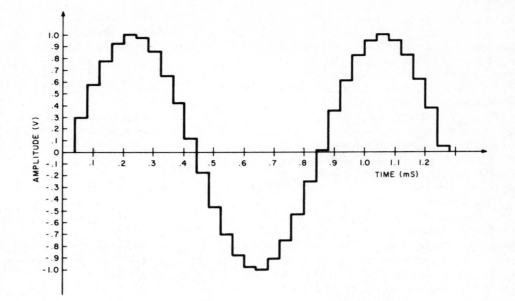

Figure 4: A sine wave as it would appear at the output from the digital to analog converter shown in figure 3. Each step in the approximation of this wave is called a sample. This particular illustration shows a 1.2 kHz sine wave sampled at a rate of 25,000 samples per second. The resulting waveform is only a very rough approximation of the original, but low pass filtering can improve accuracy (see figure 5 and text).

short of significant musical potential. The primary limitations are a narrow range of tone colors and restriction to monotonic performance. The latter difficulty may be alleviated through the use of a multitrack tape recorder to combine separate parts, but this requires an investment in noncomputer hardware and is certainly not automatic. Also, unpitched percussive sounds such as drum beats are generally not possible. Musicians, too, will probably notice a host of other limitations such as lack of vibrato and other subtle variations. All of these shortcomings may be overcome by allowing the computer to compute the entire sound waveform in detail at its own speed.

The one fundamental concept that makes direct waveform computation possible is the *sampling theorem*. Any waveform, no matter how simple or complex, can be reconstructed from a rapid series of discrete voltage values by means of a digital to analog converter such as the one used earlier. As an example, let's try to generate an accurate sine wave using a DAC. If this can be done, it follows from the Fourier (harmonic) theorem that any other waveform may also be synthesized.

Figure 4 shows a sine wave as it would appear at the DAC output. Each step on the approximation to the sine wave is termed a *sample*, and the frequency with which these samples emerge from the DAC is the *sample rate*. An attempt is being made in the

example to generate a 1.2 kHz sine wave at a sample rate of 25 kHz, or one sample every 40 μs. Obviously this is a very poor sine wave, a fact that can be easily demonstrated with a distortion analyzer.

Before giving up, let's look at the frequency spectrum of this staircase-like wave on a spectrum analyzer. The spectral plot in figure 5 shows a strong frequency component at 1.2 kHz which is the sine wave we are trying to synthesize. Also present are the distortion component frequencies due to the sampling process. Since all of the distortion components are much higher in frequency than the desired signal, they may be easily removed with a sharp low pass filter. After filtering, the distortion analyzer will confirm that a smooth, pure sine wave is all that remains.

What will happen if the sine wave frequency is increased but the sampling frequency remains constant? With even fewer samples on each sine wave cycle the waveform from the DAC will appear even more distorted. The lowest frequency distortion product is the one of concern since it is the most difficult to filter out. Its frequency is FD=(FS-f) Hertz, where FD is the lowest distortion component frequency, FS is the sampling frequency, and f is the sine wave signal frequency. Thus as f increases, FD decreases until they merge at f=FS/2. This frequency is termed the *Nyquist frequency* and is the highest theoretical frequency that

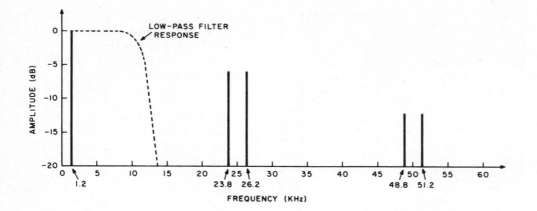

Figure 5: The spectral plot of the staircase-like sine wave approximation shown in figure 4. This frequency versus amplitude graph indicates a strong frequency component at 1.2 kHz, the frequency of the sine wave. Normally, this would be the only frequency component to appear on a plot like this, but the presence of steeply rising steps in this waveform approximation introduces distortion components at higher frequencies, as shown.

may be synthesized. Any attempt to synthesize a higher frequency will result in the desired signal being filtered out and the distortion frequency emerging instead. This situation is termed *aliasing* because the desired signal frequency has been replaced by a distortion component alias frequency. Operating close to the Nyquist frequency requires a very sharp filter to separate the signal from the distortion. With practical filters, signal frequencies up to 1/4 to 1/3 of the sampling frequency are realizable. Since any sound, whether it is a pitched tone or unpitched sound, is actually a combination of sine waves, it follows that any possible sound may be produced by a DAC. The only limitation is the upper frequency response, which may be made as high as desired by increasing the sample rate. The low frequency response has no limit, and extends down to DC.

There is another form of distortion in DAC generated sounds which cannot be filtered out, since it is spread throughout the frequency spectrum. *Quantization noise* is due to the fact that a DAC cannot generate voltages that are exact samples on the desired waveform. An 8 bit converter, for example, has only 256 possible output voltage values. When a particular voltage is needed, the nearest available value will have to be used. The theoretical signal to noise ratio when using a perfect DAC is related to the number of bits by the equation $S/N = (6 \times M) + 4$ decibels where M is the number of bits. A practical DAC may be as much as 6 db worse, but a cheap 8 bit unit can yield nearly 50 db, which is as good as many tape recorders. When using 12 bits or more, the DAC will outperform even the best profes-

sional recorders. Thus it is apparent that computed waveforms can, in theory, be used to generate very high quality music; so high, in fact, that conventional audio equipment is hard pressed to reproduce it.

Now that we have the tools, let's see how the limitations of computer music mentioned earlier can be overcome. For tones of definite pitch, the timbre is determined by the waveshape and the amplitude envelope. Concentrating on the waveshape, it should be apparent that a waveform table in memory repeatedly dumped into the DAC will produce an equivalent sound waveform. Each table entry becomes a sample, and the entire table represents one cycle of the waveform. The frequency of the resulting tone will be FS/N where FS is the sampling frequency (rate at which table entries are sent to the DAC) and N is the number of entries in the table. To get other frequencies, either the sample rate or the number of table entries must be changed.

There are a number of reasons why the sample rate should remain constant, so the answer is to change the effective table length. If the table dump routine were modified to skip every other entry, the result would be an effective halving of table size and thus doubling of the tone frequency. If the table is fairly long, such as 256 entries, a number of frequencies are possible by skipping an integer number of entries.

To get musically accurate frequencies, it is necessary to be able to skip a fractional number of table entries. At this point the concept of a *table increment* is helpful in dealing with programming such an operation. First, the table is visualized as a

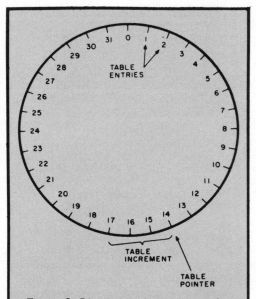

Figure 6: Diagrammatic representation of the circular table used for storing the waveform "template." The technique illustrated here is that of storing a large number of samples of one cycle of a musical waveform in memory as a table which wraps around itself in circular fashion. A pointer is used to point to the next sample to be extracted. In order to create a waveform with a given frequency, the program is designed to skip a fractional number of table entries to get the next sample value. This fractional number is called the table increment value. The process is continued around the table for one revolution to create a complete waveform. The cycle around the table is repeated until the duration counter decrements to zero.

circle with the first entry conceptually following the last as in figure 6. A pointer locates a point along the circular table which represents the sample last sent to the DAC. To find what should be sent to the DAC next, the table pointer is moved clockwise a distance equal to the table increment. The frequency of the resulting tone is now

$$\frac{FS \times I}{N}$$

where FS and N are as before and I is the increment.

With integer increments, the pointer always points squarely to an entry. With mixed number increments, the pointer also will take on a fractional part. The sensible thing to do is to interpolate between the table entries on either side of the pointer

to arrive at an accurate value to give to the DAC. This is indeed necessary to assure high quality; but simply choosing the nearest entry may be acceptable in some cases, particularly if the table is very large.

There is one elusive pitfall in this technique. The table may contain the tabulation of any waveform desired, subject to one limitation: a nonzero harmonic component of the waveform must not exceed the Nyquist frequency, FS/2. This can easily happen with the larger table increments (higher frequency tones), the result being aliasing of the upper harmonics. Theoretically this is a severe limitation. Often a small amount of aliasing is not objectionable, but a large amount sounds like gross intermodulation distortion. High sample rates reduce the possibility or magnitude of aliasing, but of course require more computation. For the moment, we will ignore this problem and restrict ourselves to relatively smooth waveforms without a lot of high frequency harmonics.

Now that the DAC is used for generating the actual waveshape, how is amplitude control accomplished? If an amplitude parameter is defined that ranges between 0 and 1.0 (corresponding to amplitudes between zero and maximum), the desired result is obtained by simply multiplying each sample from the table by this amplitude parameter and sending the product to the DAC. Things are nice and consistent if the table entries are also considered as fractions between -1 and +1 because then the product has a range between -1 and +1 which is directly compatible with the DAC. (Note that the DAC in figure 3 is unipolar. It can be considered bipolar if +2.5 V output is the zero reference and the sign bit is inverted.)

The last major hurdle is the generation of simultaneous tones. Obviously, two simultaneous tones may be generated by going through two tables, outputting to two separate DACs, and mixing the results with an audio mixer. This is relatively simple to do if the sample rates of the two tones are the same. Actually, all the audio mixer does is to *add* the two input voltages together to produce its output, but a very important realization is that the addition can also be done in the computer before the output conversion by the DAC! The two samples are simply added together with an ADD instruction, the sum is divided by two (to constrain it to the range of -1 to +1), and the result sent to a single DAC. This holds true for any number of simultaneous tones! The only requirement is that the composite samples not overflow the -1 to +1 range that the DAC can accept. Rather than dividing the sum, it is best to adjust the amplitude factors of the individual "voices" to prevent overflow. So now we have the tools necessary to generate an ensemble of tones, each one possibly having its own waveform, amplitude envelope, and loudness relative to the others. Indeed, this is all that is necessary to simulate a typical organ.

Up to this point the timbre (waveform) of a tone has been determined by the contents of a fixed waveform table. Truly interesting musical notes change their timbre during the duration of the note. A reasonable alternative to switching between similar tables for implementing this is to build the tone from harmonic components. Each harmonic component of the tone is simply a sine wave with an amplitude dependent on the waveform of the resulting tone. Giving a different amplitude envelope to each harmonic is equivalent to smoothly changing the timbre during the note. The aliasing problem mentioned earlier can also be solved by simply omitting any harmonics that become too high in frequency.

Dynamic timbre variation can also be accomplished by a *digital filter* which does the same thing to a sampled waveform that a real inductance-capacitance filter does to a normal waveform. A digital filter is simply a subroutine which accepts a sample value as an argument and gives back a sample value which represents the filtered output. The equations used in the subroutine determine the filter type, and other arguments determine the cutoff frequency, Q, etc. This is a fascinating subject which deserves its own article.

What about other, unpitched sounds? They too can be handled with a few simple techniques. Most sounds in this category are based in part on random noise. In sampled form, random white noise with a uniform frequency spectrum is simply a stream of random numbers. For example, a fairly realistic snare drum sound may be generated by simply giving the proper amplitude envelope to pure white noise. Other types of drum sounds may be generated by using a digital filter to shape the frequency spectrum of the noise. A resonant type of digital filter would be used for tom-toms and similar semipitched drums, for example. A high pass filter is useful for simulating brush and cymbal sounds. An infinite number of variations are possible. This is one area where direct computation of sound waveforms really shines.

The sampling theorem works both ways also. Any waveform may be converted into digital samples with an analog to digital converter (ADC) with no loss of information. The only requirement is that the signal being sampled have no frequency com-

Listing 2: A program which, in conjunction with tables 3, 4 and 5, generates four simultaneous musical voices, each with a different waveform and volume level. The program is designed for use with the 6502 processor coupled to an 8 bit unsigned digital to analog converter (DAC) like the one shown in figure 3.

```
            ;      THIS PROGRAM PLAYS MUSIC IN 4-PART HARMONY ON THE KIM-1 OR
            ;      OTHER 6502 BASED SYSTEM USING AN 8-BIT UNSIGNED
            ;      DIGITAL-TO-ANALOG CONVERTER CONNECTED TO AN OUTPUT PORT.  TUNED
            ;      FOR SYSTEMS WITH A 1 MHZ CRYSTAL CLOCK.  DOES NOT USE THE ROR
            ;      INSTRUCTION.
            ;      SONG TABLE IS AT "SONG"
            ;      ENTRY POINT IS AT "MUSIC"

0000                   .=    0             ; ORG AT PAGE 0 LOCATION 0

1700        DAC        =     X'1700        ; OUTPUT PORT ADDRESS WITH DAC
1701        DACDIR     =     X'1701        ; DATA DRIECTION REGISTER FOR DAC PORT
1780        AUXRAM     =     X'1780        ; ADDRESS OF EXTRA 128 BYTES OF RAM IN 6530
1C22        KIMMON     =     X'1C22        ; ENTRY POINT TO KIM KEYBOARD MONITOR

0000 00     V1PT:      .BYTE 0             ; VOICE 1 WAVE POINTER, FRACTIONAL PART
0001 0000              .WORD WAV1TB        ; INTEGER PART AND WAVE TABLE BASE
0003 00     V2PT:      .BYTE 0             ; VOICE 2
0004 0000              .WORD WAV2TB
0006 00     V3PT:      .BYTE 0             ; VOICE 3
0007 0000              .WORD WAV3TB
0009 00     V4PT:      .BYTE 0             ; VOICE 4
000A 0000              .WORD WAV4TB

000C 0000   V1IN:      .WORD 0             ; VOICE 1 INCREMENT (FREQUENCY PARAMETER)
000E 0000   V2IN:      .WORD 0             ; VOICE 2
0010 0000   V3IN:      .WORD 0             ; VOICE 3
0012 0000   V4IN:      .WORD 0             ; VOICE 4

0014 00     DUR:       .BYTE 0             ; DURATION COUNTER
0015 0000   NOTES:     .WORD 0             ; NOTES POINTER
0017 0002   SONGA:     .WORD SONG          ; ADDRESS OF SONG
0019 0000   INCPT:     .WORD 0             ; POINTER FOR LOADING UP V1INT - V4NT
001B 0C00   INCA:      .WORD V1IN          ; INITIAL VALUE OF INCPT
001D 5200   TEMPO:     .WORD 82            ; TEMPO CONTROL VALUE, TYPICAL VALUE FOR
                                           ; 3:4 TIME, 100 BEATS PER MINUTE, DUR=64
                                           ; DESIGNATES A QUARTER NOTE
0100                   .=    X'100         ; START PROGRAM CODE AT LOCATION 0100

            ;      MAIN MUSIC PLAYING PROGRAM

0100 A9FF   MUSIC:     LDA   #X'FF         ; SET PERIPHERAL A DATA DIRECTION
0102 8D0117            STA   DACDIR        ; REGISTER TO OUTPUT
0105 D8                CLD                 ; INSURE BINARY ARITHMETIC
0106 A517              LDA   SONGA         ; INITIALIZE NOTES POINTER
0108 8515              STA   NOTES         ; TO BEGINNING OF SONG
010A A518              LDA   SONGA+1
010C 8516              STA   NOTES+1
010E A000   MUSIC1:    LDY   #0            ; SET UP TO TRANSLATE 4 NOTE ID NUMBERS
0110 A51B              LDA   INCA          ; INTO FREQUENCY DETERMINING WAVEFORM TABLE
0112 8519              STA   INCPT         ; INCREMENTS AND STORE IN V1IN - V4IN
0114 B115              LDA   (NOTES),Y     ; GET DURATION FIRST
0116 F03C              BEQ   ENDSNG        ; BRANCH IF END OF SONG
0118 C901              CMP   #1            ; TEST IF END OF SONG TABLE SEGMENT
011A F029              BEQ   NXTSEG        ; BRANCH IF SO
011C 8514              STA   DUR           ; OTHERWOSE SAVE DURATION IN DUR
011E E615   MUSIC2:    INC   NOTES         ; DOUBLE INCREMENT NOTES TO POINT TO THE
0120 D002              BNE   MUSIC3        ; NOTE ID OF THE FIRST VOICE
0122 E616              INC   NOTES+1
0124 B115   MUSIC3:    LDA   (NOTES),Y     ; GET A NOTE ID NUMBER
0126 AA                TAX                 ; INTO INDEX X
0127 B520              LDA   FRQTAB+1,X    ; GET LOW BYTE OF CORRESPONDING FREQUENCY
0129 9119              STA   (INCPT),Y     ; STORE INTO LOW BYTE OF VOICE INCREMENT
012B E619              INC   INCPT         ; INDEX TO HIGH BYTE
012D B51F              LDA   FRQTAB,X      ; GET HIGH BYTE OF FREQUENCY
012F 9119              STA   (INCPT),Y     ; STORE INTO HIGH BYTE OF VOICE INCREMENT
0131 E615              INC   NOTES         ; DOUBLE INCREMENT NOTES TO POINT TO THE
0133 D002              BNE   MUSIC4        ; NOTE ID OF THE NEXT VOICE
0135 E616              INC   NOTES+1
0137 E619   MUSIC4:    INC   INCPT         ; INDEX TO NEXT VOICE INCREMENT
0139 A519              LDA   INCPT         ; TEST IF 4 VOICE INCREMENTS DONE
013B C914              CMP   #V4IN+2
013D D0E5              BNE   MUSIC3        ; LOOP IF NOT
013F 205701            JSR   PLAY          ; PLAY THIS GROUP OF NOTES
0142 4C0E01            JMP   MUSIC1        ; GO LOAD UP NEXT SET OF NOTES

0145 C8     NXTSEG:    INY                 ; END OF SEGMENT, NEXT TWO BYTES POINT TO
0146 B115              LDA   (NOTES),Y     ; BEGINNING OF THE NEXT SEGMENT
0148 48                PHA
0149 C8                INY                 ; GET BOTH SEGMENT ADDRESS BYTES
014A B115              LDA   (NOTES),Y
014C 8516              STA   NOTES+1       ; THEN STORE IN NOTES POINTER
014E 68                PLA
014F 8515              STA   NOTES
0151 4C0E01            JMP   MUSIC1        ; GO START INTERPRETING NEW SEGMENT

0154 4C221C  ENDSNG:   JMP   KIMMON        ; END OF SONG, RETURN TO MONITOR
            ;      4 VOICE PLAY SUBROUTINE
```

Listing 2, continued:

```
0157 A000      PLAY:   LDY   #0            ; SET Y TO ZERO FOR STRAIGHT INDIRECT
0159 A61D              LDX   TEMPO         ; SET X TO TEMPO COUNT
                                           ; COMPUTE AND OUTPUT A COMPOSITE SAMPLE

015B 18        PLAY1:  CLC                 ; CLEAR CARRY
015C B101              LDA   (V1PT+1),Y    ; ADD UP 4 VOICE SAMPLES
015E 7104              ADC   (V2PT+1),Y    ; USING INDIRECT ADDRESSING THROUGH VOICE
0160 7107              ADC   (V3PT+1),Y    ; POINTERS INTO WAVEFORM TABLES
0162 710A              ADC   (V4PT+1),Y    ; STRAIGHT INDIRECT WHEN Y INDEX = 0
0164 8D0017            STA   X'1700        ; SEND SUM TO DIGITAL-TO-ANALOG CONVERTER
0167 A500              LDA   V1PT          ; ADD INCREMENTS TO POINTERS FOR
0169 650C              ADC   V1IN          ; THE 4 VOICES
016B 8500              STA   V1PT          ; FIRST FRACTIONAL PART
016D A501              LDA   V1PT+1
016F 650D              ADC   V1IN+1
0171 8501              STA   V1PT+1        ; THEN INTEGER PART
0173 A503              LDA   V2PT          ; VOICE 2
0175 650E              ADC   V2IN
0177 8503              STA   V2PT
0179 A504              LDA   V2PT+1
017B 650F              ADC   V2IN+1
017D 8504              STA   V2PT+1
017F A506              LDA   V3PT          ; VOICE 3
0181 6510              ADC   V3IN
0183 8506              STA   V3PT
0185 A507              LDA   V3PT+1
0187 6511              ADC   V3IN+1
0189 8507              STA   V3PT+1
018B A509              LDA   V4PT          ; VOICE 4
018D 6512              ADC   V4IN
018F 8509              STA   V4PT
0191 A50A              LDA   V4PT+1
0193 6513              ADC   V4IN+1
0195 850A              STA   V4PT+1
0197 CA                DEX                 ; DECREMENT & CHECK TEMPO COUNT
0198 D008              BNE   TIMWAS        ; BRANCH TO TIME WASTE IF NOT RUN OUT
019A C614              DEC   DUR           ; DECREMENT & CHECK DURATION COUNTER
019C F00C              BEQ   ENDNOT        ; JUMP OUT IF END OF NOTE
019E A61D              LDX   TEMPO         ; RESTORE TEMPO COUNT
01A0 D0B9              BNE   PLAY1         ; CONTINUE PLAYING
01A2 D000      TIMWAS: BNE   .+2           ; 3   WASTE 12 STATES
01A4 D000              BNE   .+2           ; 3
01A6 D000              BNE   .+2           ; 3
01A8 D0B1              BNE   PLAY1         ; 3   CONTINUE PLAYING
01AA 60        ENDNOT: RTS                 ; RETURN
                                           ; TOTAL LOOP TIME = 114 STATES = 8770 HZ

01AB           P1END   =                   ; DEFINE BEGINNING ADDRESS FOR THIRD PART
                                           ; OF SONG TABLE
```

ponents higher than half of the sampling frequency. This may be accomplished by passing the signal to be digitized through a sharp low pass filter prior to presenting it to the ADC. Once sound is in digitized form, literally anything may be done to it. A simple (in concept) application is intricate editing of the sound with a graphic display, light pen and large capacity disk. The sound may be analyzed into harmonic components and the result or a transformation of it applied to a synthesized sound. Again, this is an area that deserves its own article.

Sampled Waveform Example

It should be obvious by now that while these sampled waveform techniques are completely general and capable of high quality, there can be a great deal of computation required. Even the most powerful computers in existence would be hard pressed to compute samples for a significant piece of music with many voices and all subtleties implemented at a rate fast enough

for direct output to a DAC and speaker. Typically the samples are computed at whatever rate the program runs and are saved on a mass storage device. After the piece has been "computed," a playback program retrieves the samples and sends them to the DAC at a uniform high rate.

Most microprocessors are fast enough to do a limited amount of sampled waveform computation in real time. The 6502 is one of the best 8 bit machines in this capacity due to its indexed and indirect addressing modes and its overall high speed. The example program shown in listing 2 has the inherent capability to generate four simultaneous voices, each with a different waveform and volume level. In order to make the whole thing fit in a basic KIM-1, however, only one waveform table is actually used.

This program could probably be considered as a variation of the timed loop technique, since the sample rate is determined by the execution time of a particular loop. The major differences are that all of the instructions in the loop perform an essential function and that the loop time is constant regardless of the notes being played. Using the program as shown on a full speed (1.0 MHz) 6502 gives a sample rate of 8.77 kHz, which results in a useful upper frequency limit of 3 kHz. The low pass filter in figure 7 coupled with the DAC in figure 3 and audio system or amplifier in figure 8 are all the specialized hardware necessary to run the program with full 4 part harmony.

The program consists of two major routines: MUSIC and PLAY. MUSIC steps through the list of notes in the song table and sets up DUR and V1IN thru V4IN for the PLAY routine. PLAY simultaneously plays the four notes specified by V1IN thru V4IN for the time period specified by DUR. Another variable, TEMPO, in page zero controls the overall tempo of the music independently of the durations specified in the song table. The waveform tables for the four voices are located at WAV1TB thru WAV4TB and require 256 bytes (one memory page) each. The actual waveform samples stored in the table have already been scaled so that when four of them are added up there is no possibility of overflow.

The song table has an entry for each musical "event" in the piece. An entry requires five bytes, the first of which is a duration parameter. By suitable choice of the TEMPO parameter in page 0, "round" (in the binary sense) numbers may be used for duration parameters of common note durations. A duration parameter of 0 signals the end of the song, in which case the program returns to the monitor. A duration parameter of 1 is used to specify a break in

Figure 7: A sharp low pass filter with 3 kHz cutoff. This circuit is used to filter out the high frequency distortion illustrated in figure 5.

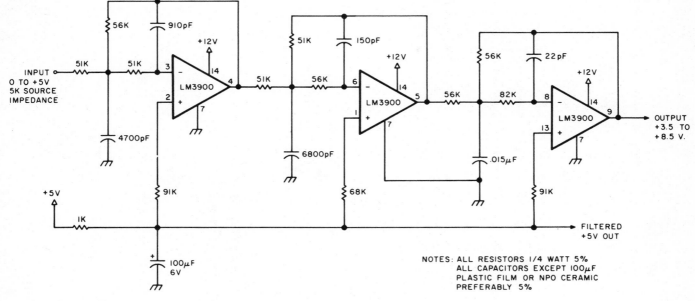

the sequential flow of the song table. In this case the next two bytes point to the continuation of the table elsewhere in memory. This feature was necessary to deal with the fragmented memory of the KIM-1, but has other uses as well. All other possible duration values are taken literally and are followed by four bytes which identify the notes to be played by each voice. Each note ID points to a location in the note frequency table which in turn contains a 2 byte frequency parameter for that note which is placed in V1IN thru V4IN.

The PLAY routine is optimized for speed, because its loop time determines the sample rate. Essentially, the routine maintains four pointers (V1PT thru V4PT) to the four waveform tables. Each pointer consists of three bytes in order of increasing significance. The first byte is the "fractional part" of the pointer, and the second byte is the integer part which is also the lower half of an address in the waveform table. The third byte is the upper address which normally remains constant. Waveform table lookup is considerably simplified by using the indirect addressing mode of the 6502 with these pointers. Note that the fractional part of the pointer is ignored when the table lookup takes place, since interpolation is much too slow for a real time routine.

During each sample, waveform table entries for each voice are fetched, added up, and sent to the digital to analog converter output port. Then the increment (VxIN) is added (double precision) to each pointer (VxPT). Wraparound from the end of a waveform table to the beginning is automatically taken care of due to the fact that

```
;          NOTE FREQUENCY TABLE FOR 8.772 KHZ SAMPLE RATE
;          RANGE FROM C2 (65.41 HZ) TO C6 (1046.5 HZ)
;                         ID NOTE  FREQ.   INCR.
001F 0000   FRQTAB:  .BYTE 0,0    ;  0  SILENCE
0021 01E9            .BYTE 1,233  ;  2  C2   65.405  1.9089
0023 0206            .BYTE 2,6    ;  4  C2#  69.295  2.0224
0025 0225            .BYTE 2,37   ;  6  D2   73.415  2.1427
0027 0245            .BYTE 2,69   ;  8  D2#  77.783  2.2701
0029 0268            .BYTE 2,104  ; 10  E2   82.408  2.4051
002B 028C            .BYTE 2,140  ; 12  F2   87.308  2.5481
002D 02B3            .BYTE 2,179  ; 14  F2#  92.498  2.6996
002F 02DC            .BYTE 2,220  ; 16  G2   97.998  2.8601
0031 0308            .BYTE 3,8    ; 18  G2#  103.83  3.0302
0033 0336            .BYTE 3,54   ; 20  A2   110.00  3.2104
0035 0367            .BYTE 3,103  ; 22  A2#  116.54  3.4013
0037 039A            .BYTE 3,154  ; 24  B2   123.47  3.6035
0039 03D1            .BYTE 3,209  ; 26  C3   130.81  3.8178
003B 040B            .BYTE 4,11   ; 28  C3#  138.59  4.0448
003D 0449            .BYTE 4,73   ; 30  D3   146.83  4.2854
003F 048A            .BYTE 4,138  ; 32  D3#  155.57  4.5402
0041 04CF            .BYTE 4,207  ; 34  E3   164.82  4.8102
0043 0519            .BYTE 5,25   ; 36  F3   174.62  5.0962
0045 0566            .BYTE 5,102  ; 38  F3#  185.00  5.3992
0047 05B8            .BYTE 5,184  ; 40  G3   196.00  5.7203
0049 060F            .BYTE 6,15   ; 42  G3#  207.65  6.0604
004B 066C            .BYTE 6,108  ; 44  A3   220.00  6.4208
004D 06CD            .BYTE 6,205  ; 46  A3#  233.08  6.8026
004F 0735            .BYTE 7,53   ; 48  B3   246.94  7.2071
0051 07A3            .BYTE 7,163  ; 50  C4   261.62  7.6356
0053 0817            .BYTE 8,23   ; 52  C4#  277.18  8.0897
0055 0892            .BYTE 8,146  ; 54  D4   293.66  8.5707
0057 0915            .BYTE 9,21   ; 56  D4#  311.13  9.0804
0059 099F            .BYTE 9,159  ; 58  E4   329.63  9.6203
005B 0A31            .BYTE 10,49  ; 60  F4   349.23  10.1924
005D 0ACC            .BYTE 10,204 ; 62  F4#  369.99  10.7984
005F 0B71            .BYTE 11,113 ; 64  G4   391.99  11.4405
0061 0C1F            .BYTE 12,31  ; 66  G4#  415.30  12.1208
0063 0CD7            .BYTE 12,215 ; 68  A4   440.00  12.8416
0065 0D9B            .BYTE 13,155 ; 70  A4#  466.16  13.6052
0067 0E6A            .BYTE 14,106 ; 72  B4   493.88  14.4142
0069 0F45            .BYTE 15,69  ; 74  C5   523.24  15.2713
006B 102E            .BYTE 16,46  ; 76  C5#  554.36  16.1794
006D 1124            .BYTE 17,36  ; 78  D5   587.32  17.1414
006F 1229            .BYTE 18,41  ; 80  D5#  622.26  18.1607
0071 133E            .BYTE 19,62  ; 82  E5   659.26  19.2406
0073 1462            .BYTE 20,98  ; 84  F5   698.46  20.3847
0075 1599            .BYTE 21,153 ; 86  F5#  739.98  21.5969
0077 16E2            .BYTE 22,226 ; 88  G5   783.98  22.8811
0079 183E            .BYTE 24,62  ; 90  G5#  830.60  24.2417
007B 19AF            .BYTE 25,175 ; 92  A5   880.00  25.6831
007D 1B36            .BYTE 27,54  ; 94  A5#  932.32  27.2103
007F 1CD4            .BYTE 28,212 ; 96  B5   987.76  28.8283
0081 1E8B            .BYTE 30,139 ; 98  C6   1046.5  30.5426
0083       POEND  =             ; DEFINE BEGINNING ADDRESS FOR SECOND PART
                                ; OF SONG TABLE
```

Table 3: Note frequency table used in conjunction with listing 2. This table is for a sample rate of 8.772 kHz. The range of the notes used is from 65.41 Hz (for C2) to 1046.5 Hz (for C6).

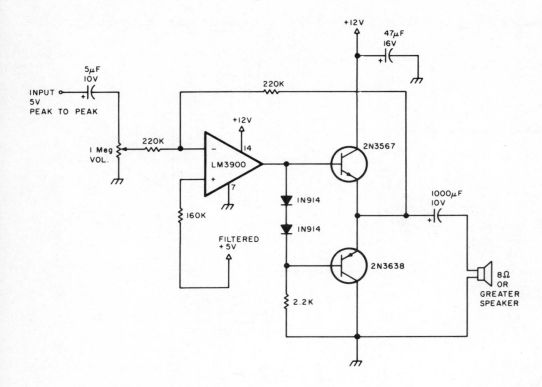

Figure 8. An inexpensive, wide band low power audio amplifier. This circuit, when coupled with the circuits in figures 3 and 7, is all the experimenter needs to create music with his or her microprocessor.

the table occupies a full memory page. Finally, the tempo counter is decremented and checked. If the tempo counter is zero, it is restored and the duration counter is decremented and checked. If it is also zero the note is finished and PLAY returns. The net result is that TxD samples are computed and sent out for the event, where T is the tempo parameter and D is the duration parameter. Note that, unlike the earlier timed loop example, there is no interaction between the duration parameter and the note frequencies being played.

How does it sound? With the waveform table shown and a reasonably good speaker system, the result sounds very much like an electronic organ, such as a Hammond. There is a noticeable background noise level due to compromises such as prescaled waveforms and lack of interpolation in the tables, but it is not objectionable. The pitches are very accurate, but there is some beating on chords due to compromises inherent in the standard equally tempered musical scale. Also there are noticeable clicks between notes due to the time taken by the MUSIC routine to set up the next set of notes. All in all the program makes a good and certainly inexpensive basis for the "family music application" mentioned earlier.

Synthesizer Control Techniques

So far we have discussed techniques in which the computer itself generates the

```
           ;          SONG TABLE
           ;          EACH MUSICAL EVENT CONSISTS OF 5 BYTES
           ;          THE FIRST IS THE DURATION OF THE EVENT IN UNITS ACCORDING TO
           ;          THE VALUE OF "TEMPO", ZERO DENOTES THE END OF THE SONG.
           ;          THE NEXT 4 BYTES CONTAIN THE NOTE ID OF THE 4 VOICES, 1 THROUGH
           ;          4.  0 INDICATES SILENCE FOR THE VOICE.

0200                  .=     X'200       ; START SONG AT 0200

           ;          SONG TABLE FOR THE STAR SPANGLED BANNER BY FRANCIS SCOTT KEY
           ;          AND J. STAFFORD SMITH
           ;          DURATION COUNT = 64 FOR QUARTER NOTE

0200 604A000032  SONG: .BYTE  96,74,0,0,50        ; 3/8    C5           C4     1
0205 104400002C        .BYTE  16,68,0,0,44        ; 1/16   A4           A3
020A 4040000024        .BYTE  64,64,0,0,36        ; 1/4    G4           F3     2
020F 4044000024        .BYTE  64,68,0,0,36        ; 1/4    A4           F3
0214 404A000022        .BYTE  64,74,0,0,34        ; 1/4    C5           E3
0219 80544E441E        .BYTE  128,84,78,68,30     ; 1/2    F5   D5  A4  D3     3
021E 305C52441C        .BYTE  48,92,82,68,28      ; 3/16   A5   E5  A4  C#3
0223 105800401C        .BYTE  16,88,0,64,28       ; 1/16   G5       G4  C#3
0228 4054003C1E        .BYTE  64,84,0,60,30       ; 1/4    F5       F4  D3     4
022D 4044003C1E        .BYTE  64,68,0,60,30       ; 1/4    A4       F4  D3
0232 4048403C28        .BYTE  64,72,64,60,40      ; 1/4    B4   G4  F4  G3
0237 804A403A32        .BYTE  128,74,64,58,50     ; 1/2    C5   G4  E4  C4     5
023C 204A000032        .BYTE  32,74,0,0,50        ; 1/8    C5           C4
0241 204A000032        .BYTE  32,74,0,0,50        ; 1/8    C5           C4
0246 605C544424        .BYTE  96,92,84,68,36      ; 3/8    A5   F5  A4  F3     6
024B 2058004028        .BYTE  32,88,0,64,40       ; 1/8    G5       G4  G3
0250 4054006044        .BYTE  64,84,0,60,44       ; 1/4    F5       F4  A3
0255 80524A4032        .BYTE  128,82,74,64,50     ; 1/2    E5   C5  G4  C4     7
025A 304E46002E        .BYTE  48,78,70,0,46       ; 3/16   D5   Bb4     Bb3
025F 10524A402E        .BYTE  16,82,74,64,46      ; 1/16   E5   C5  G4  Bb3
0264 40544A442C        .BYTE  64,84,74,68,44      ; 1/4    F5   C5  A4  A3     8
0269 405400003C        .BYTE  64,84,0,0,60        ; 1/4    F5           F4
026E 404A000032        .BYTE  64,74,0,0,50        ; 1/4    C5           C4
0273 404400002C        .BYTE  64,68,0,0,44        ; 1/4    A4           A3     9
0278 403C000024        .BYTE  64,60,0,0,36        ; 1/4    F4           F3
027D 304A000032        .BYTE  48,74,0,0,50        ; 3/16   C5           C4
0282 104400002C        .BYTE  16,68,0,0,44        ; 1/16   A4           A3
0287 403C000024        .BYTE  64,60,0,0,36        ; 1/4    F4           F3    10
028C 4044000024        .BYTE  64,68,0,0,36        ; 1/4    A4           F3
0291 404A000022        .BYTE  64,74,0,0,34        ; 1/4    C5           E3
0296 80544E441E        .BYTE  128,84,78,68,30     ; 1/2    F5   D5  A4  D3    11
029B 305C52441C        .BYTE  48,92,82,68,28      ; 3/16   A5   E5  A4  C#3
```

Table 4: This song table is an encoding of "The Star Spangled Banner" in 4 part harmony which is used by the program in listing 2. Each musical event in the table consists of five bytes. The first byte represents the duration of the event in units, according to the value of the "tempo" (0 denotes the end of the song). The next four bytes contain the note identifications of the four voices (0 indicates silence for the voice).

sound. It is also possible to interface a computer to specialized sound generation hardware and have it act as a *control* element.

The most obvious kind of equipment to control is the standard, modular, voltage controlled sound synthesizer. Since the interface characteristics of nearly all synthesizers and modules are standardized, a computer interface to such equipment could be used with nearly any synthesizer in common use.

Generally speaking, the function of a voltage controlled module is influenced by one or more DC control voltages. These are usually assumed to be in the range of 0 to +10 volts, although some modules will have a predictable response to negative voltages as well. In a voltage controlled oscillator, for example, the output frequency is determined by a control voltage. For typical tuning, 0 V would correspond to 16 Hz (a very low C), and the frequency would increase one volt per octave for higher voltages. Thus, +4 V would produce middle C, and the maximum input of +10 V would produce a nearly inaudible 16.4 kHz. A typical oscillator module has two or three control inputs and a number of outputs. The voltages at the inputs are internally summed to form the effective control value (useful for injecting vibrato), and the outputs provide several different waveforms simultaneously.

A voltage controlled amplifier has as a minimum a signal input, a control input, and a signal output. The voltage at the control input determines the gain from the signal input to the signal output. In a typical setting, +8 V would correspond to unity (0 db) gain, with lower voltages decreasing the gain by 10 db per volt.

Many other voltage controlled devices have been developed during the approximately 12 year history of this field. In order to play music, the modules are first "patched" together with patch cords (like old style telephone switchboards) according to the desired sound characteristics. Manually operated control voltage sources such as potentiometers, joysticks and specialized organ-like keyboards are then manipulated by the player. The music is generally monotonic due to difficulties in the control elements (now being largely overcome). Multitrack tape recorders are universally utilized to produce the results heard on recordings such as Walter Carlos's *Switched on Bach*.

A useful computer interface to a synthesizer can be accomplished with nothing more than a handful of digital to analog and optionally analog to digital converters. The DACs would be used to generate control

voltages under program control and the ADCs would allow operator input from the keyboard, for example, to be stored. Since control voltages vary slowly compared to the actual sound waveforms, real time control of a number of synthesizer modules is possible with the average microprocessor.

Table 4, continued:

```
02A0  105800401C      .BYTE   16,88,0,64,28       ; 1/16      G5              G4      C#3
02A5  4054003C1E      .BYTE   64,84,0,60,30       ; 1/4               F5       F4      D3    12
02AA  4044003C1E      .BYTE   64,68,0,60,30       ; 1/4               A4       F4      D3
02AF  4048403C28      .BYTE   64,72,64,60,40      ; 1/4       B4      G4       F4      G3
02B4  804A403A32      .BYTE   128,74,64,58,50     ; 1/2       C5      G4       E4      C4    13
02B9  204A000032      .BYTE   32,74,0,0,50        ; 1/8       C5                      C4
02BE  204A000032      .BYTE   32,74,0,0,50        ; 1/8       C5                      C4
02C3  605C544424      .BYTE   96,92,84,68,36      ; 3/8       A5      F5       A4      F3    14
02C8  2058004028      .BYTE   32,88,0,64,40       ; 1/8       G5              G4      G3
02CD  2054003C2C      .BYTE   32,84,0,60,44       ; 1/8       F5              F4      A3
02D2  80524A4032      .BYTE   128,82,74,64,50     ; 1/2       E5      C5       G4      C4    15
02D7  304E4A002E      .BYTE   48,78,70,0,46       ; 3/16      D5      B@4             B@3
02DC  10524A4A2E      .BYTE   16,82,74,64,46      ; 1/16      E5      C5       G4      B@3
02E1  40544A442C      .BYTE   64,84,74,68,44      ; 1/4       F5      C5       A4      A3    16
02E6  405400003C      .BYTE   64,84,0,0,60        ; 1/4       F5                      F4
02EB  404A000032      .BYTE   64,74,0,0,50        ; 1/4       C5                      C4
02F0  404400002C      .BYTE   64,68,0,0,44        ; 1/4       A4                      A3    17
02F5  403C000024      .BYTE   64,60,0,0,36        ; 1/4       F4                      F3
02FA  01              .BYTE   1                   ; DEFINE END OF THIS SEGMENT
02FB  8300            .WORD   POEND               ; ADDRESS OF BEGINNING OF NEXT
                                                  ;   SEGMENT
0083                  . =     POEND               ; ORG AT END OF PAGE 0 CODE
0083  305C544428      .BYTE   48,92,84,68,40      ; 3/16      A5      F5       A4      G3
0088  105C544428      .BYTE   16,92,84,68,40      ; 1/16      A5      F5       A4      G3
008D  405C544424      .BYTE   64,92,84,68,36      ; 1/4       A5      F5       A4      F3    18
0092  405E544628      .BYTE   64,94,84,70,40      ; 1/4       B@5     F5       B@4     G3
0097  4062544A2C      .BYTE   64,98,84,74,44      ; 1/4       C6      F5       C5      A3
009C  8062544A2C      .BYTE   128,98,84,74,44     ; 1/2       C6      F5       C5      A3    19
00A1  205E544628      .BYTE   32,94,84,70,40      ; 1/8       B@5     F5       B@4     G3
00A6  205C544A2C      .BYTE   32,92,84,74,44      ; 1/8       A5      F5       A4      A3
00AB  4058524032      .BYTE   64,88,82,64,50      ; 1/4       G5      E5       G4      C4    20
00B0  405C544430      .BYTE   64,92,84,68,48      ; 1/4       A5      F5       A4      F4
00B5  405E524640      .BYTE   64,94,82,70,64      ; 1/4       B@5     E5       B@4     G4
00BA  805E58461A      .BYTE   128,94,88,70,26     ; 1/2       B@5     G5       B@4     C3    21
00BF  405E52461A      .BYTE   64,94,82,70,26      ; 1/4       B@5     E5       B@4     C3
00C4  605C4A4424      .BYTE   96,92,74,68,36      ; 3/8       A5      C5       A4      F3    22
00C9  20584A4028      .BYTE   32,88,74,64,40      ; 1/8       G5      C5       G4      G3
00CE  40544A3C2C      .BYTE   64,84,74,60,44      ; 1/4       F5      C5       F4      A3
00D3  80524A4032      .BYTE   128,82,74,64,50     ; 1/2       E5      C5       G4      C4    23
00D8  204E00362C      .BYTE   32,78,0,54,46       ; 1/8       D5              D4      B@3
00DD  20524A3A2E      .BYTE   32,82,74,58,46      ; 1/8       E5      C5       E4      B@3
00E2  40544A3C2C      .BYTE   64,84,74,60,44      ; 1/4       F5      C5       F4      A3    24
00E7  40443C0036      .BYTE   64,68,60,0,54       ; 1/4       A4      F4               D4
00EC  01              .BYTE   1                   ; DEFINE END OF THIS SEGMENT
00ED  AB01            .WORD   P1END               ; ADDRESS OF BEGINNING OF NEXT
                                                  ;   SEGMENT
01AB                  . =     P1END               ; ORG AT END OF PAGE 1 CODE
01AB  4048403C28      .BYTE   64,72,64,60,40      ; 1/4       B4      G4       F4      G3
01B0  804A403A1A      .BYTE   128,74,64,58,26     ; 1/2       C5      G4       E4      C3    25
01B5  404A000032      .BYTE   64,74,0,0,50        ; 1/4       C5                      C4
01BA  40544A4424      .BYTE   64,84,74,68,36      ; 1/4       F5      C5       A4      F3    26
01BF  4054464028      .BYTE   64,84,70,64,40      ; 1/4       F5      B@4      G4      G3
01C4  20544A442C      .BYTE   32,84,74,68,44      ; 1/8       F5      C5       A4      A3
01C9  20524A442C      .BYTE   32,82,74,68,44      ; 1/8       E5      "        "       "
01CE  404E463C2E      .BYTE   64,78,70,60,46      ; 1/4       D5      B@4      F4      B@3   27
01D3  404E463C2E      .BYTE   64,78,70,60,46      ; 1/4       D5      B@4      F4      B@3
01D8  404E4A3E2C      .BYTE   64,78,74,62,44      ; 1/4       D5      C5       F#4     A3
01DD  4058464028      .BYTE   64,88,70,64,40      ; 1/4       G5      B@4      G4      G3    28
01E2  205E460030      .BYTE   32,94,70,0,48       ; 1/8       B@5     B@4              G3
01E7  205C44002C      .BYTE   32,92,68,0,44       ; 1/8       A5      A4               A3
01EC  205840002E      .BYTE   32,88,64,0,46       ; 1/8       G5      G4               B@3
01F1  01              .BYTE   1                   ; DEFINE END OF THIS SEGMENT
01F2  8017            .WORD   AUXRAM              ; ADDRESS OF BEGINNING OF NEXT
                                                  ;   SEGMENT (IN 6530 RAM)
1780                  . =     AUXRAM              ; ORG AT BEGINNING OF 6530 RAM
1780  20543C0030      .BYTE   32,84,60,0,48       ; 1/8       F5      F4               B3
1785  40544A4432      .BYTE   64,84,74,68,50      ; 1/4       F5      C5       A4      C4    29
178A  40524A401A      .BYTE   64,82,74,64,26      ; 1/4       E5      C5       G4       C3
178F  204A000032      .BYTE   32,74,0,0,50        ; 1/8       C5                      C4
1794  204A00002E      .BYTE   32,74,0,0,46        ; 1/8       C5                      B@3
1799  60544A442C      .BYTE   96,84,74,68,44      ; 3/8       F5      C5       A4      A3    30
179E  2058004032      .BYTE   32,88,0,64,50       ; 1/8       G5              G4      C4
17A3  205C004440      .BYTE   32,92,0,68,64       ; 1/8       A5              A4      G4
17A8  205E004640      .BYTE   32,94,0,70,64       ; 1/8       B@5             B@4     G4
17AD  80625C5444      .BYTE   128,98,92,84,68     ; 1/2       C6      A5       F5      A4    31
17B2  20544A4436      .BYTE   32,84,74,68,54      ; 1/8       F5      C5       A4      C4
17B7  2058484034      .BYTE   32,88,72,64,52      ; 1/8       G5      B4       G4      D@4
17BC  605C544A32      .BYTE   96,92,84,74,50      ; 3/8       A5      F5       C5      C4    32
17C1  205C544E32      .BYTE   32,92,84,78,50      ; 1/8       B@5     F5       D5      C4
17C6  4058524632      .BYTE   64,88,82,70,50      ; 1/4       G5      E5       B@4     C4
17CB  80544A443C      .BYTE   128,84,74,68,60     ; 1/2       F5      C5       A4      F4    33
17D0  00              .BYTE   0                   ; END OF PIECE
```

Due to the large number of DACs required and the relatively slow speeds necessary, a multiplexing scheme using one DAC and a

number of sample and hold amplifiers is appropriate. The home builder should be able to achieve costs as low as $2 per channel for a 32 channel, 12 bit unit capable of controlling a fairly large synthesizer.

The routing of patch cords can also be computerized. A matrix of reed relays or possibly CMOS bilateral switches interfaced to the computer might be used for this task. The patches used for some contemporary synthesizer sounds resemble the program patch boards of early computers and thus are difficult and time consuming to set up and verify. With computer controlled patching, a particular setup may be recalled and set up in milliseconds, thus enhancing real time performance as well as reducing the need for a large number of different modules.

Other musical instruments may be interfaced as well. One well-published feat is an interface between a PDP-8 computer and a fair sized pipe organ. There are doubtless several interfaces to electronic organs in existence also. Even piano mechanisms can be activated, as noted elsewhere in this issue.

Recently, specialized music peripherals have appeared, usually oriented toward the S-100 (Altair) bus. In some cases these are digital equivalents of analog modules of similar function. For example, a variable frequency oscillator may be implemented using a divide-by-N counter driven by a crystal clock. The output frequency is determined by the value of N loaded into a register in the device, much as a control voltage affects a voltage controlled oscillator. Such an approach bypasses the frequency drift problems and interfacing expense of analog modules. The biggest advantage, however, is availability of advanced functions not feasible with analog modules.

One of these is a programmable waveform. A small memory in the peripheral holds the waveform (either as individual sample values or Fourier coefficients), which can be changed by writing in a new waveform under program control. Another advantage is that *time multiplexing* of the logic is usually possible. This means that one set of logic may simulate the function of several digital oscillators simultaneously, thus reducing the per oscillator cost substantially. Actually, such a digital oscillator may be nothing more than a hardware implementation of the PLAY routine mentioned earlier.

Digital/analog hybrids are also possible. The speech synthesizer module produced by Computalker Consultants, for example, combines a programmable oscillator, several programmable amplifiers and filters, white

```
                ;       WAVEFORM TABLE
                ;       EXACTLY ONE PAGE LONG ON A PAGE BOUNDARY
                ;       MAXIMUM VALUE OF AN ENTRY IS 63 DECIMAL OR 3F HEX TO AVOID
                ;       OVERFLOW WHEN 4 VOICES ARE ADDED UP

0300            .=      X'300           ; START WAVEFORM TABLE AT 0300

0300    WAV1TB  =       .               ; VOICE 1 WAVEFORM TABLE
0300    WAV2TB  =       .               ; VOICE 2 WAVEFORM TABLE
0300    WAV3TB  =       .               ; VOICE 3 WAVEFORM TABLE
0300    WAV4TB  =       .               ; VOICE 4 WAVEFORM TABLE
                                        ; NOTE THAT ALL 4 VOICES USE THIS TABLE DUE
                                        ; TO LACK OF RAM IN BASIC KIM-1

                ;       FUNDAMENTAL AMPLITUDE  1.0 (REFERENCE)
                ;       SECOND HARMONIC .5, IN PHASE WITH FUNDAMENTAL
                ;       THIRD HARMONIC .5, 90 DEGREES LEADING PHASE

0300 3334353636 .BYTE  X'33,X'34,X'35,X'36,X'36,X'37,X'38,X'39
0305 373839
0308 393A3A3B3B .BYTE  X'39,X'3A,X'3A,X'3B,X'3B,X'3B,X'3C,X'3C
030D 3B3C3D
0310 3C3C3C3C3C .BYTE  X'3C,X'3C,X'3C,X'3C,X'3C,X'3C,X'3C,X'3C
0315 3C3C3C
0318 3C3C3C3B3B .BYTE  X'3C,X'3C,X'3C,X'3B,X'3B,X'3B,X'3B,X'3B
031D 3B3B3B
0320 3A3A3A3A3A .BYTE  X'3A,X'3A,X'3A,X'3A,X'3A,X'3A,X'39,X'39
0325 3A3939
0328 3939393939 .BYTE  X'39,X'39,X'39,X'39,X'39,X'39,X'39,X'39
032D 393939
0330 3A3A3A3A3A .BYTE  X'3A,X'3A,X'3A,X'3A,X'3A,X'3B,X'3B,X'3B
0335 3B3B3B
0338 3B3C3C3C3D .BYTE  X'3B,X'3C,X'3C,X'3C,X'3D,X'3D,X'3D,X'3D
033D 3D3D3D
0340 3E3E3E3E3F .BYTE  X'3E,X'3E,X'3E,X'3E,X'3F,X'3F,X'3F,X'3F
0345 3F3F3F
0348 3F3F3F3F3F .BYTE  X'3F,X'3F,X'3F,X'3F,X'3F,X'3F,X'3F,X'3F
034D 3F3F3F
0350 3E3E3E3D3D .BYTE  X'3E,X'3E,X'3E,X'3D,X'3D,X'3C,X'3C,X'3B
0355 3C3C3B
0358 3B3A393838 .BYTE  X'3B,X'3A,X'39,X'38,X'38,X'37,X'36,X'35
035D 373635
0360 3433323130 .BYTE  X'34,X'33,X'32,X'31,X'30,X'2F,X'2E,X'2D
0365 2F2E2D
0368 2C2B2A2928 .BYTE  X'2C,X'2B,X'2A,X'29,X'28,X'27,X'26,X'25
036D 272625
0370 2423222121 .BYTE  X'24,X'23,X'22,X'21,X'21,X'20,X'1F,X'1F
0375 201F1F
0378 1E1E1D1D1D .BYTE  X'1E,X'1E,X'1D,X'1D,X'1D,X'1D,X'1C,X'1C
037D 1D1C1C
0380 1C1C1D1D1D .BYTE  X'1C,X'1C,X'1D,X'1D,X'1D,X'1D,X'1D,X'1E
0385 1D1D1E
0388 1E1F1F2020 .BYTE  X'1E,X'1F,X'1F,X'20,X'20,X'21,X'21,X'22
038D 212122
0390 2323242425 .BYTE  X'23,X'23,X'24,X'24,X'25,X'26,X'26,X'27
0395 262627
0398 2828292929 .BYTE  X'28,X'28,X'29,X'29,X'29,X'2A,X'2A,X'2B
039D 2A2A2B
03A0 2B2B2B2B2B .BYTE  X'2B,X'2B,X'2B,X'2B,X'2B,X'2B,X'2B,X'2A
03A5 2B2B2A
03A8 2A2A292928 .BYTE  X'2A,X'2A,X'29,X'29,X'28,X'27,X'27,X'26
03AD 272726
03B0 2524232221 .BYTE  X'25,X'24,X'23,X'22,X'21,X'20,X'1F,X'1D
03B5 201F1D
03B8 1C1B191817 .BYTE  X'1C,X'1B,X'19,X'18,X'17,X'15,X'14,X'13
03BD 151413
03C0 11100F0D0C .BYTE  X'11,X'10,X'0F,X'0D,X'0C,X'0B,X'09,X'08
03C5 0B0908
03C8 0706050403 .BYTE  X'07,X'06,X'05,X'04,X'03,X'03,X'02,X'01
03CD 030201
03D0 0100000000 .BYTE  X'01,X'00,X'00,X'00,X'00,X'00,X'00,X'00
03D5 000000
03D8 0000010101 .BYTE  X'00,X'00,X'01,X'01,X'01,X'02,X'03,X'04
03DD 020304
03E0 0506070809 .BYTE  X'05,X'06,X'07,X'08,X'09,X'0B,X'0C,X'0D
03E5 0B0C0D
03E8 0F10121315 .BYTE  X'0F,X'10,X'12,X'13,X'15,X'16,X'18,X'1A
03ED 16181A
03F0 1B1D1F2022 .BYTE  X'1B,X'1D,X'1F,X'20,X'22,X'23,X'25,X'27
03F5 232527
03F8 282A2B2C2E .BYTE  X'28,X'2A,X'2B,X'2C,X'2E,X'2F,X'30,X'31
03FD 2F3031

                .END
```

Table 5: *This table is an encoding of the samples of the waveform used by the program in listing 2. The table is exactly one memory page long on a page boundary. The maximum value of any entry is decimal 63 or hexadecimal 3F to avoid overflow when all four voices are summed.*

noise generator, and programmable switching on one board. Although designed for producing speech, its completely programmable nature gives it significant musical potential, particularly in vocals.

How do these various control techniques compare with the direct waveform computation techniques discussed earlier? A definite advantage of course is real time playing of the music. Another advantage is simpler programming, since sound generation has already been taken care of. However, the number of voices and complexity of subtle variations is directly related to the quantity of synthesizer modules available. For example, if more voices are needed, either more modules must be purchased or a multitrack tape recording must be made, which then takes us out of the strict real time domain. On the other hand, a new voice in a direct synthesis system is nothing more than a few bytes added to some tables and a slightly lengthened execution time. Additionally, there may be effects that are simply not possible with currently available analog modules. With a direct synthesis system, one merely codes a new subroutine, assuming that an algorithm to produce the effect is known.

A separate problem for the experimenter is that a "critical mass" exists for serious work with a direct synthesis system. To achieve complexity significantly beyond the 4 voice example program described earlier, a high speed, large capacity mass storage system is needed. This means an IBM type digital tape drive or large hard surface disk drive; usually at least $3000 for a new drive less interface. Used 7 track tapes and 2311 type disks (7.5 megabytes) are often available for $500 and certainly provide a good start if the user can design his own interface. Synthesizer modules or peripheral boards, on the other hand, can be purchased one at a time as needed.

Music Languages

Ultimately, software for controlling the sound generation process, whether it be direct or real time control, is the real frontier. The very generality of computer music synthesis means that many parameters and other information must be specified in order to produce meaningful music. One function of the software package is to convert "musical units of measure" into physical sound parameters such as conversion of tempo into time durations. Another part is a language for describing music in sufficient detail to realize the control power available from music synthesis without burdening the user with too much irrelevant or

repetitious detail. With a good language, a good editor for the language, and real time (or nearly so) execution of the language, the music system becomes a powerful composition tool much as a text editing system aids writers in preparing manuscripts.

Music languages can take on two forms. One is a descriptive form. Music written in a descriptive language is analogous to a conventional score except that it has been coded in machine readable form. All information in the score necessary for proper performance of the piece is transcribed onto the computer score in a form that is meaningful to the user yet acceptable to the computer. Additional information is interspersed for control of tone color, tempo, subtle varia-

```
*    TOCCATA AND FUGUE IN D-MINOR        BACH
*
VOICE1 40,0,0,0,0,30,0,0,0,0,0,0,60,0          10          30,30
VOICE2 37,0,0,0,0,0,0,0,50,0,0,0,0,50,0        10          60,60
VOICE3 0,0,9,0,38,0,0,0,38,19,0,0,0,28,0       15          100,250
TEMPO 1/4=1200

        /-/

002 1A3,1/64; 2A2,1/64
    1A@3,1/64; 2A@2,1/64
    1A3,1/8; 2A2,1/8
    R,1/32
    1G3,1/647; 2G2,1/64.
    1F3,1/64; 2F2,1/64
    1E3,1/64; 2E2,1/64
    1D3,1/64; 2D3,1/64
    1C#3,1/32; 2C#2,1/32
    1D3,1/16; 2D2,1/16
    R,1/4
    3D2,1/1; R,1/4
    2C#3,1F2; R,1/16
    1E3,7/16; R,1/16
    1G3,7/16; R,1/16
    1B@3,5/16; R,1/16
    1C#4,4/16; R,1/16
    1E4,3/16

        /-/

140 1B@4,1/8; 1G4,1/8; 1E4,1/8; 2E3,1/8; 3C#3,1/8
    1E3,1/32
    1G3,1/32
    1B@3,1/32
    1C#4,1/32
    1B@4,1/8
    1B@4,1/8; 1G4,1/8; 1E4,1/8; 1C#4,1/8; 2E3,1/8; 3C#3,1/8
    1A4,1/8; 1F#4,1/8; 1D4,1/8; 2F#3,1/8; 3C3,1/8
TEMPO 1/4=950
    1D3,1/32
TEMPO 1/4=1050
    1A3,1/32
TEMPO 1/4=1150
    1D4,1/32
TEMPO 1/4=1200
    1F#4,1/32
    1A4,1/8
    1A4,3/8; 1F#4,1/8; 1D4,1/8; 2F#3,1/8; 3C3,1/8
141 1D4,1/2; 1B@3,1/2; 2G3,1/2; 3G2,1/4
    1G4,1/2; 3B@2,1/4
    1E4,1/4; 1C#4,1/4; 2B@3,1/4; 3E2,1/4
    1F4,1/4; 1D4,2/4; 2A3,1/4; 3F2,1/4
142 1E4,1/2; 2A3,1/2; 3A2,1/2; R,1/4
    1C4,2/4; R,1/4
    1D4,4/2; 2F3,1/4; 3B@2,1/4
    2B@3,1/4; 2G3,1/4; 3G2,1/4
143 2A3,3/2; 2F3,3/2; 3D3,3/2; 3D2,3/2
END
```

Listing 3: Bach's "Toccata and Fugue in D Minor" as encoded in NOTRAN, a music language developed by the author (NOTRAN stands for NOte TRANslation). The main function of the language is to transcribe organ music, but it will work equally well with other types of music. Program statements are used to encode duration, pitch, attack and decay rates, and loudness of each note.

tions, and other parameters available to the computer synthesist.

A simple example of such a language is NOTRAN (NOte TRANslation) which was developed by the author several years ago for transcribing organ music. Listing 3 shows a portion of Bach's "Toccata and Fugue in D Minor" coded in NOTRAN. The basic thrust of the language was simplicity of instruction (to both the user and the interpreter program), rather than minimization of typing effort.

Briefly, the language consists of statements of one line each which are executed in straight line sequence as the music plays. If the statement starts with a keyword, it is a specification statement; otherwise, it is a note statement. Specification statements simply set up parameters that influence the execution of succeeding note statements and take no time themselves.

A VOICE statement assigns the timbre described by its parameters to a voice number which is used in the note statements. In the example score, the first group of parameters describe the waveform in terms that are implementation dependent, such as harmonic amplitudes. The next, isolated parameter specifies the overall loudness of the voice in relation to other voices. The last pair of parameters specifies the attack and decay times respectively for notes using this voice. Depending on the particular implementation, other parameters may be added without limit. For example, vibrato might be described by a set of three additional parameters such as vibrato frequency, amplitude, and a delay from the beginning of a note to the start of vibrato.

A TEMPO statement relates note durations in standard fractional terms to real time in milliseconds. The effect of a tempo statement lasts until another is encountered. Although the implementation for which the example was written required a sequence of tempo statements to obtain a retard, there is no reason why an acceleration or a retard set of parameters could not be added.

Note statements consist of one or more note specifications and are indented four spaces (the measure numbers are treated as comments). Each note specification begins with a voice number followed by a note name consisting of a letter, optional sharp (#) or flat (@) sign, and an octave number. Thus C#4 is one half step above middle C. Following the comma separator is a duration fraction. Any fraction is acceptable, but conventional musical fractions are normally used. Following the duration are two optional modifiers. A period (.) indicates a "dotted" note which by convention extends the note's duration by 50%. An "S" specifies

a staccato note which is played as just an attack and decay (as specified by the corresponding voice statement) without any steady state. The presence of a semicolon (;) after a note indicates that additional notes which are intended to be part of the same statement are present, possibly extending to succeeding lines.

The execution sequence of note statements can become a little tricky due to the fact that note durations in the statement may not all be equal. The rule is that all notes in the statement start simultaneously. When the shortest one has ended, the notes in the next statement are initiated, even though some in the previous statement may be still sounding. This could continue to any depth such as the case of a whole note in the bass against a series of sixteenth notes in the melody. The actual implementation, of course, limits the maximum number of simultaneous tones that may be built up.

Also available is a rest specification which can be used like a note specification. Its primary function is to provide silent space between note statements, but it may also be used to alter the "shortest note" decision when a note statement is scanned. If the rest is the shortest then the notes in the next statement are started when the rest elapses even though none of the current notes have ended. A use of this property may be seen in the last part of measure 2 where an arpeggio is simulated.

As can be seen, NOTRAN is best suited for describing conventional organ music, although it could be extended to cover a wider area as well. One such extension which has been experimented with but not fully implemented is percussion instruments. First a set of implementation dependent parameters was chosen to define a percussive sound, and then a PRCUS statement similar to the VOICE statement was added to the language. To initiate percussive sounds, specifications such as "P3,1/4" would be interspersed with the note specifications in note statements. The "3" would refer to percussive sound number 3 and the 1/4 would be a "duration" which would be optional. All percussive sounds in the same statement would start simultaneously with the regular notes.

A much more general music language is the well-known MUSIC V. It was designed to make maximum use of the flexibility afforded by direct waveform computation without overburdening the user. It is a massive program written in FORTRAN and clearly oriented toward large computers. Much significant computer music work has been done with MUSIC V, and it is indeed powerful. An excellent book is available which describes the language in detail and includes some background material on digital sound generation (see entry 1 in the list of references at the end of this article).

A different approach to music languages is a "generative" language which describes the *structure* of the music rather than the note by note details. In use, the structure is described by "loops," "subroutines," and "conditional branches" much as an algorithm is described by a computer language. The structure is "executed" to produce detailed statements in a conventional music language which is then played to produce sound. The intermediate step need not necessarily be visible to the user. One well thought out system is described in reference 2. It was actually developed as a musicological analysis tool and so has no provisions for dynamics, timbre, etc. It could, however, be extended to include these factors. One easy way to implement such a language is to write a set of macros using a good minicomputer macroassembler.

Conclusion

By now it should be apparent that computer generated music is a broad, multidisciplinary field. People with a variety of talents can make significant contributions, even on a personal basis. In particular, clever system designers and language designers or implementers have wide open opportunities in this field. Finally, imaginative musicians are needed to realize the potential of the technique. ∎

A Short Cut to a Singing KIM. . .

Hal Chamberlin has completed the design of a board which accomplishes the digital to analog conversion and filtering functions described in this article. The board contains printed circuitry for an 8 bit digital to analog converter, low pass filter, and power amplifier. The board may be ordered either without components or completely assembled and tested from Micro Technology Unlimited, 29 Mead St, Manchester NH 03104. In addition, a software package on cassette tape for the KIM-1 computer and a 7 inch 16 ohm speaker are available, completing the required parts of a KIM's music system.

REFERENCES

1. Mathews, Max, *The Technology of Computer Music*, MIT Press, Cambridge MA, 1969. Contains a detailed description of MUSIC V, the high level music language.

2. Oppenheim, A and Schafer, R, *Digital Signal Processing*, Prentice-Hall, NJ, 1975.

3. Smoliar, Stephen, "A Parallel Processing Model of Musical Structures," PhD dissertation, Massachusetts Institute of Technology, September 1971.

Walsh Functions:

A Digital Fourier Series

Benjamin Jacoby PhD

Using a mathematical technique called Fourier analysis, it is possible to build arbitrary wave forms by adding together various "components."

While a full appreciation of the inner workings of the Fourier series requires a knowledge of advanced mathematics far beyond the capacity of many persons interested in electronics, that in no way deters them from using the concepts or even simplified portions of the math in practical applications. Even beginners are aware that wave forms can be broken into a set of harmonics and that a set of sinewaves of integer multiple frequencies can be summed to build up a complex wave form. In a like manner, Walsh function concepts can be put to work once a few fundamental ideas are mastered. A key to generating complicated sounds in computerized music and voice outputs is the ability to generate arbitrary wave forms from digital codes.

In these days of digital computers, a person familiar with Fourier concepts might ask the question: Is it possible to build up any wave form out of a sum of square waves of some type? Such a system would be ideal for use with digital logic. This question has been answered in the affirmative by the German mathematician H Rademacher, not in 1972 or 1962, but in 1922. His set of square waves, called "Rademacher functions," consists of a fundamental square wave of 50% duty cycle at some frequency plus harmonics of square waves of 2,4,8,16,32 and higher powers of two times the fundamental frequency. A deficiency of this system, however, is that it is not possible to generate any arbitrary wave shape from only a simple sum of these square wave harmonics.

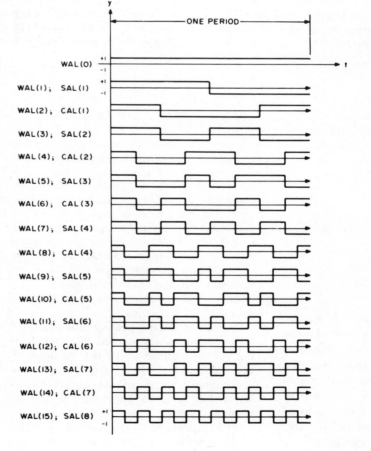

Figure 1: The Walsh Functions WAL(0) through WAL(15). The fact that Walsh functions lend themselves to digital generation is evident in the nature of the basic wave forms. The notations SAL and CAL emphasize the resemblance of Walsh functions to the Fourier series trigonometric functions SIN and COS.

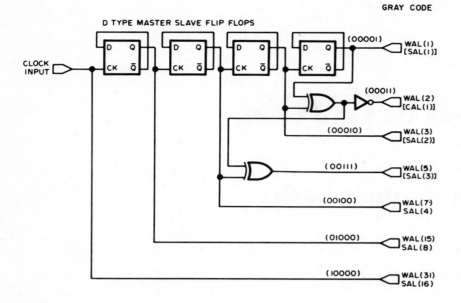

Figure 2: The logic of a digital circuit which generates a set of Walsh functions using a string of flip flops and some external gating. The flip flops are connected as toggles (division by 2 at each stage). The exclusive OR gates combine terms to produce the more complicated Walsh wave forms indicated.

Fourier series are used to create wave forms as the sum of pure sine and cosine waves at selected frequencies; this leads to the obvious question: Is it possible to use a similar mechanism which builds a complex wave form out of digital wave forms with sharp edges?

Walsh functions are the digital answer to sines and cosines used in Fourier analysis.

In translating a mathematical summation into a physical circuit, the operational amplifier provides the summing element and the resistors from inputs to the summing node form the coefficients of the component signals.

Also in 1922, J L Walsh presented his independently developed system to the American Mathematical Society. His system was later shown by the Polish mathematician Kaczmarz in 1929 to include the Rademacher system as a subset of the Walsh complete set of orthonormal functions, which, in plain English, says that some of the Walsh functions are square waves and that if all Walsh functions are allowed (you may not need to use them all, however) then any arbitrary periodic wave form can be built up by adding them together in a manner totally analogous to sinewave summation in Fourier series.

Interest in the engineering applications of Walsh functions was sparked by an article in the IEEE *Spectrum* by Dr H F Harmuth of the University of Maryland in 1968 and is continuing because of the suitability of Walsh functions to generation by digital systems.

The fastest way to understand what Walsh functions are is simply to look at a picture of some wave forms. Figure 1 shows the Walsh functions WAL(0) through WAL(15). It is seen that WAL(0) is merely a DC level which we will usually ignore in practical applications since offsets are easily handled by other means and that WAL(1), WAL(3), WAL(7), and WAL(15) are really the square wave Rademacher functions. You will note that in addition to the WAL(n)

designation, the functions are also labeled with CAL or SAL. These labels are also commonly used and are acronyms for the terms Cosine wALsh and Sine wALsh by analogy to Fourier analysis. In short all WAL (even n) are called CAL and all WAL (odd n) are called SAL. CAL and SAL are also numbered but the numbers do not correspond to the WAL designation though they are easy to figure out. Also by analogy to Fourier analysis, a Walsh spectrum is called a sequency spectrum as opposed to a Fourier frequency spectrum.

Enter Mr Gray and His Code

However, knowing what Walsh functions look like and knowing how to generate them digitally are two different things. It is clear that the generation of WAL(1), WAL(3), WAL(7), WAL(15), etc, is a snap since they are simple square waves. A string of flip flops does the job, as shown in figure 2. The generation of the remaining functions, while a little more difficult, is not impossibly complex once the mathematics is shaken down into a few simple rules:

1. To generate WAL(n), first write the number n in Gray code. Gray code is a modified binary code having only one bit changing at a time when going to the next higher or next lower number. A table of Gray code numbers is

Table 1: Gray Code Bit Patterns for the Walsh Functions WAL(0) Through WAL(31). The corresponding SAL and CAL notation of each WAL function is shown down the right hand column of the table.

WALSH FUNCTION	DIGIT	WAL(31)	WAL(15)	WAL(7)	WAL(3)	WAL(1)	WALSH FUNCTION
WAL(0)	0	0	0	0	0	0	
WAL(1)	1	0	0	0	0	1	SAL(1)
WAL(2)	2	0	0	0	1	1	CAL(1)
WAL(3)	3	0	0	0	1	0	SAL(2)
WAL(4)	4	0	0	1	1	0	CAL(2)
WAL(5)	5	0	0	1	1	1	SAL(3)
WAL(6)	6	0	0	1	0	1	CAL(3)
WAL(7)	7	0	0	1	0	0	SAL(4)
WAL(8)	8	0	1	1	0	0	CAL(4)
WAL(9)	9	0	1	1	0	1	SAL(5)
WAL(10)	10	0	1	1	1	1	CAL(5)
WAL(11)	11	0	1	1	1	0	SAL(6)
WAL(12)	12	0	1	0	1	0	CAL(6)
WAL(13)	13	0	1	0	1	1	SAL(7)
WAL(14)	14	0	1	0	0	1	CAL(7)
WAL(15)	15	0	1	0	0	0	SAL(8)
WAL(16)	16	1	1	0	0	0	CAL(8)
WAL(17)	17	1	1	0	0	1	SAL(9)
WAL(18)	18	1	1	0	1	0	CAL(9)
WAL(19)	19	1	1	0	1	0	SAL(10)
WAL(20)	20	1	1	1	1	0	CAL(10)
WAL(21)	21	1	1	1	1	1	SAL(11)
WAL(22)	22	1	1	1	0	1	CAL(11)
WAL(23)	23	1	1	1	0	0	SAL(12)
WAL(24)	24	1	0	1	0	0	CAL(12)
WAL(25)	25	1	0	1	0	1	SAL(13)
WAL(26)	26	1	0	1	1	1	CAL(13)
WAL(27)	27	1	0	1	1	0	SAL(14)
WAL(28)	28	1	0	0	1	0	CAL(14)
WAL(29)	29	1	0	0	1	1	SAL(15)
WAL(30)	30	1	0	0	0	1	CAL(15)
WAL(31)	31	1	0	0	0	0	SAL(16)

GRAY CODE

shown in table 1; and with a little study, the pattern can easily be extended to any value.

2. Starting with the least significant bit, assign a square wave Rademacher function to each bit. Assign WAL(1) to the LSB, WAL(3) to the next, WAL(7) to the next, etc.

3. Any Rademacher function whose bit is 0 is not used. Those whose bits are 1 are combined by modulo 2 addition, which is to say by exclusive OR gates to give the Walsh output of that order.

4. All Walsh functions must begin positive so that the composite Walsh output may need to be inverted depending upon how many exclusive OR gates were used to produce it.

A couple of examples are shown in figure 2 and a complete generator producing all Walsh functions from WAL(1) through WAL(15) is shown in figure 3.

It should be noted that although a Walsh function is mathematically defined as going from +1 to −1, and it is possible to obtain positive and negative swings with CMOS logic with positive and negative supplies, in practice little is gained by going this route since all that is involved is a DC offset which is easily handled by the summing amplifier. Thus, 0–5 volt TTL logic outputs are fine.

Now that a set of Walsh functions has been generated, it only remains to add them in a summing amplifier with appropriate magnitudes and signs to simulate any wave form with a stair step approximation. The general expression of a Walsh function representation is a summation analogous to that found in Fourier analysis:

$$\text{Arbitrary wave form} \equiv X(t) = A_0 + \sum_{i=1}^{\infty} (A_i \, SAL(i) + B_i \, CAL(i))$$

where A_i and B_i are weighting constants which correspond to the resistors used in the summing amplifier inputs. The size of the steps and the number present will be determined by how many harmonics are combined. The more you use, the smaller and more numerous the steps, hence the better will be your approximation to your original wave form. The determination of these combining coefficients from the wave form desired requires a bit more detailed consideration.

Wave Form Synthesis

Before proceeding any further into the theoretical aspects of Walsh applications, a review of what we are attempting to do and how we intend to do it will help get our feet on solid ground. The device we wish to build using Walsh functions could be called "a square wave to arbitrary wave form converter." It will be a circuit into which you put a square wave of some frequency and out of which comes a periodic analog signal with a frequency related to that of the input wave (perhaps some submultiple) and a wave form that can be made to take any shape desired by adjusting a set of controls, switches or internal resistors. With such a device, digital logic could be used to synthesize a frequency and the converter could then be set to produce a sinewave for use in standard applications, or given sufficient accuracy of conversion, a computer could be made to talk or even sing. Both have been done by engineers working in this area.

The converter consists of two parts: The

So you want to produce a sine wave? Calculate the values at 16 evenly spaced locations in the period, then use these values to calculate the Walsh coefficients using a tabulator method. Then wire in resistors of values derived from the Walsh coefficients and the output of the circuit will be a step function approximation of the desired sine wave.

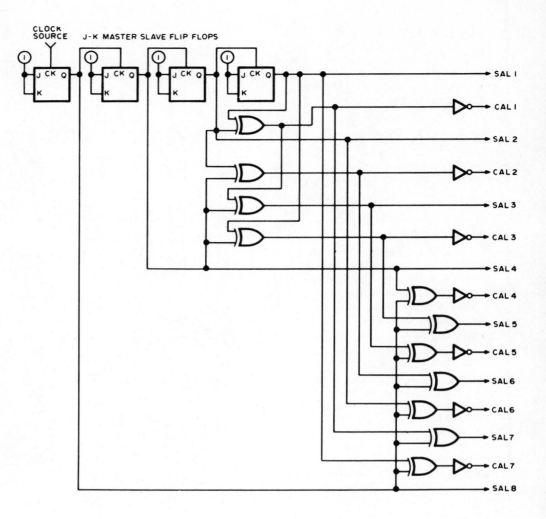

Figure 3: Extending the logic of figure 2, this circuit generates all the Walsh functions WAL(1) through WAL(15) as illustrated in figure 1. This circuit uses an alternate kind of flip flop, the JK master slave flip flop connected as a toggle. This circuit could be built with two 7473 ICs, three 7486 ICs and one 7404 circuit. (One of the 12 exclusive OR sections is used as an inverter.)

When Walsh function analysis is applied to a linear ramp, what's the result? A set of resistor values which form an ordinary DA converter operating upon the binary value in the counter used for the Walsh function generator.

first is the digital expander which expands the input square wave into a variety of digital wave forms, and the second is the analog combiner which adds up these wave forms to produce the periodic analog output. The expander is, of course, the Walsh generator shown earlier and the combiner will be dicussed below.

All of the Walsh outputs will be fed into the summing junction of an operational amplifier, but they will not have the same strength or sign. It is the strength and sign of each component which will determine the net analog output so that once we have chosen the analog output we desire, the relative strength and sign of each Walsh harmonic must be calculated from that desired wave form. Once these values are known, a negative sign can be handled with a digital inverter and the magnitude by the choice of the resistor value into the summing junction. The net output will then be a stair step approximation to the desired output which can then be made more perfect by low pass filtering to smooth the wave shape.

Theoretically, the calculation of the coefficients from the analog wave form desired

involves complex operations with the integral calculus; but it turns out that it is possible to shortcut the high powered math by starting, not with the analog signal, but rather with the stair step approximating function itself. This function can be easily determined by eyeball or by just taking the height of each step to be the value of the analog output at the center of each time interval. Figure 4 shows two examples: a linear ramp and a sinewave with 16 step approximations. The height of each step is shown.

Before proceeding to an actual calculation we will give some time and work saving rules, which are illustrated in figure 5.

1. The waveform to be synthesized must be repetitive (as in Fourier synthesis), although it is easy to start and stop at any point by control of the digital input.
2. It is especially advantageous to use 2^n steps in one period as this gives an automatic cutoff to the number of Walsh harmonics required.

Thus: With a 4 step output no functions

beyond WAL(3) are required, with an 8 step output no functions beyond WAL(7) are required, with a 16 step output no functions beyond WAL(15) are required . . .etc.

3. If the coefficients for a higher order approximation are calculated (say 16 steps), and a less accurate approximation can be used (say 8 steps) then one only need disconnect WAL(8) through WAL(15) since the lower order coefficients will have the same value in either case (or nearly so). This effect is demonstrated in the sine generator circuit.

If your wave form to be synthesized possesses certain symmetries or can be made to do so by a DC baseline shift, many Walsh component coefficients will be zero which will not only simplify the calculations, but the circuitry as well.

4. If the wave form to be synthesized is even, which is to say that any value that the function takes to the left of center is the same as the value an equal distance to the right of center, then only CAL functions will be used and all SAL coefficients will be zero.

5. If the wave form is odd, or can be made so by a baseline shift, then only SAL functions will be used and all CAL coefficients will be zero. Here any value to the left of center equals minus the value to the right of center.

6A. If the wave form is even as in point 4 above and in addition it is even about the 1/4 point, then only CAL(k) where k is an even number will be present and all CAL(k) where k is an odd number will be zero.

6B. If the wave form is even as in point 4 above and in addition is odd about the 1/4 point, then only CAL(k) where k is an odd number will be present and all CAL(k) with k an even number will be zero.

7A. If the wave form is odd as in point 5 above and in addition is even about the 1/4 point, then only SAL(k) where k is an odd number will be present and all SAL(k) where k is an even number will be zero.

7B. If the wave form is odd as in point 5, and in addition is odd about the 1/4 point, then only SAL(k) with k an even number will be present and all SAL(k) where k is an odd number will be zero.

In the calculations that follow it will also be observed that if a wave form is even or odd, the signed sums of the step values need only be calculated for the first half of the

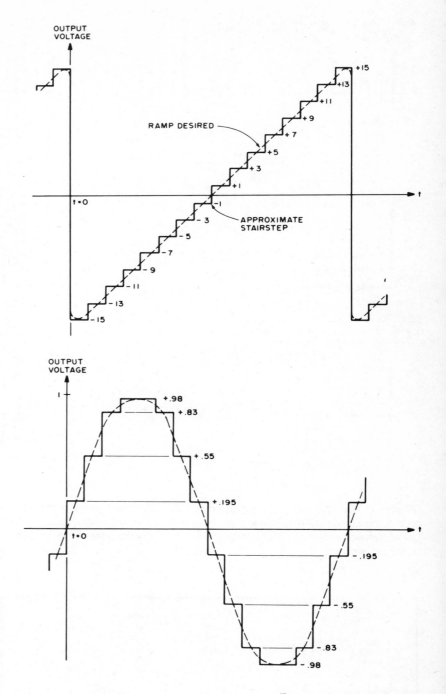

wave form since that value will be exactly half the sum of all steps. This is probably best understood by examining some practical examples.

Two Examples

The first example will be the linear ramp. This function can be made odd by adjusting the baseline, so by rule 5 it is seen that only SAL coefficients need be calculated and no CAL functions need be generated.

The best way to get your mind right in calculating coefficients is to make a table as shown in table 2. The value desired for each

Figure 4: By picking a series of weighting constants for each Walsh function term, the outputs of figure 3 can be summed by an operational amplifier to produce arbitrary wave forms. Here are examples of the ramp and sine wave approximations generated by the Walsh function method. The smooth curve is the desired one in each case, obtained by filtering the output of the summing amplifier.

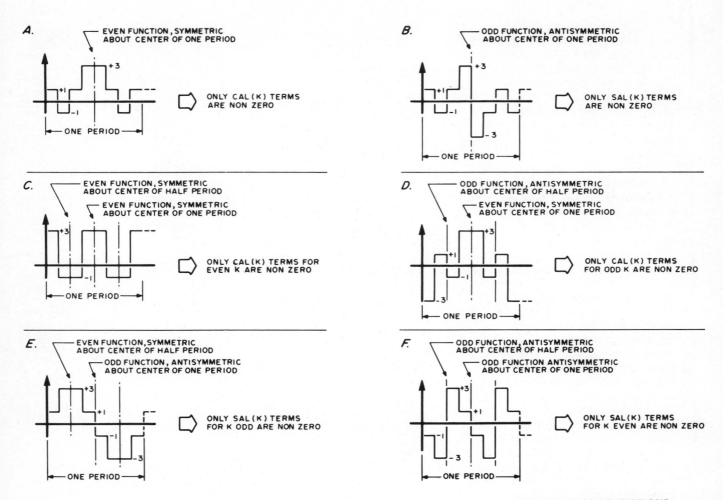

Figure 5: The properties of even and odd functions give constraints on the weighting constants needed for a given wave form. Here are illustrations of six different special cases of symmetry which give zero terms in the Walsh function sum.

Desired Function Values	-15	-13	-11	-9	-7	-5	-3	-1	+1	+3	+5	+7	+9	+11	+13	+15	Signed Sum
						ONE PERIOD											
SAL(1)	P	P	P	P	P	P	P	P	N	N	N	N	N	N	N	N	−128
SAL(2)	P	P	P	P	N	N	N	N	P	P	P	P	N	N	N	N	− 64
SAL(3)	P	P	N	N	N	N	P	P	N	N	P	P	P	P	N	N	0
SAL(4)	P	P	N	N	P	P	N	N	P	P	N	N	P	P	N	N	− 32
SAL(5)	P	N	N	P	P	N	N	P	N	P	P	N	N	P	P	N	0
SAL(6)	P	N	N	P	N	P	P	N	P	N	N	P	N	P	P	N	0
SAL(7)	P	N	P	N	N	P	N	P	N	P	N	P	P	N	P	N	0
SAL(8)	P	N	P	N	P	N	P	N	P	N	P	N	P	N	P	N	− 16

Table 2: A computational table used to help determine the Walsh function coefficients for the linear ramp. The relative strength of the SAL or CAL term in question is obtained by summing horizontally the +1(P) or −1(N) Walsh function value multiplied by the actual waveform value desired for that element of time. After figuring out the value of the signed sum for each term, the values should be normalized so that the largest magnitude is 1 (regardless of sign). Thus the normalized ratios shown below this picture were computed assuming −128 corresponded to −1.

step comprising the output function is written in order along the top of the table. Since we are attempting to produce a linear ramp, our output will be a rising staircase with a fixed increase with each step (we used two units per step). This staircase will eventually be filtered to remove the jogs and give a linear ramp.

The body of the table shows the sign (positive or negative) each particular Walsh function takes in each of the 16 time intervals into which one period of the output wave form has been divided. As indicated earlier, we need not go past WAL(15) in this case. The Walsh sign values can be taken from the wave forms of figure 1 or from table 3 which is good for up to 32 segment approximations.

The numbers to the far right are the sums

of the upper values when all signs are taken into account. Thus, for WAL(1) we see that it is positive in the first half period, but the step values are negative, so we get:

$(-15) + (-13) + (-11) + (-9) + (-7) + (-5) + (-3) + (-1) = -64$ and in the second half period where WAL(1) is negative and the values positive we get:

$-(+1) - (+3) - (+5) - (+7) - (+9) - (+11) - (+13) - (+15) = -64$ or a total of -128. This number gives the relative strength of WAL(1) in the output summation. We repeat the process for each Walsh function.

If we divide all nonzero values by the largest (WAL(1)), it is observed that the weighting is binary and further it is seen that only the square wave Rademacher functions are nonzero. Thus, it is seen that the way to generate a ramp is with a counter feeding a standard digital to analog converter. (So here we have a long, complicated way of arriving at an "obvious" result, but it also should be noted that D to A binary weighting is *only* "matched" to a ramp output.)

If another wave form such as a sinewave is desired, a D to A converter could be used, but a more accurate method would be to switch between 16 voltages of appropriate values. The Walsh system is just as accurate and is simpler for the more general case.

If we divide a sinewave into 16 portions, the value at the center of the first interval will be Sin (11.25°) = 0.19509 and the next will be Sin (33.75°) = 0.55557 and the next Sin (56.25°) = 0.83147, etc. This produces the top row of our table. Since Sin(x) is an odd function, even about the 1/4 point, only SAL(1), SAL(3), SAL(5) and SAL(7) are calculated over the first half period. Our chart with the calculated coefficient values is shown in table 4. Since in a standard operational amplifier summing circuit (we won't go into details here as they can be found in any book on operational amplifiers), the relative summing ratios are related to the inverse of the summing resistor values, we divide each normalized value into 1 and multiply by the feedback resistor value to obtain

The Sign of CAL and SAL in Each 1/32 Interval of Their Period

WAL(0)	PPPP	PPPP	PPPP	PPPP	PPPP	PPPP	PPPP	PPPP
SAL(1)	PPPP	PPPP	PPPP	PPPP	NNNN	NNNN	NNNN	NNNN
CAL(1)	PPPP	PPPP	NNNN	NNNN	NNNN	NNNN	PPPP	PPPP
SAL(2)	PPPP	PPPP	NNNN	NNNN	PPPP	PPPP	NNNN	NNNN
CAL(2)	PPPP	NNNN	NNNN	PPPP	PPPP	NNNN	NNNN	PPPP
SAL(3)	PPPP	NNNN	NNNN	PPPP	NNNN	PPPP	PPPP	NNNN
CAL(3)	PPPP	NNNN	PPPP	NNNN	NNNN	PPPP	NNNN	PPPP
SAL(4)	PPPP	NNNN	PPPP	NNNN	PPPP	NNNN	PPPP	NNNN
CAL(4)	PPNN	NNPP	PPNN	NNPP	PPNN	NNPP	PPNN	NNPP
SAL(5)	PPNN	NNPP	PPNN	NNPP	NNPP	PPNN	NNPP	PPNN
CAL(5)	PPNN	NNPP	NNPP	PPNN	NNPP	PPNN	PPNN	NNPP
SAL(6)	PPNN	NNPP	NNPP	PPNN	PPNN	NNPP	NNPP	PPNN
CAL(6)	PPNN	PPNN	NNPP	NNPP	PPNN	PPNN	NNPP	NNPP
SAL(7)	PPNN	PPNN	NNPP	NNPP	NNPP	NNPP	PPNN	PPNN
CAL(7)	PPNN	PPNN	PPNN	PPNN	NNPP	NNPP	NNPP	NNPP
SAL(8)	PPNN	PPNN	PPNN	PPNN	PPNN	PPNN	PPNN	PPNN
CAL(8)	PNNP	PNNP	PNNP	PNNP	PNNP	PNNP	PNNP	PNNP
SAL(9)	PNNP	PNNP	PNNP	PNNP	NPPN	NPPN	NPPN	NPPN
CAL(9)	PNNP	PNNP	NPPN	NPPN	NPPN	NPPN	PNNP	PNNP
SAL(10)	PNNP	PNNP	NPPN	NPPN	PNNP	PNNP	NPPN	NPPN
CAL(10)	PNNP	NPPN	NPPN	PNNP	PNNP	NPPN	NPPN	PNNP
SAL(11)	PNNP	NPPN	NPPN	PNNP	NPPN	PNNP	PNNP	NPPN
CAL(11)	PNNP	NPPN	PNNP	NPPN	NPPN	PNNP	NPPN	PNNP
SAL(12)	PNNP	NPPN	PNNP	NPPN	PNNP	NPPN	PNNP	NPPN
CAL(12)	PNPN	NPNP	PNPN	NPNP	PNPN	NPNP	PNPN	NPNP
SAL(13)	PNPN	NPNP	PNPN	NPNP	NPNP	PNPN	NPNP	PNPN
CAL(13)	PNPN	NPNP	NPNP	PNPN	NPNP	PNPN	PNPN	NPNP
SAL(14)	PNPN	NPNP	NPNP	PNPN	PNPN	NPNP	NPNP	PNPN
CAL(14)	PNPN	PNPN	NPNP	NPNP	PNPN	PNPN	NPNP	NPNP
SAL(15)	PNPN	PNPN	NPNP	NPNP	NPNP	NPNP	PNPN	PNPN
CAL(15)	PNPN	PNPN	PNPN	PNPN	NPNP	NPNP	NPNP	NPNP
SAL(16)	PNPN	PNPN	PNPN	PNPN	PNPN	PNPN	PNPN	PNPN

|← 1 Period →|

P = Positive   N = Negative

(Columns only for ease of reading.)

Table 3: A larger computational table giving 32 Walsh function components and their signs during a 32 interval period.

$\frac{1}{A_i}$ x 10k	1%	5% EIA
10.00k	10.0k	10k
24.14k	24.3k	24k
121.4 k	121 k	120k
50.27k	49.9k	51k

Table 5: The EIA resistor equivalents for the calculated values of table 4. The 5% tolerance resistance values shown at the right were used in the circuit of figure 6.

	SIN(11.25°) = 0.19509	SIN(33.75°) = 0.55557	SIN(56.25°) = 0.83147	SIN(78.75°) = 0.98078	SIN(101.25°) = 0.98078	SIN(123.75°) = 0.83147	SIN(146.25°) = 0.55557	SIN(168.75°) = 0.19509	signed sum	Normalized coefficients = A_i
SAL(1)	P	P	P	P	P	P	P	P	−5.1258	−1
SAL(3)	P	P	N	N	N	N	P	P	+2.1232	+0.4142
SAL(5)	P	N	N	P	P	N	N	P	+0.4223	+0.08239
SAL(7)	P	N	P	N	N	P	N	P	+1.0196	+0.1989

|← 1/2 period →|

Table 4: Using the computational table to calculate the resistor values for a 16 step sine wave approximation. The specialized sine wave generator of figure 6 uses these results, subject to a further approximation shown in table 5. Note that the signs of the coefficients take into account the inverting op amp configuration and thus appear reversed.

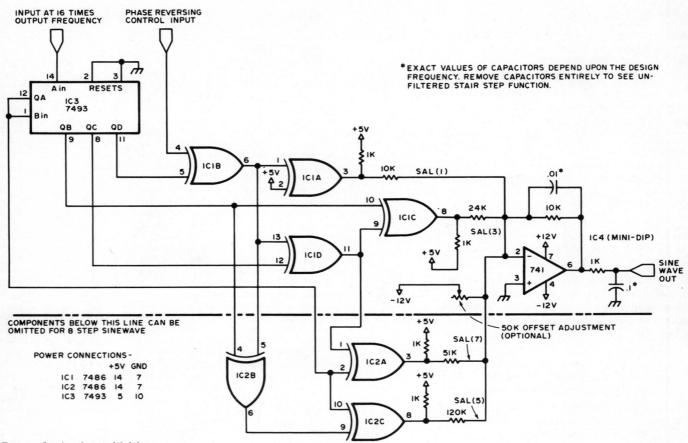

INPUT AT 16 TIMES OUTPUT FREQUENCY

PHASE REVERSING CONTROL INPUT

*EXACT VALUES OF CAPACITORS DEPEND UPON THE DESIGN FREQUENCY. REMOVE CAPACITORS ENTIRELY TO SEE UN-FILTERED STAIR STEP FUNCTION.

COMPONENTS BELOW THIS LINE CAN BE OMITTED FOR 8 STEP SINEWAVE

POWER CONNECTIONS -

	+5V	GND
IC1 7486	14	7
IC2 7486	14	7
IC3 7493	5	10

Figure 6: Applying Walsh Functions. Here is the circuit of a sine wave generator which produces a Walsh function approximation of the sine function. The frequency of the sine wave is set by the input to pin 14 of the 7493. Filtering components of the operational amplifier help smooth out the staircase wave form generated by summing the Walsh function components as weighted by resistors.

each summing resistor value in ohms. Table 5 shows the calculated values compared to 1% and 5% EIA resistor standard values.

The total sinewave converter circuit is shown in figure 6. While three of the co-efficients were negative, a single inverter was used on the lone positive Walsh output since the op amp inverts the wave form. In addition, a gate has been added by which the phase of the entire output wave form can be inverted by simultaneously inverting all Walsh components. It is interesting to also note that if the components below the dotted line are removed, an 8 step sinewave approximation results. The feedback capacitor and output low pass filter can be added to smooth up the wave form to give a nearly perfect sinewave.

The Walsh methods presented here would seem to have wide application for experimentation and engineering. Although these concepts are based on advanced mathematics, nevertheless, as the philosopher Seneca observed so many years ago, "The language of truth is simple."

Walsh Functions for Music Synthesis?

Some background information on the use of orthogonal functions in music wave form

synthesis has been generated by Hal Chamberlin, and published in *Electronotes Newsletter*, Volume 4, Number 25, July 20 1973. Hal also sent along a copy of a portion of a report by B A Hutchins, 60 Sheraton Dr, Ithaca NY 14850, on the use of Walsh functions in wave form generation. According to Hal, there was considerable analysis of Walsh functions in electronic music circles during a period of time approximately centered on 1973, but complexities of controlling the Walsh harmonic amplitudes digitally led to the demise of that interest. Hal's current approach is to employ a real time Fourier series evaluation module which digitally sums terms of the first 32 components of a Fourier series, specified to 8 bit accuracy both in amplitude and phase.

GLOSSARY

The following terms may be unfamiliar to some readers and are highlighted with further explanations.

Baseline: It is possible to add a fixed DC level to an analog signal, which will not affect its wave form. Using the 0 V and +5 V levels obtained with TTL circuits (using pull up resistors) as "Walsh functions" corresponds to a baseline adjustment of +2.5 volts to the ideal case of a symmetric positive or negative voltage value.

CAL: An acronym derived from Cosine wALsh. The CAL functions are the "even" Walsh functions, analogous to the Fourier cosine functions.

Duty cycle: For a digital wave form, the duty cycle is the percentage of time spent in the high state relative to the full period of the wave form.

Even function: An even function (or wave form) is one which is symmetric about the center point of its period. This means that its value a certain distance to the left of center is the same as its value the same distance to the right of center.

Fundamental: The lowest frequency in a Fourier or Walsh function summation.

Gray code: A binary code modified so that only one bit changes when going to the next higher or lower number. It is often used to deglitch position encoders.

Harmonic: A frequency which is a multiple of the fundamental frequency.

Integral calculus: The mathematical formalism used to calculate the area under a curve. The integral calculus is used together with the theory of orthogonal functions to evaluate analytically the coefficients of Fourier and Walsh function expansions. The example of Walsh function coefficient calculation in this article uses properties of Walsh functions to simplify the process of calculating integrals required for the coefficients. There is no such simplification for the Fourier coefficients of a wave form, thus making the application of Fourier analysis a more complicated problem.

Odd function: An odd function (or wave form) is one which is antisymmetric with respect to the center point of its period. This means that if at a fixed interval before the center point its value is X, then at the same interval past the centerpoint the value will be $-X$.

Orthonormal functions: The mathematical theory of orthonormal functions is one of the most powerful tools used by physicists, theoretical chemists and engineers. Among other applications, it provides the tools needed to analyze complex wave forms and synthesize such wave forms using the principle of superposition: That the whole is a linear sum of its parts. Fourier series and Walsh function analysis mentioned here are two particular choices of a set of orthonormal functions which have useful practical applications. (See also **spectrum** below.)

Periodic wave form: A periodic wave form is one which has a fixed shape which is constantly re-peated. A simple example would be the clock oscillator signal of a typical home brew central processor. A more complicated example (subject to imperfections) would be a long steady tone played on a musical instrument.

Rademacher functions: The subset of Walsh components consisting of only the unmodified square waves.

SAL: An acronym derived from Sine wALsh. The SAL functions are the "odd" Walsh functions, analogous to the Fourier sine functions.

Sequency: Walsh function terminology referring to the Walsh components of a wave form in exactly the same way that frequency is used to refer to the Fourier components. Example: Sequency spectrum.

Spectrum: When orthonormal functions are used to analyze a wave form, the result frequently is a set of coefficients which weigh each of the basic functions found in a (theoretically) infinite sum which represents the wave form. Each coefficient corresponds to some parameter of the orthonormal functions, which might be, for example, a number "n." Whatever the parameter is, a spectrum for the analysis is obtained by plotting the coefficient values versus the parameter value for a large number of coefficients. For a Fourier analysis, the result is a plot of coefficient versus frequency (which at the low end corresponds to a small integer value). A Walsh spectrum would plot the coefficient of WAL (n) versus n.

Wave form: For the purposes of this article, a signal's wave form is a value of (for example) voltage as a function of time.■

REFERENCES

1. Corrington, M S, "Solution of Differential and Integral Equations with Walsh Functions," *IEEE Transactions on Circuit Theory,* volume CT-20, number 5, September 1973.
2. Harmuth, H F, "Applications of Walsh Functions in Communications," *IEEE Spectrum,* November 1969.
3. Rademacher, H, "Einige-Saltze von allegemeinen Orthogonalfunktionen," *Math Annalen,* volume 87, 1922, pages 112 to 138.
4. Walmsley, W M, "Walsh functions, transforms and their applications," *Electronic Engineering,* June 1974.
5. Walsh, J L, "A Closed Set of Orthonormal Functions," *American Journal of Math,* volume 45, 1923, pages 5 to 24.

Simple Approaches

to Computer Music Synthesis

Thomas G Sneider

In order to produce a musical output, we must at least create a pitch output under control. This is but a starting point, since more complicated waveform and envelope generation is also useful in music.

The block diagram of a basic note and octave synthesis system is shown in figure 1. The top octave generator produces a square wave whose frequency (pitch) is determined by data sent out on the computer's data bus. Since the output of the top octave generator is a square wave, it can easily be divided by digital circuitry. Each time we divide the frequency by two, we end up with a note whose pitch is one octave lower than the input frequency. By using an ordinary TTL data selector as an octave selector, we can generate a musical scale covering many octaves, and we can also produce more than one pitch at a time, although these extra outputs will always be octave related to one another. The octave selector can also be controlled by data sent out on the computer's data bus, giving us more flexibility.

The octave selector can be easily implemented using an n-stage divider and several NAND gates. However, there are several methods of generating the top octave. We need 12 notes to produce a 1 octave chromatic scale. These notes must be accurate in frequency and drift free in order to produce a true chromatic or "equally tempered" scale useful in music.

One way of synthesizing the top octave is to use a digital to analog (D/A) converter controlling an oscillator. An 8 bit converter limits both resolution and range so that we cannot produce an acceptably accurate chromatic scale. If we use a converter of 10 bits or more, resolution and range are suitable, but such units are expensive and require stable voltage controlled oscillators for this type of application. This method of pitch generation is shown in figure 1. The one nice feature of the digital to analog converter method is that we have a continuously variable output frequency. This permits nifty frequency sweeping effects (known as "portamento" or "glide" effects to the musician).

To save money we can construct a rather crude digital to analog converter which, in conjunction with the voltage controlled

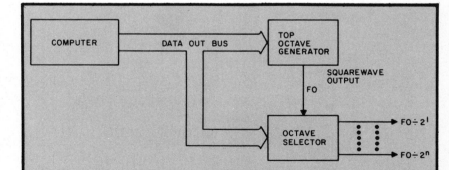

Figure 1: Block diagram of a pitch synthesis subsystem for use in electronic music experiments under computer control. The top octave generator produces a repetitive digital waveform selected under computer control from one of 12 well tempered pitches. This in turn drives octave generation logic consisting of a chain of toggles dividing frequency by two at each stage, and a selector to pick which of the octave related frequencies appear in the output.

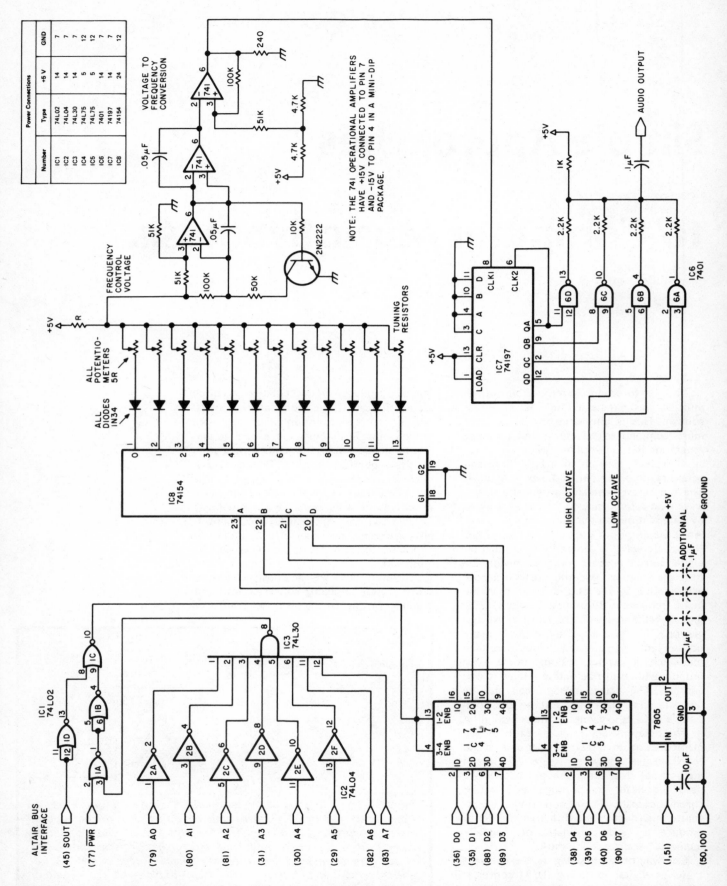

Figure 2: An Altair bus interface and frequency selection logic for the tunable digital to analog conversion method of generation of pitches. This circuit can be constructed on a general purpose prototyping card for the Altair (S-100) bus.

oscillator, will produce the 12 notes required for the full top octave. This method is shown in detail in figure 2. By using surplus 10 turn trimpots and the voltage controlled oscillator, we can construct an inexpensive top octave generator. However, this method has its disadvantages: tuning the trimpots is a critical operation, and once the pots are tuned, they can easily detune themselves because of vibration or temperature variations. My present synthesizer uses this method and needs to be retuned about every two months or so.

A good alternate method of generating the top octave is to use an integrated circuit top octave generator such as the MOSTEK MK50240P. This chip can be had for under $10 and is second-sourced by General Instrument Corporation as the AY-3-0215.

There are several advantages to be had by using this chip. The chip nominally requires a 2.000240 MHz reference frequency which is approximated by the central processor clock's circuitry of most Altair (S-100) bus systems. (The frequency is not exactly 2.000240 MHz, but will be close enough for this application.) This chip eliminates both the voltage controlled oscillator and digital to analog converter, and therefore puts an end to stability and tuning complications. The MK50240P generates the top 13 notes of the well-tempered music scale with an accuracy better than can be determined by the best musician.

Hardware Considerations for Two Working Circuits

The circuit used for the pitch generator, using the tunable digital to analog converter with an Altair bus is shown in figure 2. Bus timing and address decoding are performed by IC1, IC2, and IC3. IC4 and IC5 latch and hold data sent to the board on the data out bus. IC8 is a 4 to 16 decoder with active low outputs. These outputs select which 10 turn trimpot is selected as the bottom leg of the voltage divider whose top leg is resistor R. These trimpots should all have a value about 5 R. The voltage produced by this divider is connected to the input of the voltage controlled oscillator. The output of the voltage controlled oscillator is divided by IC7. The outputs of counter IC7 are gated onto the output bus by IC6, the quad open collector NAND gates. IC8 and the voltage controlled oscillator comprise the top octave generator and IC6 and IC7 comprise the octave selector.

The circuit using the MK50240P for top octave generation is shown in figure 3. The board address, bus timing and latch circuitry are identical to the circuit of figure 2. The

Note	Octal Code	Hexadecimal Code
C	000	00
C#	001	01
D	002	02
D#	003	03
E	004	04
F	005	05
F#	006	06
G	007	07
G#	010	08
A	011	09
A#	012	0A
B	013	0B

Table 1: Octal and hexadecimal representations of note selections, in the low order bits, for these pitch generation circuits.

octave selector is also identical to the one in figure 2. The MK50240P, IC6, is a 12 V device and requires input signal conditioning and output buffering. The 2N2222 transistor and associated resistors bring the TTL level clock signal from the bus up to the 12 V level required by the MK50240P. The outputs of this chip are buffered by IC7 and IC8 before going to IC9 which is the data selector and multiplexer. The MK50240P generates all the notes in the top octave simultaneously and IC9 selects any one of these outputs depending on what data is present at the outputs of IC4. The output of IC9 is then connected to the two chips (IC10 and IC11) comprising the octave selector. An additional voltage regulator, a 7812, has been provided to supply the 12 V needed for the MK50240P. Note that for additional music channels, additional copies of the note selector IC9 and octave selector can be driven off the buffered outputs of the MK50240P.

A word of caution: the audio output of the circuits in figures 2 and 3 swings about 2 V peak to peak and should be attenuated with a potentiometer before you plug it into your stereo system or amplifier.

Software Considerations

From a software point of view, the circuits of figures 2 and 3 are identical. Both circuits have an IO device address of 300 octal. Outputting the proper data to 8080 port 300 octal will cause the synthesizer to audibly produce the note and octave(s) represented by that data.

The synthesizer can be considered as having two input nybbles, each nybble containing four bits. The least significant nybble determines what note is to be selected and the most significant nybble determines what one of four possible octave(s) is to be selected. One byte contains all the information necessary to set up any note and octave(s).

Bear in mind that the synthesizer will continue to produce the note and octave(s)

77

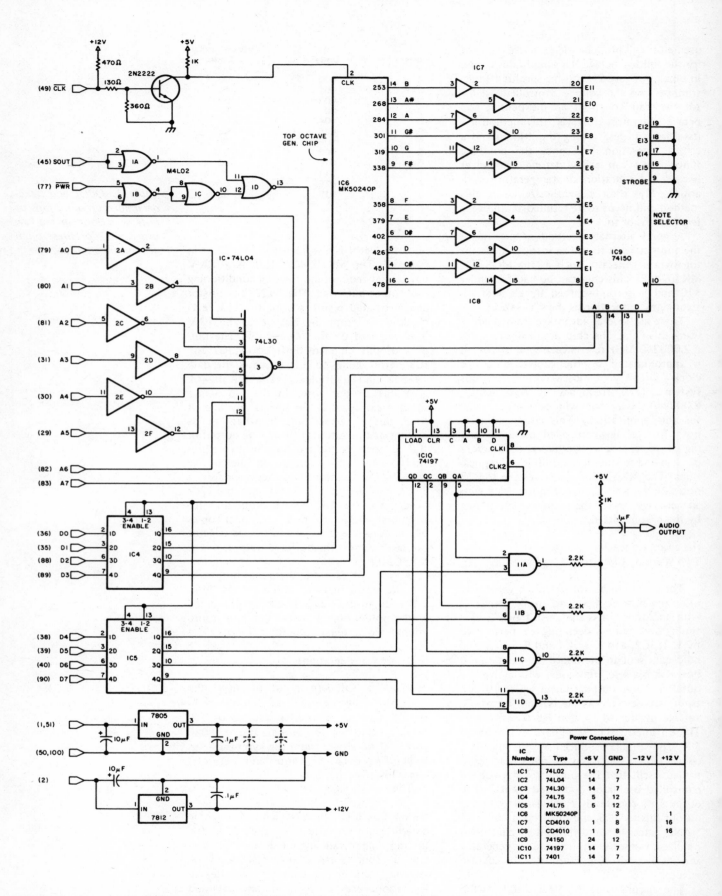

Figure 3: The complete circuit for an equivalent of figure 2, which uses the top octave generator chip with an Altair bus interface. This method uses the top octave generator and a note selector to drive the octave selection logic, while the digital to analog converter method uses a voltage controlled oscillator with a diode resistance selection of pitch.

Octave	Octal Code	Hexadecimal Code
4 (highest)	020	10
3	040	20
2	100	40
1 (lowest)	200	80

Table 2: Octal and hexadecimal notation for octave enabling bits sent to the interface in the high order nybble of the 8 bit word. Note that one or more of the octaves may be enabled simultaneously simply by adding the codes together (or using the logical OR).

you have selected until you send it new data. To clear the synthesizer (no audible output) all you need do is output a 0 on data lines D4 thru D7, the most significant nybble.

Table 1 shows what the octal representations are for each note in the top octave. Table 2 shows the octal representations for each octave. To pack these two codes into one byte, they can either be added or ORed. Table 3 shows a series of codes that, when moved to port 300 octal in sequence, will produce a 12 note musical scale in the synthesizer's highest octave. However, if you wish to hear this scale, you must insert a software time delay in between each note. Otherwise all you will hear is a very short "click" because of the processor's high speed of program execution. If you wish to hear this scale in four octaves simultaneously, all you need to do is keep all four bits in the octave enabling nybble in the high state.

Armed with this information and some simple software routines, you and your trusty computer are now capable of synthesizing all of J S Bach's "B Minor Mass," to

Octal	Hexadecimal
020	10
021	11
022	12
023	13
024	14
025	15
026	16
027	17
030	18
031	19
032	1A
033	1B

Table 3: Octal and hexadecimal representations of the notes of a chromatic scale in the highest octave of this interface. The codes for any given pitch can be generated by adding the note code of table 1 to one or more of the octave codes of table 2, providing a multiple frequency output in the summing resistor network of these circuits. In these examples, only one octave selection is enabled, the high octave.

say nothing of the many new types of musical expression you now have at your fingertips. I myself have synthesized Haydn's "Minuet in G," parts of Bach's "Toccata and Fugue in D Minor," Henry Mancini's "Pink Panther Theme," and "Hot Rod Lincoln!"■

Notes on Anatomy:

Chris Morgan

Photo 1: The Duo-Art reproducing player piano as it is currently displayed in my home. Notice the electric motor at bottom center. It is original equipment. The vacuum pump is at the right; it is connected to the motor by a 1968 V8 Buick fan belt, which just happens to be a perfect fit. The piano was built in 1925 and required extensive renovations. The binary dynamics control system is located at bottom left (see photos 3a and 3b).

The Piano's Reproductive System

When was the binary number system first used for control purposes in a mass produced machine? The early nineteenth century Jacquard punch card controlled loom comes immediately to mind; but, surprisingly enough, a more widespread application occurred in the first quarter of this century: the reproducing player piano!

The reproducer was so-called because it went one step beyond the player piano in its ability to "reproduce" the dynamics and subtle shadings of the pianist who recorded the roll.

I have owned a Duo-Art upright reproducing piano for five years now (see photo 1), during which time I have restored it so that it can now play the specially encoded Duo-Art rolls which were made for it. The Duo-Art roll catalog was remarkably extensive, featuring such items as Chopin etudes and Beethoven sonatas in addition to a large selection of popular titles. (The pièce de résistance was a complete set of themes from Wagner's Ring cycle comprising some 30 odd rolls!)

Reproducers were a luxury item during the 1920s, and for good reason: they were built like fine watches and contained some fairly sophisticated features (for the time) to control dynamics, operate the pedals, and so on.

Photo 1 shows the Duo-Art with the bottom cover removed for clarity. The spool box (photos 2a and 2b) is located at the top and is the place where the piano roll is inserted. Immediately below the keyboard are the levers which are used to control the speed of the roll as it plays, as well as volume and roll rewind. At the bottom center is the original electric motor (built in 1925) which drives the vacuum pump at the right. No pedalling is required on this

Photo 2a: The spool box, showing the brass tracker bar. There are 88 holes across the bar, corresponding to the notes of the piano. There are additional holes at each end to input two 4 bit "nybbles" of information to the dynamics (volume) control system from the paper roll.

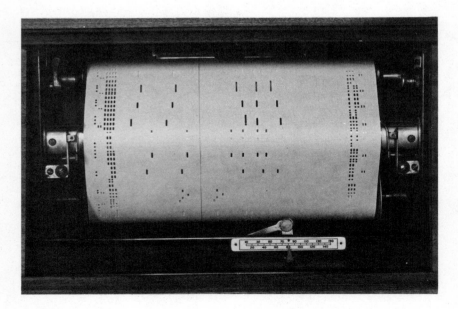

Photo 2b: A view of the spool box with a Duo-Art roll installed. Note the dense groups of holes at each side of the roll; these contain binary encoded information about the volume of the notes which are being played. All four dynamics holes are about to be uncovered on the left side as the roll paper moves downward across the tracker bar. (Thus maximum volume is about to be set up.) The dynamics holes appear as groups of holes rather than long slots so that the paper will not fall apart. The tracker bar holes underneath are long enough so that the small paper bridges left for mechanical strength do not close up the holes as they pass over them.

model, a boon for the lazy experimenter. Like most player pianos, the Duo-Art works on a vacuum actuated system which opens and closes cloth covered "pneumatics," or bellows. These in turn do all the mechanical work inside the piano, such as playing keys and operating pedals.

But what makes the Duo-Art so interesting is its binary-based volume control system located in the lower left section of the piano (see photos 3a and 3b for a close-up). There are two independent volume control systems built into the Duo-Art. They are controlled by two sets of four holes per set, located above the main row of holes near each end of the tracker bar. Photo 4 shows the right-hand set of holes in enlargement. Notice that they are vertically in line with the four highest note sensing holes on the tracker bar. When a Duo-Art roll is played, therefore, a special pneumatic 8 pole double throw switch must be thrown to disable the lower two sets of four holes and allow the upper two sets of four holes to control piano dynamics (the volume of sound heard).

Each set of holes is connected to a set of "accordion" pneumatics, so-called because they open and close like vertical accordion bellows. A rod at the top of each pneumatic is connected to an air governor. As the pneumatics close, the governor admits more and more air to the system and the volume of the notes played on the controlled side of the keyboard goes up.

The spacings of the four sections of the pneumatics are 1/2, 1/4, 1/8 and 1/16 inch, so that 16 different volume levels can be achieved. This bellows is in fact a form of mechanical digital to analog converter. So we have two nybbles (or one byte) of information to control volume in a Duo-Art reproducer piano. Photo 3b shows a level corresponding to 1/2 + 1/8, or 10/16ths of maximum volume, and photo 3a shows a zero level for comparison. Photo 5 shows the roll positioned to produce the level of photo 3b; the most significant bit is to the left. Since an opening (hole) corresponds to a binary 1 level, the binary number here is 1010.

Counting from the right in photo 4, the first 3 holes are mute pedal control, automatic reroll and the "theme" hole. The theme hole is an ingenious feature. There are often cases when the piano must suddenly change volume levels for isolated notes or chords and then return to the previous level. It takes a finite time for this sort of change, so the rolls are designed to allow the left-hand accompaniment dynamics control system to control the entire keyboard range,

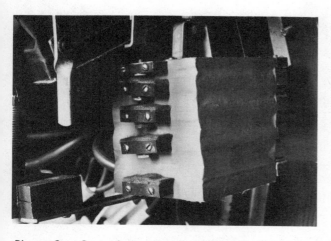

Photo 4: A closeup illustrating the four right hand dynamics control holes, located slightly above the center line of the rest of the holes.

Photo 3a: One of the two Duo-Art accordion pneumatics used to control the volume of one half of the piano keyboard. Each of the four chambers can be individually exhausted under control of the piano roll. The pneumatic is connected by a rod on top to an air governor. The four chambers close by 1/2, 1/4, 1/8 and 1/16 inches, so that the air governor can be set to any of 16 different vacuum levels to power the keyboard pneumatics. The roll's 4 bit binary "word" is thus translated into a vacuum level: in effect, this is a digital (vacuum lines from tracker bar) to analog (mechanical position of governor) converter.

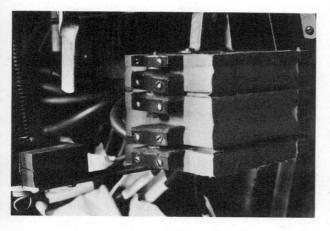

Photo 3b: The accordion pneumatic shown converting the integer value 10 into one of 16 possible mechanical positions. This corresponds to the binary number 1010 on the roll. See photo 5.

Photo 5: The roll in this case is outputting level ten to the accordion pneumatics. Photo 3b indicates the resulting mechanical position output of the pneumatics.

Photo 6: A Duo-Art roll of Chopin's "Polonaise, Opus 40, Number 1," as played by Paderewski, in position over the tracker bar. Note the extensive ornamentation, both visually and verbally, in the form of the performer's authorization of the work. This roll is approximately 55 years old. Paderewski was a link in a liszt of salon pianists which began in America with Louis Moreau Gottschalk, and which continues to this day with certain candelabra wielding virtuosos.

while the right-hand theme system "charges" itself with vacuum for the upcoming volume change. When the roll triggers either or both of these holes, control of the respective sides of the keyboard is transferred for that instant to the theme control. Details of this theme control system are essential to the design of software drivers for Duo-Art players converted to computer control.

Numerous other fascinating features abound on this instrument. Take for example the automatic roll-centering negative feedback system. The curved vertical "finger" shown in photo 5 is one of two which are positioned to just touch the edges of the roll. If the roll wanders off to the right or left, the fingers tilt back, uncovering air tubes which are under vacuum. This sends a signal to a set of opposing bellows with a high damping ratio, which push the roll spool back until the air tube is covered again. The design is simple, yet effective. Long before Norbert Wiener made it explicit, servomechanisms as control systems were in practical daily use.

Just how good does the Duo-Art sound? Well, it has some obvious limitations (limited dynamic range, for one), but on the whole

it sounds remarkably good. The sound quality is several orders of magnitude better than the "new fangled" phonograph which eventually supplanted it commercially.

In its heyday, the Duo-Art Company could afford to hire some of the most famous pianists of the age to record for them: Paderewski (see photo 6), Wanda Landowska, Vladimir Horowitz (when he was in his twenties), Igor Stravinsky (!), George Gershwin (playing his own four-hand arrangement of "Rhapsody in Blue" by overdubbing), and on and on. The rolls were beautifully decorated, too (see photo 6).

Readers wishing to find out more about the fascinating hobby of reproducing pianos should write to the Vestal Press, POB 97, Vestal NY 13850, and ask for their catalog. The Vestal Press specializes in books about player pianos and other musical automata. The Player Piano Company in Wichita KS is an excellent source of supplies for the do-it-yourself restorer. The current bible in the field is *Rebuilding the Player Piano*, by Larry Givens, published by Vestal. In it you'll find valuable material about the Duo-Art and about the other brands of competing reproducers like the Ampico and Wurlitzer models. But that's another story.■

Photo 1: The object of the design exercise documented in this article is an interface between the computer in the basement and the Steinway baby grand player piano shown at the left in this picture. Using the interface of figure 1, and the solenoid valves of photo 2, electronic control of the restored piano will be completed by adding a motor driven bellows unit of later vintage than this 1910 piano. In the picture, various subassemblies have been placed at skewed angles atop the keyboard (spool box and 3 phase wind motor) and underneath (foot operated bellows and pedals). In the restoration of this piano, all the original mechanisms will be preserved, with the electronics interface consisting of an addition to the basic design.

Notes on
Interfacing Pneumatic
Player Pianos

Carl Helmers

Everyone is familiar with the concept of the player piano, a complex mechanical monstrosity which had its heyday in the early part of this century as the prime home entertainment device before the invention of electronic media which now dominate the home entertainment scene. But player pianos are far from dead. Just as there is an active subculture of computer aficionados, there is a whole cult of player piano and mechanical music freaks. Thanks largely to these people a working player piano is not an uncommon sight in the parlors, dens and

living rooms of contemporary suburbia.

Many of the owners of player pianos may not recognize that these instruments can be a most interesting output device for a personal computer, an output device whose interface can be achieved with very little woodworking and mechanical skill as well as the usual hardware and software skills of the experienced computer hacker.

I have long had an interest in electronic music as generated and controlled by computers. It is this interest which started me on the road to learning electronics hard-

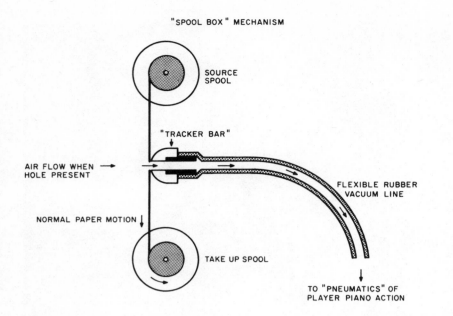

"SPOOL BOX" MECHANISM

SOURCE SPOOL

"TRACKER BAR"

AIR FLOW WHEN HOLE PRESENT →

FLEXIBLE RUBBER VACUUM LINE

NORMAL PAPER MOTION ↓

TAKE UP SPOOL

TO "PNEUMATICS" OF PLAYER PIANO ACTION

Figure 1: The normal arrangement of a player piano's vacuum control system is illustrated here. A player piano roll moving past a "tracker bar," analogous to a magnetic tape recorder's read head, turns on and turns off a flow of air into the evacuated control line which goes to one of the pneumatic controls of the piano. For the key mechanisms, the leading edge of loss of vacuum cues the striking of a key, which is held down until vacuum is restored. This occurs when the roll passes to a point which closes off the particular line. For control of a full 88 notes, there are 88 separate "channels" in the tracker bars of the more sophisticated players, not counting additional channels to control dynamics, pedals and other special effects.

ware skills needed to build computers for music control.

I also knew that player pianos existed, and would eventually make an interesting experiment for use with electronic music in programmed performances of concerto style works with orchestral background for the solo instrument provided by electronics. But I had never turned my attention to the details of the piano interface problem until one day in October of 1976 when I went to an estate auction in nearby Milford NH at which a 1910 Steinway-DuoArt baby grand player piano (in unplayable condition) was put on the block. After outbidding a mechanical music box museum owner from Maine, I had the potential for the ultimate piano. When the piano is eventually restored, it will provide my personal and computer music systems with a piano output device which, incidentally, can be used for normal piano rolls, normal practice under direct manual control of the keys, and under computer control using an interface to be described in this article.

The piano, which is shown in photo 1, gave me the impetus needed to examine in more detail the problem of controlling a

pneumatic vacuum line with the output of a computer. Figure 1 shows a schematic illustration of the essence of the typical player piano's control mechanism. The player piano roll passes over what is called the "tracker bar" in the jargon of that technology. This tracker bar has one hole for each active key of the piano as well as auxiliary holes for various other types of information which may be encoded on the rolls. When a hole in the roll passes the hole in the tracker bar, the vacuum line associated with the hole is opened to outside air. This release of the vacuum in the line triggers one of the "pneumatics" in a bank under the piano, which is basically a vacuum operated buffer amplifier with enough output power to toggle a key or actuate some other mechanism. The operation of the "pneumatic" is of no great concern at this point, since all we need to know is that if the vacuum line is opened, the key will be struck, and that if the vacuum line is closed, the key will be released and the device will charge up with vacuum, waiting for the next time that key is to be actuated. The conversion to electronic control is simplest if we just adapt the existing mechanism by plugging up the tracker bar holes (temporarily during electronic performance) and adding a "T" junction to each control line so that an electronic control valve can simulate the opening of the vacuum line. Figure 2 shows this adaptation of the usual vacuum line arrangement for electronic control.

Figure 2 also shows schematically the physical arrangement of a flap valve. As I began looking into the problem of controlling air flow, I quickly learned about the existence of electrically controlled pneumatic devices used in pipe organ and piano technology. It turns out that there is a company called Reisner Inc, which among other items makes a specialty of manufacturing and selling control valves for player pianos and pipe organs. Photo 2 shows the model for the schematic rendition in figure 2, a Reisner No 601-90 magnet with 5/8 inch valve mounted for the purpose of testing on a scrap of pine board, with a metal standoff used as the junction fitting to connect to the vacuum line. The Reisner subassembly consists of everything you see attached to the metal frame which is screwed to the top of the wood block: the magnet, the upper valve seal with cushions for sound dampening, and the return spring. In adapting this unit to a player piano's purposes, a bank of these valves is required, with a number depending upon the details of the particular piano. (For more complete information on these valves, contact Reisner Inc, 240 N Prospect St, POB 71,

Hagerstown MD 21740.) The physical mounting of the valve magnets, tubing, etc, depends upon the particular piano being converted. In the case of my baby grand player, an equipment chest will probably be attached under the sounding board in back of the presently installed pneumatics chest. Some woodworking ability and some mechanical handiwork are required in the fabrication of a bank of valves and in making the interconnections to the vacuum lines.

Electrical Drive and Interface

The era of integrated circuits simplifies the basic problem of controlling the sole-

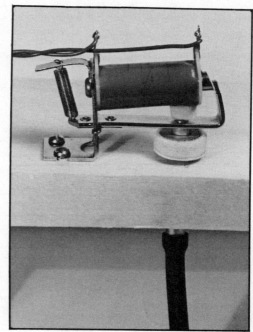

Photo 2: A test jig used to try out the magnetic control valve concept. The Reisner No. 601-90 magnet with 5/8 inch valve is mounted on a wood block using wood screws. In a final installation as part of a multiple valve attachment to a player piano's penumatics, one such valve would be assigned to each control tube of the piano.

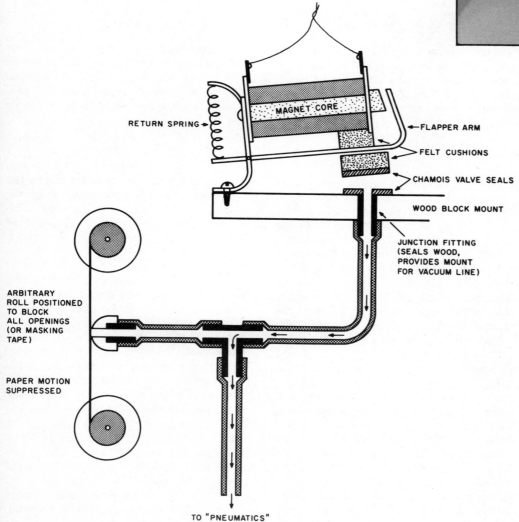

Figure 2: Adapting the player piano mechanisms for computer control is accomplished using Reisner magnets and flapper valves. Each tube from the tracker bar is modified with a "T" junction which allows an alternate control point on the vacuum line. When the piano is run in computer control mode, all the holes in the tracker bar are sealed and the solenoid controlled valves simulate the effects of the roll's passage over the bar. The sealing of the bar can be accomplished by pasting a run of masking tape over the bar or by disabling the spools box's drive motor and positioning a roll's leader over the tracker bar to close all the holes. For details of the valve, see photo 2. A basic interface drive circuit for the solenoid is shown in figure 3.

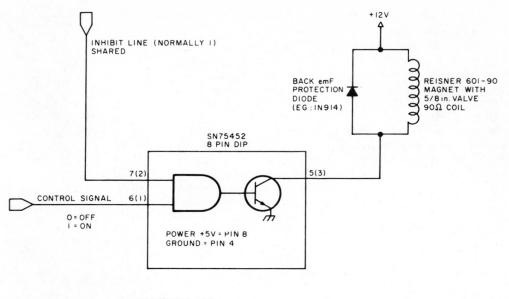

Figure 3: The basic magnet drive circuit used for the pneumatic player piano interface. The driver circuit shown here is a Texas Instruments SN75452, a dual peripheral driver which comes in a miniature 8 pin dual inline package. Each driver has a maximum capability of sinking 300 mA in the low level output state (logical 1 input which "turns on" the magnet). With the nominal 90 ohm coil and a low level output of 0.25 V the coil will have 11.75 V across it. The current through the coil is thus 130 mA, more than enough to actuate the valve based on experiments with the unit shown in photo 1 which was tested against a vacuum applied to valve through the rubber hose.

noids of the Reisner magnet valves. The solenoid coil has a resistance of nominally 90 ohms, and from the specification sheet (confirmed by tests in my laboratory) the valves can be actuated under load with a current higher than about 100 mA (about 9 V across the magnet). Using the *Texas Instruments Linear and Interface Circuits Data Book* as the source of information, it soon became apparent that the 75452 peripheral driver circuit (or its cousin, the 75451) would prove quite adequate for the job since it can sink 300 mA and has a maximum voltage rating well above the voltage required for the actuation of the magnets. The basic circuit for driving a solenoid with the 75452 integrated circuit is shown in figure 3. In this illustration, I have shown one of the two gate inputs as an inhibit signal (normally at logic level 1) and the other input pin as the control signal defined so that if it is low (logic 0) the magnet is off (valve closed) and if it is high (logic 1) the magnet is on (valve open). The diode mounted on the solenoid coil is an absolute requirement. These magnets have a considerable inductance, and as a result when the current is removed will generate a substantial back EMF which can damage the 75452 output transistor if it is not shorted out by the diode. (The inductance is suffi-

cient to cause an impulse which can be felt by the observer if fingers are held across the coil while the voltage is removed. This suggests a minimum of 50 to 100 V of inductive "kick.")

Logic of a Practical Interface

The brute force technique of interfacing the piano would be to simply put one wire from a latched output bit to each driver of the piano magnets, resulting in roughly 80 to 100 twisted pair interface data paths in a monstrously thick cable. This is an unwieldy mess. The problem is shared by pipe organ aficionados, as I found out from Jeff Raskin's lecture at the First West Coast Computer Faire's session on computers and music(see page 20). At that time he suggested the use of a serial technique to define the state of a bank of control valves. Basically, the technique consists of using serial synchronous transmission from the computer to cut down on the immense number of lines which would otherwise be required. Figure 4 shows a detailed sketch of the logic I designed which will enable this method of interfacing to be employed with three signal lines from a parallel output port of the control computer. In this scheme, each group of four valves is assigned one 4 bit shift register segment and a latch which can be loaded

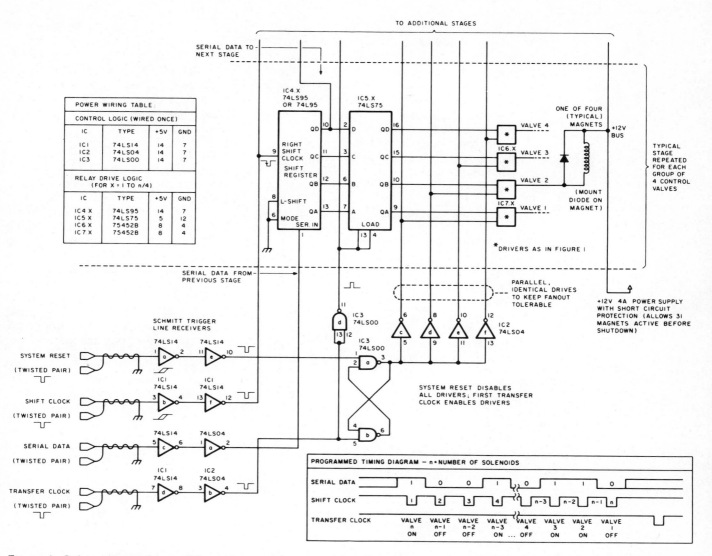

Figure 4: Solving the problem of heavy interconnection cables. This diagram shows a synchronous serial transmission scheme which requires four twisted pair wires to connect a parallel output port with the piano for programmed serial transfers. One twisted pair cable is dedicated to the system reset line so that the local electronics in the piano will turn off all drivers when the system is reset. The other three lines are connected to three output bits. One bit is programmed with the successive bits of data for the various valves when an output transfer is done. After each data bit is defined, the shift clock line is toggled to push its value down the 88-100 or so shift register stages assigned to control the 88 to 100 valves used in the piano. Then, when all the bits have been defined in successive operations, the transfer clock line is toggled to parallel load all the control latches and define the state of the solenoids. With a programmed transfer loop on a typical microprocessor, no more than 50 μs per bit should be required, or an update time of 5 ms per 100 solenoid data transfer under program control. This gives the processor a limiting resolution of 1/200th of a second, well within the timing accuracy needed for music. Using specialized transmission hardware to automatically serialize the data from 8 bit bytes would speed up the typical data rates if needed.

from the shift register. This module of four bits works out very well with the widely available TTL MSI technology shown. The entire bank of n/4 such modules defines an n bit shift register with an n bit latch in parallel. Transfers of new information are accomplished (see timing diagram) under program control by shifting out n bit values with the data line and shift clock line, after which the now valid outputs of the n bit shift register can be transferred into the n bit

latch to set the state of the valves.

As conceived here, the unit can be directly plugged into an existing parallel output port which has 3 available lines. The timing diagram shown in figure 4 is implemented in software by programming the states of the bits when transferring the current data for the piano, which might be derived from a music interpreter program, or from a real time keyboard source. When programming the low level transfer routine, each bit in turn is shifted and is used to control how the "serial data" line will be set at the output port. After the bit is defined, the "shift clock" bit is turned off, then turned back on, to clock the data into the shift register. After all the control bits have been transferred by "n" operations, the output bit which controls the "transfer clock" line is toggled off, then on, accomplishing the transfer of the shift register's contents to the latches and thus defining the state of the various solenoids.

System Reset and Inhibit

The state of the solenoid drivers must be set in software in the control computer; however, if the system is first turned on, or if garbage is left over from previous use, the result could be a crashing dissonance on the piano output device. To account for bad initial values, the circuit incorporates IC3, which drives the inhibit lines as a set-reset flip flop. When system reset occurs (low level on that line) all the solenoid drivers are disabled by a low level on the "inhibit" input (see figure 3). When the first transfer of data under program control defines a valid solenoid drive state, the inhibit condition is removed by the transfer clock pulse, and does not recur until another system reset.

Summary

In these notes, I have outlined the essentials of the low level details needed to interface a pneumatic player piano with a typical computer system's parallel output lines. This can lead to some very interesting personal use applications of computers, as new piano music is programmed and played using the mass storage facilities of a personal computer instead of the traditional piano roll. These notes are by no means complete, and I leave the software of control of the piano system to the tastes and judgement of the individual user.∎

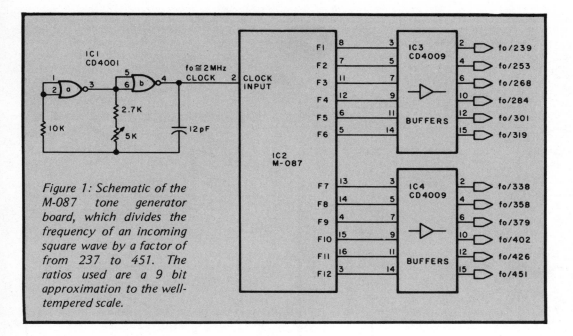

Figure 1: Schematic of the M-087 tone generator board, which divides the frequency of an incoming square wave by a factor of from 237 to 451. The ratios used are a 9 bit approximation to the well-tempered scale.

Electronic Organ Chips For Use in Computer Music Synthesis

Robert Grappel

Generation of music by the use of computers has intrigued many people over the years, and a number of schemes have been published. It appears to me, however, that those involved in computer music may be missing a potentially rich source of special components for their systems: the electronic organ. There are a substantial number of large scale integrated circuits made specially for electronic organ applications, many of which can be readily adapted to computer music use. This article describes some of these special components and shows how one might apply them in a computer context. The chips described are made by the SGS-ATES Semiconductor Corp, 79 Massasoit St, Waltham MA 02154. They are modestly priced and are available in single units or small quantities to experimenters. Much of the data in this article comes from the SGS-ATES data sheets associated with their chips. The article has three subsections: pitch generation, rhythm and accompaniment generation.

Pitch Generation

Programmed computer music generators typically generate pitches using carefully timed delay loops. Unfortunately, the typical processor must work nearly full time to generate a typical musical note. Tuning such loops can be a tedious and time consuming process. The use of organ chips allows a relatively simple pitch generator to be built that can produce 96 different pitches (a piano has only 88) in perfect tune. The computer need only output a byte that selects the appropriate note. Many different notes can be generated in parallel using several output ports. This frees the computer from the time consuming generation of pitch in order to control timing, waveshaping, etc.

The heart of the pitch generator is the M-087 upper octave chip. This $9 LSI package accepts a clock and divides it by 12 different divisors. These divisors are chosen to produce 12 even-tempered musical notes. Thus, one tuned clock frequency produces an entire octave of perfectly tuned notes. A circuit to use the M-087 is shown in figure 1. The M-087 is a CMOS device, so it is used with CMOS logic. The logic runs from +5 to −5 V supplies to obtain a symmetrical waveform about ground potential. The M-087 also requires a −12 V supply. The input clock is generated by an astable multi-

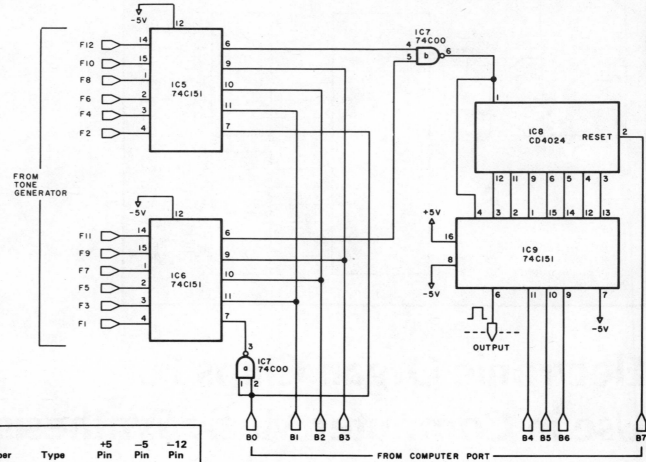

IC Number	Type	+5 Pin	−5 Pin	−12 Pin
IC1	CD4001	14	7	—
IC2	M-087	1	10	9
IC3	CD4009	1, 16	8	—
IC4	CD4009	1, 16	8	—
IC5	74C151	16	8	—
IC6	74C151	16	8	—
IC7	74C00	14	7	—
IC8	CD4024	14	7	—
IC9	74C151	16	8	—
IC10	M-252AD	9	—	10

Table 1: Power wiring table for figures 1, 2 and 5.

Figure 2: Schematic of the note board. Two multiplexers (IC5 and IC6) form a 1 of 16 selector. The low order four bits of the input from the computer select either no note or one of the twelve notes from the tone board (figure 1). The note is then transformed to the correct octave by IC8, a 7 stage binary counter. IC9 selects either the fundamental note or one of the seven other octaves based on the B4-B6 lines from the computer. The output of the board is a square wave ranging from +5 to −5 V.

vibrator composed of two gates. A crystal oscillator could also be used. The output of the clock should be a square wave of frequency 2.0024 MHz for perfect tune. The 12 outputs of the M-087 are square waves swinging between +5 and −5 V. The frequency divisions are shown in the figure. CMOS buffers are shown on the outputs for extra drive capacity. The idea is that only one tone generator board can drive many note boards; each note board produces an output pitch.

Figure 2 shows a note board schematic. The two 74C151 multiplexers on the left form a 1 of 16 selector. The low order four bits of the input from the computer select either no note or one of the 12 notes from the tone board. Once the note is selected, it must be transformed to the desired octave. The CD4024 7 stage binary counter performs this task. Since each octave is simply one half the frequency of the higher octave, this divides the input note at seven different octaves. The 74C151 on the right selects either the fundamental note or one of the seven other octaves, based on the B4 thru B6 bits from the computer. Thus, the note board can select silence or one of 12 notes in one of eight octaves. The output is a square wave between +5 and −5 V. This signal may be shaped, filtered, etc, and mixed with signals from other note boards. With the appropriate bit pattern at the computer port, the note board will generate the note with no further computer aid.

One point remains, however. This circuit produces a transient during changes in pitch because the dividers in the octave generator are not cleared. To fix this, a reset line is brought from the divider to the port. A brief positive pulse on the reset line generated whenever the port is accessed will clear the dividers and eliminate the transient.

Rhythm Generation

After generating pitch, the next important step in music is timing, or rhythm. Music has been defined as "time ordered sound." This section describes a circuit to ease this part of music making. Musicians often use timing aids such as metronomes to produce periodic signals as cues to the musician. The M-252 circuit provides cues to the computer music synthesizer.

The M-252 chip is one of a family of rhythm generators made by SGS-ATES. It provides a set of 15 rhythms for $13.50 (a block diagram of this chip is shown in figure 3). The M-252 takes a clock input that forms the basis of the rhythm. This clock is divided down to provide the musical subdivisions of the rhythm. A measure can have up to 32 subdivisions. The rhythms themselves are produced by a read only memory in the chip containing 3840 bits. This memory has 32 rows, corresponding to the 32 elementary times. It has 120 columns (15 groups of 8). The 15 groups correspond to the 15 input states of the four rhythm select lines (the sixteenth state turns the generator off). The eight outputs are driven by the bits thus selected in the memory. Rhythms having fewer than 32 elementary units reset the input clock divider at the appropriate time for their meter. This reset signal is output as a "downbeat" signal to indicate the beginning of a new musical measure.

Figure 4 shows the rhythms preprogrammed into the M-252. These are the standard programs available, but, if you buy a lot of them, the chip can be custom programmed. Contact the manufacturer for programming details. M-252 chips may be used in combination to increase the number of rhythms, the number of outputs, or the number of elementary times (see the data sheets for these circuits). Figure 5 shows a simple circuit for using the M-252. An external reset signal is provided, as well as an LED driven by the downbeat output. The eight outputs are shown driving instrument circuits. These circuits are triggered by the memory outputs in the proper order for the desired rhythm. Figure 6 shows the timing of this chip.

The M-252 requires two power sources, +5 V and −12 V. The clock is TTL compatible, as are the rhythm selects and reset. The outputs provide a roughly symmetrical swing

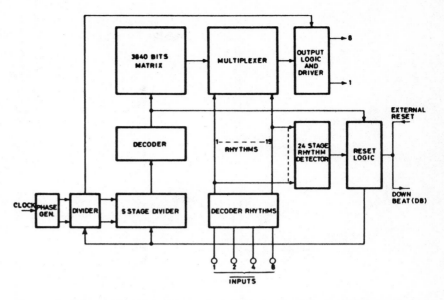

Figure 3: Block diagram of the M-252 rhythm generator. Supplied courtesy of SGS-ATES.

RHYTHM	CODE				STANDARD CONTENT-AA		STANDARD CONTENT-AD	
	INPUT 8	INPUT 4	INPUT 2	INPUT 1				
1	1	1	1	0	Waltz	3/4	Waltz	3/4
2	1	1	0	1	Jazz Waltz	3/4	Tango	2/4
3	1	1	0	0	Tango	2/4	March	2/4
4	1	0	1	1	March	2/4	Swing	4/4
5	1	0	1	0	Swing	4/4	Mambo	4/4
6	1	0	0	1	Foxtrot	4/4	Slow Rock	6/8
7	1	0	0	0	Slow Rock	6/8	Beat	4/4
8	0	1	1	1	Pop Rock	4/4	Samba	4/4
9	0	1	1	0	Shuffle	2/4	Bossa Nova	4/4
10	0	1	0	1	Mambo	4/4	Cha Cha	4/4
11	0	1	0	0	Beguine	4/4	Rhumba	4/4
12	0	0	1	1	Cha Cha	4/4	Beguine	4/4
13	0	0	1	0	Bajon	4/4	Bajon	4/4
14	0	0	0	1	Samba	4/4	Foxtrot	4/4
15	0	0	0	0	Bossa Nova	4/4	Shuffle	2/4
No selected rhythm	1	1	1	1				

Figure 4: Rhythm selection logic chart for the M-252 rhythm generator. Supplied courtesy of SGS-ATES.

from +5 to −5 V. In a computer application, these, in addition to the downbeat signal, would provide interrupt or input signals to the computer. They give the computer musician cues, like an electronic conductor. The computer can control the input clock rate, the rhythm selected, and the reset. These provide the range of control necessary for musicality. The inherent flexibility of this system makes it a strong competitor to the timing loop approach often used in computer music applications.

Accompaniment Generation

Generating accompaniments is a complicated process. SGS-ATES sells a sophisticated chip, the M-251, which can generate

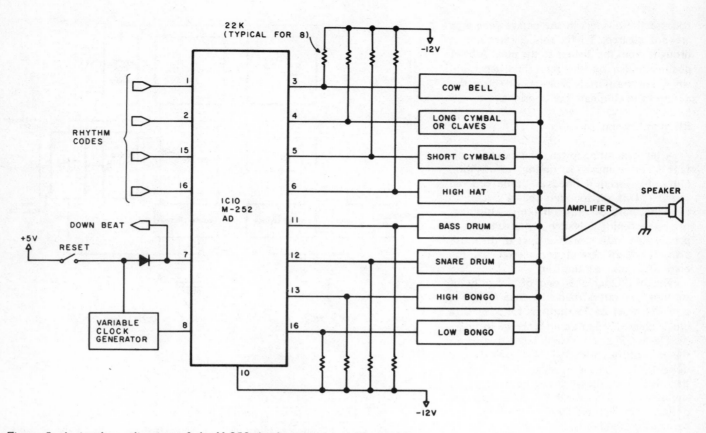

Figure 5: A simple application of the M-252 rhythm generator. The circuit is shown here driving eight "instrument" circuits.

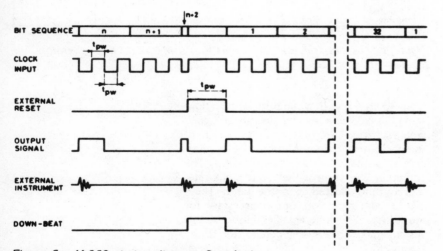

Figure 6a: M-252 timing diagram. Supplied courtesy of SGS-ATES. In these timing waveforms it has been assumed, for example, that in the truth table bits n + 1 and 2 have not been programmed, ie: the musical instrument has not been introduced. All the other bits have been programmed for the introduction of the instruments.

many types of musical accompaniment. The chip sells for $36. There are more than 20 data sheets of diagrams and charts. This section briefly outlines the capabilities of this chip and how it might be used in a computer context.

Referring to the block diagram in figure 7, we see that the M-251 generates three types of accompaniment: chords, arpeggios, and bass. Chords are simultaneous combinations of several notes chosen to form a particular harmony. Arpeggios are like chords except that the notes are played sequentially instead of simultaneously. Bass accompaniments use sequences of low notes chosen to form harmonious relationships with higher melody notes. The M-251 is capable of forming chords, arpeggios, etc, with these proper relationships.

The M-251 takes 12 frequency inputs. These come from the tone generator board or another octave generator. It also takes 24 note inputs. These cover two octaves of the frequency range of the instrument. The computer switches these to ground when that note is to be played (similar to the keys of an organ). The M-251 uses these signals to decide how to form an accompaniment. The M-251 also requires eight rhythm inputs to control bass lines, chords, and arpeggios. These are derived from a rhythm generator, such as the M-252. These inputs are labelled

O1 thru O8. O1 is not shown in figure 7. It is used to trigger the envelope formation circuitry for chords (external to the M-251). Bass and arpeggio have their own trigger outputs. There are also three command inputs that control the formation of chords, etc. Some of the variables allow choice of major or minor chords, sixth or seventh chords, diminished or augmented chords, etc. The notes of the bass accompaniment are also chosen by these signals. Thus, the M-251 examines the note inputs to see what is being played, then builds chords and bass and arpeggios based upon the input notes, but subject to the control of the command inputs. The rhythm inputs control the time sequence of the outputs, and the M-251 then forms the outputs and provides trigger signals. Not bad for a single chip! For further information on the many modes of operation of the M-251, please refer to the data sheet. The M-251 makes quite a good musician once you give it the necessary inputs.

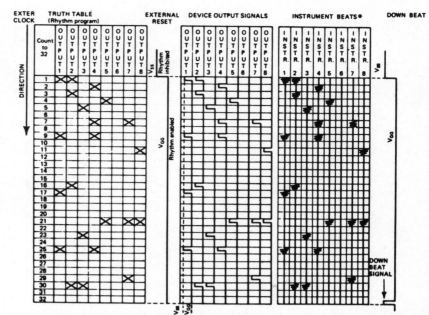

* The lowering of the music signals depends on the intrinsic decay time of the sound generator and not on the length of the enable pulses. Each beat can therefore last for more than one elementary time

Figure 6b: M-252 beat chart. Supplied courtesy of SGS-ATES.

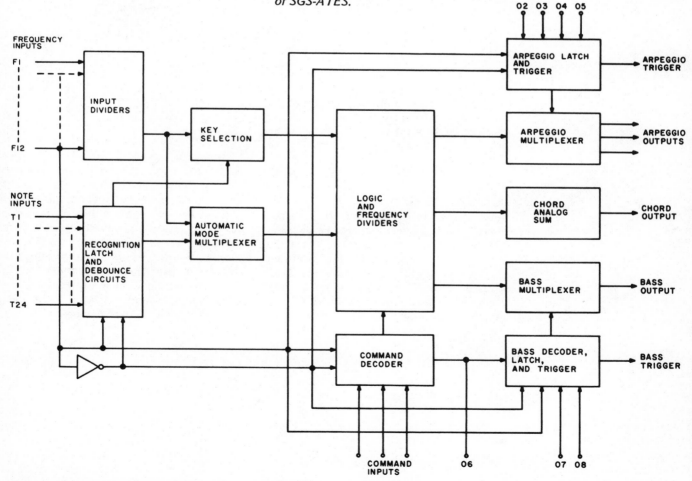

Figure 7: Block diagram of the M-251 accompaniment generator. This circuit can generate three types of accompaniment: chords, arpeggios and bass. This complex circuit requires 12 frequency inputs, 24 note inputs, 8 rhythm inputs, and 3 command inputs.

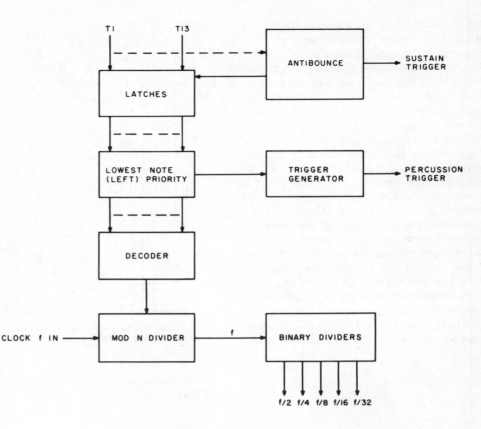

Figure 8: Block diagram of the M-147 pedal sustain generator circuit. It can play up to 13 different bass notes in any combination to serve as an accompaniment.

SGS-ATES makes one other accompanist: the M-147 pedal-sustain chip. This circuit is much simpler, and sells for $9.75. It is intended to form a sustained or percussive bass accompaniment using the pedals of an organ. Figure 8 shows the block diagram of the M-147.

The M-147 takes a clock input of about 2 MHz (this clock should be the same one that drives the tone generator, or the bass notes will not be in tune with the melody). There are also 13 note inputs to be switched by the computer or musician to select the bass note. The lowest pitch selected will gain priority and will lock out higher notes until released. Two trigger outputs are formed, one which detects changes in note selected, and the other which fires on each note de-

pression. The M-147 provides five outputs. These are five octaves of the bass note selected.

Summary

I hope this quick discussion of a family of electronic organ chips and their application will prove useful to those attempting to make their computers into playable instruments. The built-in musicality of these chips can go a long way toward this goal. With the problems of pitch generation, rhythm, and accompaniment eased by automation, the computer programmer can work on the more interesting problem of teaching a computer music instead of laboring with timing loops and huge tables of numbers.■

Fast Fourier Transforms on Your Home Computer

William D Stanley
Steven J Peterson

The advent of the home computer makes possible many new and varied applications both of a general nature and of a scientific or mathematical nature. One of the latter applications we have successfully implemented on a personal computer is the *fast Fourier transform,* which we will subsequently refer to as the FFT, according to standard usage. Some of the most important properties of the FFT are described in this article, and an FFT program written for the Digital Group Z-80 System using BASIC is provided.

Continuous Fourier Transform

Before discussing the FFT in particular, it is desirable to briefly survey some of the general concepts of the classical continuous Fourier (pronounced "foor-yay") transform. The terminology used refers to *time* and *frequency* since they are among the most common variables of interest in many applications, although the theory involved applies to a variety of different types of physical phenomena.

Consider the waveform x(t) shown in figure 1a which is displayed as a function of *time* (denoted by t). The waveform can also be described by the *frequencies* present in the signal. This description is called the *spectrum* of the time signal and, mathematically, it is the *Fourier transform* of the time function. The process of Fourier transformation is represented by the mathematical function

$$X(f) = \int_{-\infty}^{\infty} x(t)e^{-j2\pi ft}\,dt$$

where X(f) is the Fourier transform of x(t).

[The constant j is used in electrical engineering to denote $\sqrt{-1}$, also called i. The number e, 2.71828, is the base of the natural algorithms. . . .CM] For all but fairly simple functions, this mathematical process represented a formidable operation for many years. Prior to the development of the digital computer, many analytical and experimental methods were investigated for determining the approximate spectra of functions that arose in physical systems.

The magnitude of a typical spectrum is shown in figure 1b and is denoted by |X(f)|, where f represents the frequency in Hertz (Hz). For example, if x(t) were a music signal, strong peaks of the spectrum at low frequencies would be characteristic of a significant amount of bass content such as

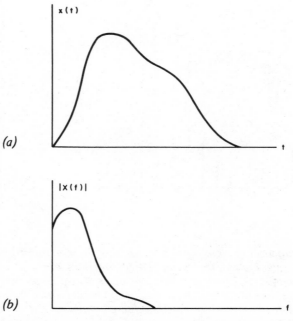

(a)

(b)

Figure 1: An arbitrary continuous signal x(t) expressed as a function of time (a) may also be described by its spectrum or Fourier transform X(f), which is expressed as a function of frequency (b). The relative strength of the spectrum at different frequencies is a measure of the frequency content that comprises the given signal. The concept of spectrum finds numerous applications in many varied disciplines including music waveform analysis, communications signal analysis, mechanical vibrations, oceanography, statistics, and others. In signal analysis, the function x(t) is said to be a time domain *representation, and X(f) is said to be a* frequency domain *representation.*

drums or tubas. Conversely, many string instruments such as the violin display stronger peaks at higher frequencies in the audio spectrum. The frequency spectrum (or Fourier transform) thus provides a plot of the relative weight of different frequencies that comprise or represent the given signal.

If the Fourier transform or spectrum of a signal is known, the time function may be determined from the inverse transformation which is given by

$$x(t) = \int_{-\infty}^{\infty} X(f)e^{j2\pi ft} \, df$$

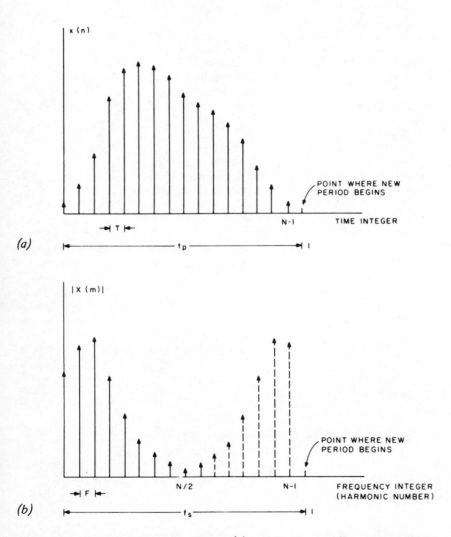

(a)

(b)

Figure 2: A sampled function of time (a) and its discrete Fourier transform spectrum (b). The discrete Fourier transform (DFT) functions are used to approximate the continuous transform functions whenever digital implementation is to be used. The time function is sampled at N points separated by an increment T over an interval $t_p = NT$ to create a discrete function $x(n)$. The resulting spectrum $X(m)$ is periodic with a period $f_s = 1/T$ and contains N components within one period with spacing between components $F = 1/t_p$. If $x(n)$ is a real function, only half or N/2 of the spectral components are unique. The integers n and m represent the time and frequency integers which identify the location in the sequence of the time sample ($t = nT$) and the frequency component or harmonic number ($f = mF$).

Observe that the inverse transform has essentially the same general form as the direct transform except for the sign of the exponential argument.

The concept of the frequency spectrum has long played a most important role in numerous scientific applications and has been of interest to mathematicians, engineers and scientists of many different disciplines. Among the areas where spectral analysis has been employed are sound and music analysis, communications systems design, analysis of mechanical vibrations, ocean wave analysis, statistics and many others.

Discrete Fourier Transform

The heart of the FFT is a mathematical operation known as the *discrete Fourier transform* (DFT). In the DFT, a set of integers n and m are defined to represent the equivalent in a sense of the time and frequency variables, respectively, of the continuous Fourier transform. This correspondence is best seen by observing the sampled signal $x(n)$ shown in figure 2a. There are assumed to be N samples of the signal spaced T seconds apart. Thus, as n varies from 0 to N−1, the N samples of the time signal are generated. The duration of the time signal is $t_p = NT$.

The DFT of $x(n)$ is defined by the finite summation

$$X(m) = \frac{1}{N} \sum_{n=0}^{N-1} x(n)W^{mn}$$

where

$$W = e^{\frac{-j2\pi}{N}}$$

The function $X(m)$ represents a discrete spectrum with m serving the same purpose in frequency as n did in time. The frequency increment between successive components is $F = 1/t_p$ so that the spectral component at a frequency mF is $X(m)$. For $x(n)$ real and for N time points, a unique spectrum can be computed only at N/2 frequency points. Actually, $X(m)$ is periodic in m with N points in each period, but only N/2 are unique. $X(m)$ is, in general, a complex function consisting of a real and an imaginary part at each frequency. For many applications, the magnitude spectrum $|X(m)|$ is the quantity of most significance. Some of the preceding points are illustrated in figure 2b.

As in the case of continuous signals, an *inverse discrete Fourier transform* (IDFT) can be defined. In this case, the inverse transformation is

$$x(n) = \sum_{m=0}^{N-1} X(m)W^{-mn}$$

The resulting function is periodic in the variable n and has N points in one period. Thus, even if the original time signal were not periodic, the operation of the IDFT produces a function capable of providing the desired results in one cycle, but the pattern continues to repeat itself if the interval is extended outside of the basic range.

Observation of the definition of the DFT reveals that there are approximately N complex multiplications and about the same number of complex additions required to compute the spectrum at one particular value of m. Since there are N/2 unique spectral components, the total number of computations required to generate a complete spectrum is of the order of N^2. The Cooley-Tukey algorithm, published in 1965, demonstrates one way to perform this transformation with a number of computations of the order of $N \log_2(N)$, which turns out to be an enormous savings in computational time for long signal records. The Cooley-Tukey algorithm, along with subsequent variations, is referred to as the *fast Fourier transform* (FFT). Thus, the FFT is a high speed algorithm for computing the discrete Fourier transform.

While the DFT is a finite summation and the classical Fourier transform is an integral transform, the DFT may be used to closely approximate the continuous function under many circumstances. Some of the concepts involved with such an approximation are considered later in this article.

The various FFT algorithms work best when the number of points in the sample record is an integer power of 2, ie: $N = 2^k$, where k is an integer. The form of one of the basic algorithms is shown in figure 3 for the case of N = 8. Obviously, N = 8 is far too small for most applications, but the flow graph is of interest in understanding the form of the general computational algorithm. This particular algorithm is referred to as an *in place* algorithm since at each stage of the computation, the data may be stored in the same memory locations from which they were obtained.

Implementation of In Place Algorithm

The in place algorithm previously discussed was implemented on the Digital Group Z-80 System using BASIC. The program is given in listing 1. The particular system used had 18 K bytes of memory, of which about 12 K bytes were required for the BASIC software. It was determined

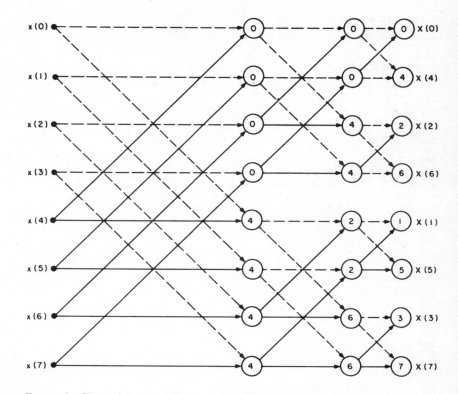

Figure 3: Flow diagram indicating the computations involved in an 8 point fast Fourier transform (FFT) implementation of the discrete Fourier transform (DFT) function. Significant reductions in computation time are achieved with FFT realizations of large arrays. For example, the computation time for a 1024 (2^{10}) sequence of samples using an FFT is approximately 1 percent of the time required by direct application of the DFT. In the chart, two paths merging together in a given column represent a combination of two quantities in the preceding column. For example, the first quantity in the second column is obtained by forming x(0) + W^0x(4). The first term is indicated by the dashed line and the second is indicated by the solid line. The integer in the circle is the power of W. (See text for definition of W.) The pattern continues until the spectrum appears in the last column. This particular algorithm for the FFT results in a scrambled order for the spectral coefficients as can be seen from the chart. Some variations result in a natural order but require more internal memory.

that a 256 point transform could be computed with this system and the program listed uses this capacity. It could be readily expanded or contracted as the available memory size dictates. However, the size selected should be chosen as an integer power of 2 as previously noted. Thus, the next smaller size should be 128 and the next larger size should be 512.

In order to reduce the memory requirements, the trigonometric functions are generated as they are required in the program. This approach is not nearly as efficient from the standpoint of computation time as would be the process of initially generating and storing the functions in

```
2 DIM X1(256),X2(256)
4 N=256 : L=8 : P1=3.14159
6 REM -- GENERATE TIME FUNCTION --
10 REM
20 REM   LINE NUMBERS 10-499 ARE USED TO
30 REM   GENERATE OR INPUT THE TIME FUNCTION
40 REM
500 PRINT "DO YOU WANT A LISTING OF THE GENERATED TIME FUNCTION ";
510 INPUT A$
520 IF A$="NO" THEN 640
530 IF A$<>"YES" THEN 500
540 B=X1(0)
550 FOR Z=0 TO N-1
560 IF ABS(X1(Z))>B THEN B=ABS(X1(Z))
580 NEXT Z
600 FOR Z=0 TO N-1
610 PRINT X1(Z);TAB(41+20*X1(Z)/B);"*"
620 NEXT Z
630 REM  - SCALE INPUT TIME FUNCTION -
640 FOR Z=0 TO N-1
650 X1(Z)=X1(Z)/N
660 NEXT Z
670 REM - - FFT IN-PLACE ALGORITHM - -
675 PRINT" - FFT CALCULATION IN PROGRESS -"
680 I1=N/2 : I2=1 : V=2*P1/N
690 FOR I=1 TO L
700 I3=0 : I4=I1
710 FOR K=1 TO I2
720 X=INT(I3/I1)
730 GOSUB 1300
740 I5=Y
750 Z1=COS(V*I5)
760 Z2=-SIN(V*I5)
770 FOR M=I3 TO I4-1
780 A1=X1(M) : A2=X2(M)
790 B1=Z1*X1(M+I1)-Z2*X2(M+I1)
800 B2=Z2*X1(M+I1)+Z1*X2(M+I1)
810 X1(M)=A1+B1 : X2(M)=A2+B2
820 X1(M+I1)=A1-B1 : X2(M+I1)=A2-B2
830 NEXT M
840 I3=I3+2*I1 : I4=I4+2*I1
850 NEXT K
860 I1=I1/2 : I2=2*I2
870 NEXT I
880 REM - OUTPUT RESULTS -
890 PRINT"IN WHAT FORM DO YOU WANT THE OUTPUT ?"
900 PRINT"   MAGNITUDE SPECTRUM PLOT     (1)"
910 PRINT"   TABLE OF VALUES             (2)"
920 INPUT A
930 IF A=1 THEN 970
940 IF A=2 THEN 1130
950 PRINT"INCORRECT INPUT (1 OR 2)" : GOTO 890
960 REM - OUTPUT MAGNITUDE SPECTRUM PLOT -
970 B=0
975 PRINT" - CALCULATIONS IN PROGRESS  "
980 FOR Z=0 TO N/2
985 X=Z
990 GOSUB 1390
1000 IF X3>B THEN B=X3
1010 NEXT Z
1020 FOR Z=0 TO N/2
1025 X=Z
1030 GOSUB 1390
1040 X4=INT(55*X3/B)
1050 C=0
1060 PRINT Z;TAB(5);"!";
1070 C=C+1
1080 IF C<X4 THEN PRINT"=", : GOTO 1070
1090 PRINT ""
1100 NEXT Z
1110 GOTO 1240
1120 REM - OUTPUT TABLE OF VALUES -
1130 U=0
1140 Z=0
1150 PRINT"HARMONIC";TAB(14);"REAL";TAB(30);
1160 PRINT"IMAGINARY";TAB(50);"MAGNITUDE"
1165 X=U
1170 GOSUB 1390
1180 PRINT U;TAB(10);X1(Y);TAB(30);X2(Y);TAB(50);X3
1190 U=U+1 : Z=Z+1
1200 IF Z>9 THEN 1140
1210 IF U>N/2 THEN 1240
1220 GOTO 1165
1230 REM - TERMINATE ? -
1240 PRINT"DO YOU WANT ANOTHER OUTPUT (YES, NO)";
1250 INPUT A$
1260 IF A$="YES" THEN 890
1270 IF A$<>"NO" THEN 1240
1280 END
1290 REM - SCRAMBLER SUBROUTINE -
1300 Y=0 : N1=N
1310 FOR W=1 TO L
1320 N1=N1/2
1330 IF X<N1 THEN 1360
1340 Y=Y+2^(W-1)
1350 X=X-N1
1360 NEXT W
1370 RETURN
1380 REM - MAGNITUDE (X3) SUBROUTINE -
1390 GOSUB 1300
1400 X3=SQRT(X1(Y)^2 + X2(Y)^2)
1410 RETURN
1420 END
```

memory so that they can simply be called as required. However, where speed is not a major priority, this approach minimizes the total memory required.

Statements 10 through 499 in the program represent the particular input signal for which the transform is being computed. The time function may be generated by appropriate equations or an algorithm as will be demonstrated for several cases later. For experimental data, the values could be listed point by point if the function cannot be readily described by an equation.

Applying the Program

In order to effectively utilize an FFT program for spectral analysis, it is necessary to understand some of the peculiarities of the DFT and its relationship to the continuous Fourier transform. Although the time signal may or may not be periodic in nature, the mathematical form of the DFT treats the signal as if it were periodic. The total duration of the time signal is the period t_p, and for the program being considered, this period contains 256 points. If T is the time increment between samples, then $t_p = 256\,T$. The spectrum obtained from the DFT is also periodic and contains N (or 256) spectral components. However, for a time function that is real (which incidentally is the case for all signals considered in this article), it can be shown that half of the components are ambiguous; ie: they are similar to the other half and do not represent any actual spectral information. Thus, there are N/2 (or 128) meaningful complex spectral components that are obtained with the FFT. These components are spaced apart in frequency by $F = 1/t_p$. The value for m = 0 corresponds to the DC component, m = 1 is the fundamental, m = 2 is the second harmonic, etc. According to sampling theory, a time signal must be sampled at a rate at least equal to (practically speaking, greater than) twice the highest frequency contained in the spectrum. Thus, if the highest frequency contained in a spectrum is known to be no greater than f_h, the maximum time between samples (T) should be chosen to satisfy $T < \frac{1}{2f_h}$. If this condition is not met, there will be a spectral overlap or *aliasing* effect which will distort the spectrum.

For a fixed number of points (such as 256 for the program under discussion), there is a trade-off between the high frequency capability and the spectral resolution. In order to analyze higher frequencies, a shorter sampling time is required, but this necessitates a shorter overall period and a larger increment between successive frequencies. Specifically for 256 points, N/2 = 128; and since N = 0 corresponds to DC, the highest frequency that can be measured is 127 times the spectral resolution. It is very important that the sampling rate be chosen to be greater than twice the highest frequency in the spectrum even if the higher frequencies are not of interest. If the minimum sampling rate requirement is not met, erroneous spectral components may appear at various places in the spectrum.

There are various other properties of the DFT that may be important in applying an FFT program in various situations. The reader is encouraged to consult one of the references listed at the end of this article or the many other available sources for more extensive details, since this article provides only a brief overview of the theory along with the details of a workable program for a home computer.

Examples

Several examples that illustrate some of the properties of the FFT are now considered. The various function programs for these waveforms are shown in listing 2. The first example is that of a single rectangular pulse whose duration is 25 percent of the total period corresponding to 256/4, or 64 points as illustrated in figure 4. (Due to the large number of points, the function is shown as a continuous curve.) The video display of the first 14 spectral components in tabular form is shown in photo 1, and the first 15 components of the magnitude spectrum are displayed in photo 2. Henceforth,

```
10 REM - GENERATE 25% PULSE
20 FOR Z=0 TO N/4
30 X1(Z)=1
40 NEXT Z
50 FOR Z=N/4 TO N
60 X1(Z)=0
70 NEXT Z


10 REM - GENERATE 12.5% PULSE
20 FOR Z=0 TO N/8
30 X1(Z)=1
40 NEXT Z
50 FOR Z=N/8 TO N
60 X1(Z)=0
70 NEXT Z


10 REM - GENERATE 1000HZ SINE WAVE
20 T=0
30 FOR Z=0 TO N-1
40 X1(Z)=SIN(2*3.14159*1000*T)
50 T=T+1.953125E-4
60 NEXT Z


10 REM - GENERATE 1010HZ SINE WAVE
20 T=0
30 FOR Z=0 TO N-1
40 X1(Z)=SIN(2*3.14159*1010*T)
50 T=T+1.953125E-4
60 NEXT Z
```

Listing 2: Three different generating routines that can be used with listing 1 as the time functions. The first routine generates a pulse function that lasts 25 percent of the time that is being analyzed. The second routine also generates a pulse but half as long as the first routine. The third and fourth routines generate sine waves which are only slightly different.

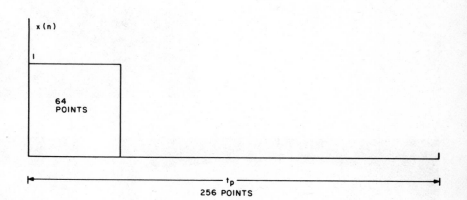

Figure 4: Rectangular pulse for which the FFT is partially displayed in photos 1 and 2. The pulse is unity for 64 of the 256 points in the time record and zero for the remainder.

Figure 5: Rectangular pulse for which the FFT is partially displayed in photo 3. The pulse is unity for 32 of the 256 points in the time record and zero for the remainder. Since this pulse is shorter than the one of figure 4, the spectrum is broader. In general, there is an inverse relationship between the width of a pulse-like time function and the width of the frequency spectrum. This property is an important concept in signal transmission and results in the requirement of larger bandwidths for transmitting shorter pulse signals.

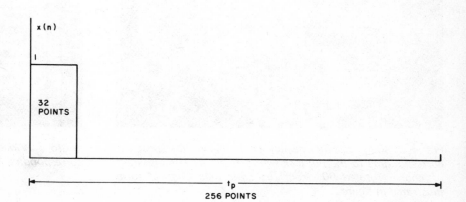

only the magnitude spectra will be shown.

When the pulse duration is changed to 12.5 percent of the period or 32 points as indicated in figure 5, the magnitude spectrum changes to the form shown in photo 3.

It should be pointed out that the bandwidth of a rectangular pulse is theoretically infinite in extent and so there is some aliasing error in each of these cases. However, the effects of aliasing are not pronounced in these two examples over the frequency range shown in the photos. At larger harmonic values for the given signals and at shorter pulse widths for the given frequency range, the aliasing errors would be more significant.

A sine wave representing an assumed frequency of 1000 Hz and an assumed sampling time of T = 0.1953 ms was generated and analyzed. The resulting spectrum is shown in photo 4. Note that the frequency resolution is F = 1/(0.1953 x 10^{-3} x 256) = 20 Hz so that 1000 Hz corresponds to harmonic number 50. Observe that an ideal single line appears as one might hope. On the other

Photo 1: The first 14 components (DC and harmonics up through the 13th) of the FFT spectrum corresponding to the pulse shown in figure 4. The program lists the real part of X(m), the imaginary part of X(m) and the magnitude |X(m)|.

HARMONIC	REAL	IMAGINARY	MAGNITUDE
0	.25	0	.25
1	.16110021	-.15719375	.22500477
2	3.906457SE-03	-.15912311	.15917106
3	-5.1074587E-02	-5.498105ZE-02	7.50435I8E-02
4	0	0	0
5	3.3744231E-02	-2.9837863E-02	4.504410ZE-02
6	3.906392SE-03	-.05295584	5.3099726E-02
7	-2.072739SE-02	-2.4633799E-02	3.2193922E-02
8	0	0	0
9	1.956507SE-02	-1.5658766E-02	2.5059713E-02
10	3.906333SE-03	-.03167107	3.191106SE-02
11	-1.242750SE-02	-1.6333864E-02	2.052400SE-02
12	0	0	0
13	.01409184	-1.0185506E-02	1.7307401E-02

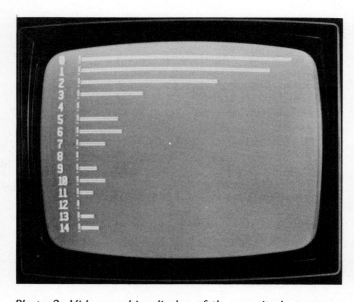

Photo 2: Video graphics display of the magnitude spectrum corresponding to the pulse shown in figure 4. The display is of course rotated 90° from the basic mathematical form illustrated in figure 2.

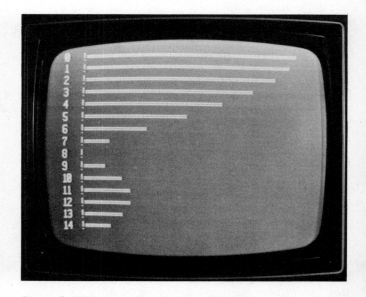

Photo 3: Video graphics display of the magnitude spectrum corresponding to the pulse shown in figure 5.

hand, when the frequency is changed to 1010 Hz while maintaining the same value of T, the spectrum changes to the form shown in photo 5. The reasons for the striking difference are as follows: In the first case, the frequency corresponds exactly to one of the harmonic numbers (50th harmonic), and a property of the DFT is that no other line components appear in this case. However, in the second case, the component would theoretically appear halfway between the 50th and 51st harmonics so that the imperfections of the finite time duration of the observed sinusoid are now apparent. The phenomenon observed is called *leakage*. It can also be readily verified that the first sinusoid was observed over an exact integer number of cycles, while in the second case, the sinusoid was truncated during a cycle.

This example illustrates the necessity of understanding some of the limitations of the truncation and sampling processes in order to properly evaluate results. The phenomena just noted can be reduced by smoothing the data to be transformed with certain *window functions* before computing the FFT. Window functions smooth the beginning and end of a record length and reduce the effects of leakage on the spectrum.

More Examples

Other applications include the use of an analog to digital converter to sample speech and music waveforms or the waveforms encountered in electronic systems. The sample points could be stored for later spectral analysis using the FFT program. We hope readers will be encouraged to experiment with the program on their own computers.■

REFERENCES

1. Bergland, G D, "A Guided Tour of the Fast Fourier Transform," *IEEE Spectrum,* July 1969, pages 41 thru 52.
2. Brigham, E O, *The Fast Fourier Transform,* Prentice-Hall, Englewood Cliffs NJ, 1975.
3. Cooley, J W, and Tukey, J W, "An Algorithm for the Machine Calculation of Complex Fourier Series," *Math of Computation,* volume 19, April 1965, pages 297 thru 301.
4. Stanley, W D, *Digital Signal Processing,* Reston Publishing Co (a division of Prentice-Hall), Englewood Cliffs NJ, 1975.

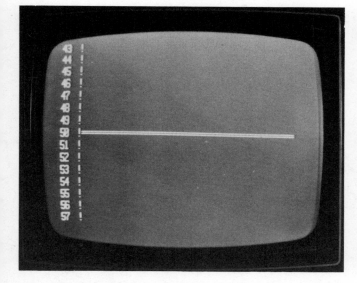

Photo 4: Video graphics display of the magnitude spectrum corresponding to a sine wave whose assumed frequency is 1000 Hz with a sampling interval T = 0.1953 ms. This assumption results in an integer number of cycles (50) in the record duration t_p, which corresponds to 50 ms. The frequency then corresponds exactly to the 50th harmonic and the spectrum appears as a single line.

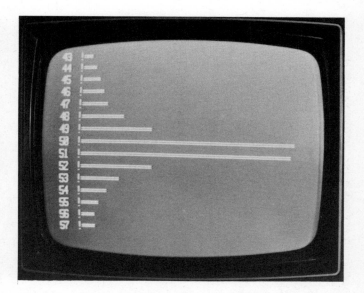

Photo 5: Video graphics display of the magnitude spectrum corresponding to a sine wave whose assumed frequency is 1010 Hz with a sampling interval T = 0.1953 ms. This frequency corresponds to the midpoint between the 50th and 51st harmonics, and the imperfections of the DFT in representing a continuous time signal now can be seen.

Fast Fourier Transforms for the 6800

Richard Lord

If you're involved with music or speech processing applications with your computer, you've probably wished you could look at the frequency spectrum of your sampled signals. This may not be as difficult as you might guess, because here is a simple, straightforward fast Fourier transform (FFT) subroutine that can do the trick in just a few seconds.

A Microhistory of the Fast Fourier Transform

The analysis of waveforms for harmonic content has a long and fascinating history. Bernoulli and Euler developed the mathematics of the transform while experimenting with musical strings in 1728, nearly a hundred years before Jean Baptiste Fourier gave his name to the equations. Interest in prediction of the tides led Lord Kelvin to build a mechanical harmonic synthesizer that inspired the construction of increasingly complex mechanical harmonic analyzing machines. This trend culminated in the Mader-Ott machine of 1931, which is on display at the Smithsonian Institute in Washington DC.

With the growth of the telephone and the communication industry came sampling theory and the *discrete Fourier transform*. At first, discrete Fourier transforms were hand calculated and tabular forms called "schedules" were soon employed to speed the process. With the development of digital computers in the 1940s this task became somewhat easier to perform. The number of calculations required still made the concept of real time discrete Fourier transforms unlikely even on the ever faster new computers.

Then in the 1960's a number of matrix theory mathematicians, including J W Cooley and J W Tukey, went back to the "schedules" and discovered that a great many of the terms were redundant and

could be factored out. The procedure they evolved became known as the *fast Fourier transform*, which reduces the number of calculations to the point that special hardware can be built to perform the transform in real time and display the frequency spectrum continuously on a video display.

The Basic Concepts

A number of books have been published describing the mathematics of the fast Fourier transform in some detail. A few of these contain sample programs in FORTRAN, ALGOL, or BASIC. However, the use of a high level language to perform this computation not only costs a great deal in speed and efficiency, but also obscures the simple binary processes that characterize the algorithm. Since high level languages do not usually support bit manipulation, these processes can become almost as time consuming as the arithmetic.

Clearly, assembly language programming of the fast Fourier transform offers many advantages, but the literature seldom provides any examples of assembly level code to illustrate how the equations are implemented. Thus the program described in this article may well be the reinvention of someone else's "wheel."

The details of the inner workings of the fast Fourier transforms are left to the technical references, but the basic concepts are not difficult to grasp. The transform involves complex products which behave in the manner of the coordinates of a rotating vector. When this vector is at angles which are multiples of 90 degrees, the sine and cosine terms of the equations become +1, 0, or -1. Since terms containing these values do not require computed multiplication, the arithmetic becomes very simple. Other terms cancel each other out in order to simplify the equations at other angles. By factoring

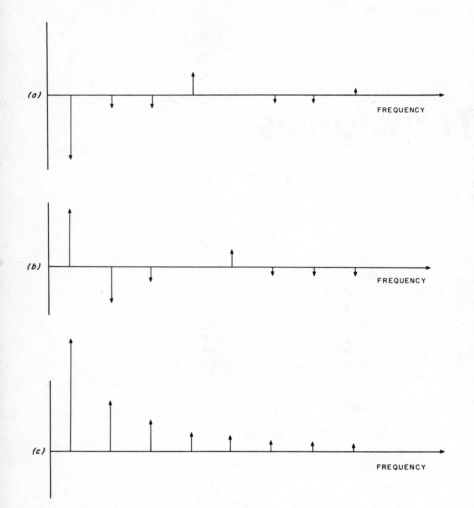

Figure 1: Fast Fourier transform of a square wave using the author's technique. The real (or sine) part of the transform is shown in (a). The imaginary (or cosine) part of the transform is shown in (b). The resulting transform is at (c). The resulting transform values are normally found by taking the square root of the sum of the squares of the cosine and sine elements. In order to save computational time, however, the author takes the sum of the absolute values of the terms, which introduces slight errors into the relative magnitudes of the components.

realized as the number of points increases.

Each of the simplified transforms operates on the data in pairs of complex points. The real and imaginary parts of a pair are transformed and the new values placed back in the array so that the transform is performed "in place." The algorithm then moves on to the next pair until all pairs have been transformed. The process is repeated for each of the eight stages of our 256 point transform, but on each pass the distance between pairs is changed.

On the first pass, adjacent points are paired. After completing a pair the algorithm skips down to the next. In a sense, the data has been split into 128 adjacent 2 point transforms. These 128 groups are known as cells. On each subsequent pass the distance between elements of the pair is doubled. In the second pass there are 64 cells, each four elements wide. On the final pass there is only one cell containing all 256 elements.

This process of forming pairs and cells causes the elements of the array to become scrambled. On the final pass the data is completely mixed up and must be sorted out before it can be used. The way it is scrambled is very interesting, though. If each element is assigned a binary number that represents its location in the array, the scrambled data makes it appear that the computer has read this binary address backwards. It is as if the binary word were swapped end for end so that the most significant bit (MSB) appears where the least significant bit (LSB) should be.

This rearrangement of the data may be corrected by swapping each data point with its bit reverse addressed mate. The procedure is called "bit swapping" and may be performed either at the end of the fast Fourier transform or before it is begun. The pre-transform swap is more convenient because less points need be swapped and because the vector rotation within each cell is simpler. In the posttransform version the vector angles would also have to be bit swapped.

Implementation

Now that we have looked at the concept, let us look at how it can be implemented. The algorithm has been written as a subroutine (see listing 1) to be called by a signal gathering and display program. It assumes that this program has stored some time dependent data in 2's complement form and that a 256 byte sample of this is to be transformed to the frequency domain.

The fast Fourier transform subroutine begins with an address lookup table for the data areas. This table makes the reassignment of these areas very simple. The INPUT data area may be anywhere in memory, but

these terms out of the transform, many unnecessary calculations may be eliminated.

The input data may be thought of as elements of an input matrix which will be multiplied by a transform matrix. The product is a matrix containing the transformed data. The redundant elements may be factored out of the transform matrix, converting it to the product of a number of simpler transforms. For an input array of 256 points, a discrete Fourier transform would require 256 by 256 complex products or 262,144 binary multiplications. The fast Fourier transform reduces this to eight simpler transforms and ultimately requires 8 by 2 by 256 complex products, or 16,384 binary multiplications (1/16 the number of previous multiplications). Even greater savings are

the SINE, REAL, and IMAG arrays must be at address page boundaries (ie: at hexadecimal XX00), and REAL and IMAG must be in adjacent pages forming a continuous 512 byte block. These restrictions greatly simplify address calculation within the program. SINE is the address of a 256 byte sine and cosine lookup table which must be loaded in with the transform subroutine (see listing 2).

The first instruction of the subroutine clears the variable SCLFCT which keeps track of the number of times the data has to be scaled to prevent overflow. The IMAG array is then cleared and at MOVE the INPUT data is copied into REAL, where the transform will take place. The data is then prescrambled to put it in bit reverse order for the transform process. The bit reversed address is calculated by rotating the least significant bit of the address into the carry and rotating the reversed address out in the opposite direction. The new address is compared with the first address to prevent swapping the data back to the original order, and the two array elements are then exchanged.

Once the swapping is complete, the data is ready to be transformed. The fast Fourier transform is performed in eight separate passes; before each pass begins, the data is tested by SCALE to prevent any overflow. For the first pass there are 128 cells formed by adjacent pairs of data. In this pass the vector angle steps in multiples of 180 degrees. This means that all the sine terms are 0 and the cosine terms are either +1 or -1. Also there is no data yet in the IMAG array. The general equations thus become greatly simplified and the pass is reduced to addition and subtraction among elements of the REAL array. Considerable time is saved by making this pass separate and bypassing the unneeded table lookup and multiply routines.

Once this pass is completed, the arithmetic gets much more complex. The remaining seven passes are performed by a general fast Fourier transform algorithm. It begins at FPASS by setting up 64 cells of four elements with the pairs separated by two units. The vector angle is set to increment by 90 degrees by setting DELTA to 64. At NPASS the pointers are set up for the first cell and the pass then begins with a sine and cosine table lookup. The complex data pair is then processed using the standard fast Fourier transform equations:

$$TR = RN \cos(w) + IN \sin(w)$$
$$TI = IN \cos(w) - RN \sin(w)$$

$$RM' = RM + TR \quad RN' = RM - TR$$
$$IM' = IM + TI \quad IN' = IM - TI$$

After each pair has been transformed the angle is incremented by DELTA and the next pair processed. When all pairs in a cell have been transformed the routine moves down to the next cell and returns to NCELL to continue the process. When the last cell has been done, CELCT becomes 0 and the pass is complete.

At the end of each pass the number of cells and the angle increment are divided in half and the pair separation and number of pairs per cell are doubled. The whole process is then repeated by branching to NPASS until the end of the last pass when the number of cells becomes 0. The routine then branches to DONE and returns to the calling program.

The SCALE subroutine is used to anticipate and prevent overflow of the 8 bit data. It is called before each pass and begins by testing the value of each data point. If any point exceeds the range of -64 to +64 the subroutine branches to SCL4 where the entire array is scaled down by a factor of 2. The variable SCLFCT is incremented to indicate the total number of times the data has been scaled.

The multiply routine has been placed at the end of the program to make substitution of other versions easy. The original program was written for a hardware multiplier similar to the device described in an article by Bryant and Swasdee (see references).). To eliminate the need for such exotic hardware, a software multiply routine has been substituted with some increase in transform time. After the multiplication is completed the data must be scaled up by a factor of two. This is because the sine and cosine terms represent fractional binary values. The least significant bit is shifted in from the lower byte to preserve accuracy.

Analyzing the Results

After working with all this mathematics and software, what do you end up with? We started with a 256 point time domain sample in REAL. The fast Fourier transform converts this to a frequency domain sample corresponding to the spectrum of the input. The first element of each array represents the DC component of the input. The next element represents the sine wave with period equal to the duration of the input sample. Each remaining element depicts a multiple of this frequency until the middle of the array is reached, representing 128 cycles per period. The remainder of the array is symmetrical to the first 128 points.

Each element in the REAL and IMAG arrays represents information about one frequency component of the input sample. But why do we end up with two arrays, and what do the cosine terms of REAL and the sine terms of IMAG really mean to us? Usually this information is described in terms of amplitude and phase of the component, and often the phase information is of little interest. The cosine and sine terms represent the X and Y components of a vector with length and angle equal to the amplitude and phase terms that we are after. All we have to do is find the length of the vector from the square root of the sum of squares of the cosine and sine terms.

The only problem is that this calculation requires almost as much time as the transform, due to the square root. If we bypass the root and display the sum of squares (the power spectrum) we miss most of the detail of the lesser components. I have found that the highly unmathematical solution of displaying the sum of the absolute values is fairly satisfactory, although it introduces some error in the relative amplitude of peaks. This value is then sent to a digital to analog converter for display on an oscilloscope.

Putting the Fast Fourier Transform to Work

This program has a number of interesting applications for speech recognition, image processing, and the synthesis of musical instruments. A recent issue of *The Computer Music Journal* even describes a program for transcribing recordings back into sheet music (see references).

To get meaningful information from the transform, the input data must be sampled judiciously. While this program in theory is capable of analyzing 128 harmonics of a given sample, this is only true when the input represents exactly one complete cycle of the waveform being analyzed. Most data just doesn't come packaged that way.

To accurately measure the pitch of a sound you must sample many cycles. To analyze harmonics you want to sample few. The best result for real data will always be a compromise between range (bandwidth) and resolution. Both can be increased only by analyzing more points, which takes more time.

After experimenting with one sample at a time you will probably want to try continuous analysis. The input data pointer at hexadecimal address 0202 can be moved through an input buffer by the program that calls the transform. At roughly three seconds per transform, the data cannot suitably be analyzed in real time. A sample of a few seconds of data can be continuously analyzed and the changes slowly displayed. This is probably most easily accomplished by transferring the "sum of absolute value" data to a display buffer which is then scanned by an interrupt driven display program.

Bigger, Better, and Faster

Like most software, this program exists to be rewritten. No attempt was made to optimize execution speed. Preliminary experiments with an MMI-67558 hardware multiplier took slightly under one second. This relatively minor improvement was probably due to the time wasted in moving the data in and out of the multiplier. Perhaps it can be streamlined to the extent that a continuous display can be created. I plan to try a version for the 6502 microprocessor with hope of adding still more speed.

The algorithm is simple enough so that conversion should be easy. Enterprising 8080 and Z-80 enthusiasts shouldn't have too much trouble adapting the principles to their computers, either. Conversion to double precision or 512 to 1024 points should also be possible, although the present addressing scheme would have to be abandoned.

I hope this program will provide you with a tool that will be a lot of fun to play with. Please write and tell me what uses you find for it and any improvements you would like to suggest. ∎

REFERENCES

1. Brigham, E Oran, *The Fast Fourier Transform,* Prentice-Hall, Englewood Cliffs NJ, 1974.
2. Bryant, J and Swasdee, M, "How to Multiply in a Wet Climate," BYTE, volume 3, number 4, April 1978, page 28.
3. Cooper, James W, *The Minicomputer in the Laboratory,* John Wiley and Sons Inc, New York, 1977.
4. Moorer, J, "On the Transcription of Musical Sound by Computer," *Computer Music Journal,* volume 1, number 4, November 1977, page 32.
5. Stearns, Samuel D, *Digital Signal Analysis,* Hayden Book Co Inc, Rochelle Park NJ, 1975.

```
00001                         NAM    FFT#2
00002                         OPT    O,S,NOGEN
00003                  ************************
00004                  **   FAST FOURIER    **
00005                  **    TRANSFORM      **
00006                  **    SUBROUTINE     **
00007                  ************************
00008                  **    BY R.H.LORD    **
00009                  **   21 APRIL, 1978  **
00010                  ************************
00011                  **
00012                  ** THIS SUBROUTINE PERFORMS A 256 POINT FFT
00013                  ** ON THE DATA IN THE INPUT DATA TABLE.
00014                  ** INPUT DATA IS ASSUMED TO BE TWO'S COMPLEMENT.
00015                  ** THE SUBROUTINE GENERATES A COSINE (REAL) AND SINE
00016                  ** (IMAGINARY) DATA TABLE AT "REAL" AND "IMAG"
00017                  ** THE RESULTANT TRANSFORM DATA IS 128 POINTS
00018                  ** SYMMETRICALLY REFLECTED ABOUT THE CENTER OF
00019                  ** THE 256 POINT TABLE.
00020                  **
00021                  ** THE SUBROUTINE ASSUMES THAT THE INPUT DATA
00022                  ** IS ALL REAL AND THEREFORE DOES NOT MANIPULATE
00023                  ** THE IMAGINARY PORTION UNTIL AFTER THE FIRST
00024                  ** PASS.
00025                  **
00026                  ** ALL DATA AREAS MUST BE ON PAGE BOUNDARIES (XX00)
00027                  ** SINCE THE ROUTINE MANIPULATES ONLY THE LSB'S.
00028                  **
00029                  ** THE TWO'S COMPLEMENT MULTIPLICATION IS KEPT AS A
00030                  ** SEPARATE SUBROUTINE.   IT MAY BE PERFORMED WITH
00031                  ** A CONVENTIONAL SOFTWARE MULTIPLY SUBROUTINE
00032                  ** OR WITH A HARDWARE MULTIPLIER FOR HIGHER SPEED.
00033                  **
00034                  ** THE SUBROUTINE SCALES THE DATA WHENEVER
00035                  ** IT ANTICIPATES OVERFLOW. THE SCALE FACTOR
00036                  ** COUNT IS AVAILABLE IN "SCLFCT".
00037                  **
00038                  **
00039                  **
00040                  **
00041                  ************************
00042                  **     DATA AREAS     **
00043                  ************************
00044      0800       INPUT  EQU    $0800        INPUT DATA TABLE
00045      0500       REALT  EQU    $0500        "REAL" DATA TABLE
00046      0600       IMAGT  EQU    $0600        "IMAG" DATA TABLE
00047      0400       SINET  EQU    $0400        SINE LOOKUP TABLE
00048                  ************************
00050 0020                   ORG    $0020
00051                  ************************
00052                  **   BASE PAGE PTRS   **
00053                  ************************
00054 0020 0002       RLPT1  RMB    2            "REAL" DATA POINTERS
00055 0022 0002       RLPT2  RMB    2
00056 0024 0002       IMPT1  RMB    2            "IMAG. " DATA POINTERS
00057 0026 0002       IMPT2  RMB    2
00058 0028 0002       SINPT  RMB    2            SINE TABLE POINTER
00059 002A 0001       CELNUM RMB    1            CELLS FOR THIS PASS
00060 002B 0001       CELCT  RMB    1            CELL COUNTER FOR PASS
00061 002C 0001       PAIRNM RMB    1            PAIRS/CELL
00062 002D 0001       CELDIS RMB    1            CELL OFFSET(DISTANCE)
00063 002E 0001       DELTA  RMB    1            ANGLE INCREMENT
00064 002F 0001       SCLFCT RMB    1            SCALE FACTOR CTR.
00065 0030 0001       COSA   RMB    1            TEMPORARY COSINE
00066 0031 0001       SINA   RMB    1            TEMPORARY SINE
00067 0032 0001       TREAL  RMB    1            TEMP. REAL DATA
00068 0033 0001       TIMAG  RMB    1            TEMP. IMAG DATA
00069 0034 0001       MSBY   RMB    1            MULTIPLY MSB
00070 0035 0001       LSBY   RMB    1            MULTIPLY LSB
00071 0036 0004       MPA    RMB    4            SOFTWARE MPY ACCUM.
```

```
00072                    ********************************
00073                    **   START OF TRANSFORM     **
00074                    ********************************
00075 0200                        ORG     $0200
00076 0200 20 08                   BRA     START     JUMP AROUND PARAMETERS
00077                    ********************************
00078                    **   ADDRESS LOOK-UP TABLE   **
00079                    **     FOR DATA AREAS         **
00080                    ********************************
00081 0202 0800 INPD     FDB     INPUT     SET UP DATA AREAS
00082 0204 0500 REAL     FDB     REALT
00083 0206 0600 IMAG     FDB     IMAGT
00084 0208 0400 SINE     FDB     SINET
00085                    ********************************
00086                    **
00087 020A 7F 002F START CLR     SCLFCT    NOTHING SCALED YET
00088                    **
00089                    ********************************
00090                    **   INPUT DATA SET-UP        **
00091                    ********************************
00092 020D FE 0206 CLEAR LDX     IMAG      CLEAR OUT IMAG.
00093 0210 5F             CLR B             SET UP COUNTER
00094 0211 6F 00   CLR1  CLR     0,X       CLEAR MEMORY
00095 0213 08             INX
00096 0214 5A             DEC B
00097 0215 26 FA          BNE     CLR1
00098 0217 FE 0202 MOVE   LDX     INPD      SET UP POINTERS
00099 021A DF 20          STX     RLPT1
00100 021C FE 0204        LDX     REAL
00101 021F DF 22          STX     RLPT2
00102 0221 DE 20   MOV1   LDX     RLPT1     MOVE INPUT DATA
00103 0223 A6 00          LDA A   0,X       TO "REAL" ARRAY
00104 0225 08             INX
00105 0226 DF 20          STX     RLPT1
00106 0228 DE 22          LDX     RLPT2
00107 022A A7 00          STA A   0,X
00108 022C 7C 0023        INC     RLPT2+1
00109 022F 26 F0          BNE     MOV1      TEST PAGE OVERFLOW
00110                    ********************************
00111                    **   PRE-TRANSFORM BIT SWAP **
00112                    ********************************
00113 0231 FE 0204        LDX     REAL      SET UP DATA POINTERS
00114 0234 DF 20          STX     RLPT1
00115 0236 DF 22          STX     RLPT2
00116 0238 C6 08   BITREV LDA B   #8        SET BIT COUNTER
00117 023A 96 21          LDA A   RLPT1+1   GET POINTER 1
00118 023C 46     BRV1    ROR A             REVERSE BIT ORDER
00119 023D 79 0023        ROL     RLPT2+1   FOR SECOND POINTER
00120 0240 5A             DEC B             COUNT BITS
00121 0241 26 F9          BNE     BRV1
00122 0243 96 23          LDA A   RLPT2+1   GET REVERSED BYTE
00123 0245 91 21          CMP A   RLPT1+1   COMPARE WITH #1
00124 0247 25 0E          BCS     SWP1      BRANCH IF ALREADY SWAPPED
00125 0249 DE 20   SWAP   LDX     RLPT1     GET POINTER 1
00126 024B A6 00          LDA A   0,X       GET VAL 1
00127 024D DE 22          LDX     RLPT2     GET POINTER 2
00128 024F E6 00          LDA B   0,X       GET VAL 2
00129 0251 A7 00          STA A   0,X       REPLACE WITH VAL 1
00130 0253 DE 20          LDX     RLPT1     GET FIRST POINTER
00131 0255 E7 00          STA B   0,X       COMPLETE SWAP
00132 0257 7C 0021 SWP1   INC     RLPT1+1   DO NEXT POINT PAIR
00133 025A 26 DC          BNE     BITREV    UNLESS ALL ARE DONE
00134                    ********************************
00135                    **      FFT   FIRST PASS      **
00136                    ********************************
00137                    **  SINCE IN PASS 1 ALL ANGLES  **
00138                    **    ARE MULTIPLES OF 180 DEG.  **
00139                    **  THERE ARE NO PRODUCT TERMS.  **
00140                    **    AND NO IMAGINARY TERMS YET **
00141                    **  HENCE A FAST VERSION OF PASS 1 **
00142                    ********************************
00143 025C BD 0333 PASS1  JSR     SCALE     SCALE IF ANY OVER-RANGE DATA
00144 025F FE 0204        LDX     REAL      SET UP POINTERS
00145 0262 DF 20          STX     RLPT1
00146 0264 DE 20   PA1    LDX     RLPT1     GET POINTER
```

```
00147 0266 A6 00          LDA A  0,X      GET RM
00148 0268 E6 01          LDA B  1,X      AND RN
00149 026A 36             PSH A           SAVE RM
00150 026B 1B             ABA             RM'=RM+RN
00151 026C A7 00          STA A  0,X      STORE NEW RM'
00152 026E 32             PUL A           GET OLD RM
00153 026F 10             SBA             RN'=RM-RN
00154 0270 A7 01          STA A  1,X      STORE RN'
00155 0272 7C 0021        INC    RLPT1+1  MOVE TO NEXT PAIR
00156 0275 7C 0021        INC    RLPT1+1
00157 0278 26 EA          BNE    PR1      KEEP GOING TILL DONE
00158              ********************************
00159              **   COMPUTATION OF FFT       **
00160              **     PASS 2 THRU N          **
00161              ********************************
00162 027A 86 40   FPASS  LDA A  #64      SET UP PARAMETERS
00163 027C 97 2A          STA A  CELNUM   FOR CELL COUNT
00164 027E 97 2E          STA A  DELTA    AND ANGLE
00165 0280 86 02          LDA A  #2       AND FOR
00166 0282 97 2C          STA A  PAIRNM   PAIRS/CELL
00167 0284 97 2D          STA A  CELDIS   DISTANCE BETWEEN PAIRS
00168 0286 BD 0333 NPASS  JSR    SCALE    KEEP DATA IN RANGE
00169 0289 96 2A          LDA A  CELNUM   GET NUMBER OF CELLS
00170 028B 97 2B          STA A  CELCT    PUT IN COUNTER
00171 028D FE 0204        LDX    REAL     SET UP POINTERS
00172 0290 DF 20          STX    RLPT1
00173 0292 DF 22          STX    RLPT2
00174 0294 FE 0206        LDX    IMAG
00175 0297 DF 24          STX    IMPT1
00176 0299 DF 26          STX    IMPT2
00177 029B FE 0208 NCELL  LDX    SINE
00178 029E DF 28          STX    SINPT
00179 02A0 D6 2C          LDA B  PAIRNM   GET PAIRS/CELL CTR.
00180 02A2 96 21   NC1    LDA A  RLPT1+1  GET POINTER 1 LSBY
00181 02A4 9B 2D          ADD A  CELDIS   ADD PAIR OFFSET
00182 02A6 97 23          STA A  RLPT2+1  SET BOTH POINTER 2'S
00183 02A8 97 27          STA A  IMPT2+1
00184 02AA 37             PSH B           SAVE PAIR CTR
00185 02AB DE 28          LDX    SINPT    SET UP SINE LOOKUP
00186 02AD A6 00          LDA A  0,X      GET COSINE OF ANGLE
00187 02AF 97 30          STA A  COSA     SAVE ON BASE PAGE
00188 02B1 A6 40          LDA A  64,X     GET SINE
00189 02B3 97 31          STA A  SINA     AND SAVE IT
00190 02B5 DE 22          LDX    RLPT2    GET "REAL" POINTER 2
00191 02B7 A6 00          LDA A  0,X      GET RN
00192 02B9 36             PSH A           SAVE IT
00193 02BA D6 30          LDA B  COSA     GET COSINE
00194 02BC BD 036A        JSR    MPY      MAKE RN*COS(A)
00195 02BF 97 32          STA A  TREAL    SAVE IT
00196 02C1 32             PUL A           RESTORE RN
00197 02C2 D6 31          LDA B  SINA     GET SINE
00198 02C4 BD 036A        JSR    MPY      RN*SIN(A)
00199 02C7 97 33          STA A  TIMAG
00200 02C9 DE 26          LDX    IMPT2    GET IMAG. POINTER 2
00201 02CB A6 00          LDA A  0,X      GET IN
00202 02CD 36             PSH A           SAVE IT
00203 02CE D6 31          LDA B  SINA     GET SINE
00204 02D0 BD 036A        JSR    MPY      IN*SIN(A)
00205 02D3 9B 32          ADD A  TREAL    TR=RN*COS+IN*SIN
00206 02D5 97 32          STA A  TREAL
00207 02D7 32             PUL A           RESTORE IN
00208 02D8 D6 30          LDA B  COSA     GET COSINE
00209 02DA BD 036A        JSR    MPY      IN*COS(A)
00210 02DD 90 33          SUB A  TIMAG    TI=IN*COS-RN*SIN
00211 02DF 97 33          STA A  TIMAG
00212 02E1 DE 20          LDX    RLPT1
00213 02E3 A6 00          LDA A  0,X      GET RM
00214 02E5 16             TAB             SAVE IT
00215 02E6 9B 32          ADD A  TREAL    RM'=RM+TR
00216 02E8 A7 00          STA A  0,X
00217 02EA DE 22          LDX    RLPT2
00218 02EC D0 32          SUB B  TREAL    RN'=RM-TR
00219 02EE E7 00          STA B  0,X
00220 02F0 DE 24          LDX    IMPT1
00221 02F2 A6 00          LDA A  0,X      GET IM
```

```
00222 02F4 16            TAB                SAVE IT
00223 02F5 9B 33         ADD A   TIMAG      IM´=IM+TI
00224 02F7 A7 00         STA A   0,X
00225 02F9 DE 26         LDX     IMPT2
00226 02FB D0 33         SUB B   TIMAG      IN´=IM-TI
00227 02FD E7 00         STA B   0,X
00228 02FF 96 29         LDA A   SINPT+1    INCREMENT ANGLE
00229 0301 9B 2E         ADD A   DELTA
00230 0303 97 29         STA A   SINPT+1
00231 0305 7C 0021       INC     RLPT1+1    INCREMENT POINTERS
00232 0308 7C 0025       INC     IMPT1+1
00233 030B 33            PUL B              GET PAIR COUNTER
00234 030C 5A            DEC B              DECREMENT
00235 030D 26 93         BNE     NC1        DO NEXT PAIR
00236 030F 96 21         LDA A   RLPT1+1    GET POINTERS
00237 0311 9B 2D         ADD A   CELDIS     ADD CELL OFFSET
00238 0313 97 21         STA A   RLPT1+1
00239 0315 97 25         STA A   IMPT1+1
00240 0317 7A 002B       DEC     CELCT      DECR. CELL COUNTER
00241 031A 27 03         BEQ     NP1        NEXT PASS?
00242 031C 7E 029B       JMP     NCELL      NO, DO NEXT CELL
00243              **
00244              ** CHANGE PARAMETERS FOR NEXT PASS **
00245              **
00246 031F 74 002A NP1   LSR     CELNUM     HALF AS MANY CELLS
00247 0322 27 0C         BEQ     DONE       NO MORE CELLS
00248 0324 78 002C       ASL     PAIRNM     TWICE AS MANY PAIRS
00249 0327 78 002D       ASL     CELDIS     TWICE AS FAR APART
00250 032A 74 002E       LSR     DELTA      HALF THE ANGLE
00251 032D 7E 0286       JMP     NPASS      DO NEXT PASS
00252              ******************************
00253              **    END OF FFT ROUTINE     **
00254              ******************************
00255              **
00256 0330 39      DONE  RTS                EXIT FFT SUBROUTINE
00257 0331 0002          RMB     2          ROOM FOR JUMP EXIT
00258              **
00259              ******************************
00260              **    OVER-RANGE DATA SCALE  **
00261              ******************************
00262 0333 FE 0204 SCALE LDX     REAL       SET UP DATA POINTER
00263 0336 5F            CLR B              SET UP PAIR CTR
00264 0337 37     SCL1   PSH B              SAVE PAIR CTR.
00265 0338 C6 02         LDA B   #2         SET UP PAIR
00266 033A A6 00  SCL2   LDA A   0,X        GET DATA
00267 033C 08            INX                BUMP POINTER
00268 033D 81 C0         CMP A   #$C0       TEST LOWER LIMIT
00269 033F 22 04         BHI     SCL3       SKIP TO NEXT POINT
00270 0341 81 40         CMP A   #$40       TEST UPPER LIMIT
00271 0343 24 08         BCC     SCL4       SCALE IF OUT OF RANGE
00272 0345 5A     SCL3   DEC B              TEST NEXT POINT
00273 0346 26 F2         BNE     SCL2
00274 0348 33            PUL B
00275 0349 5A            DEC B
00276 034A 26 EB         BNE     SCL1
00277 034C 39            RTS                DONE TESTING
00278 034D 33     SCL4   PUL B              RESTORE STACK
00279 034E 7C 002F       INC     SCLFCT     BUMP SCALE FACTOR COUNT
00280 0351 FE 0204       LDX     REAL       SET UP TABLE PTR.
00281 0354 5F            CLR B              SET UP PAIR CTR
00282 0355 37     SCL5   PSH B              SAVE IT
00283 0356 C6 02         LDA B   #2         SET UP PAIR
00284 0358 A6 00  SCL6   LDA A   0,X        GET DATA
00285 035A 8B 80         ADD A   #$80       MAKE IT ABSOLUTE
00286 035C 44            LSR A              DIVIDE IT BY 2
00287 035D 80 40         SUB A   #$40       MAKE IT 2´S COMP.
00288 035F A7 00         STA A   0,X
00289 0361 08            INX                BUMP POINTER
00290 0362 5A            DEC B              NEXT POINT
00291 0363 26 F3         BNE     SCL6
00292 0365 33            PUL B
00293 0366 5A            DEC B              NEXT PAIR
00294 0367 26 EC         BNE     SCL5
00295 0369 39            RTS                RETURN
```

```
00296                 ********************************
00297                 **  2'S COMP.  MULTIPLY SUBR.   **
00298                 ********************************
00299 036A 97 37  MPY     STA A  MPA+1    STORE MULTIPLIER
00300 036C D7 39          STA B  MPA+3    AND MULTIPLICAND
00301 036E 4F             CLR A
00302 036F 97 36          STA A  MPA      CLEAR MSB'S
00303 0371 97 38          STA A  MPA+2
00304 0373 97 34          STA A  MSBY     CLEAR PRODUCT
00305 0375 97 35          STA A  LSBY
00306 0377 5D             TST B
00307 0378 2C 03          BGE    MPY1     NEGATIVE MULTIPLICAND ?
00308 037A 73 0038        COM    MPA+2    EXTEND NEG TO MSB
00309 037D 7D 0037 MPY1   TST    MPA+1
00310 0380 2C 03          BGE    MPY2     NEG MULTIPLIER ?
00311 0382 73 0036        COM    MPA      EXTEND NEG TO MSB
00312 0385 C6 0F   MPY2   LDA B  #15      SET UP COUNTER
00313 0387 77 0036 MPY3   ASR    MPA      SHIFT X RIGHT
00314 038A 76 0037        ROR    MPA+1
00315 038D 24 0C          BCC    MPY4     BIT WAS ZERO
00316 038F 96 39          LDA A  MPA+3    ADD Y TO PRODUCT
00317 0391 9B 35          ADD A  LSBY
00318 0393 97 35          STA A  LSBY
00319 0395 96 38          LDA A  MPA+2    MSB'S
00320 0397 99 34          ADC A  MSBY
00321 0399 97 34          STA A  MSBY
00322 039B 78 0039 MPY4   ASL    MPA+3    SHIFT Y LEFT
00323 039E 79 0038        ROL    MPA+2
00324 03A1 5A             DEC B
00325 03A2 26 E3          BNE    MPY3
00326                 **
00327                 ** SCALE IT UP **
00328                 **
00329 03A4 96 34          LDA A  MSBY
00330 03A6 79 0035        ROL    LSBY
00331 03A9 49             ROL A
00332                 **
00333                 ** RETURN WITH PRODUCT IN A
00334                 **
00335 03AA 39             RTS
00336                 ********************************
00337                 **    END OF FFT PROGRAM      **
00338                 ********************************
00339                     END
```

INPUT	0800	REALT	0500	IMAGT	0600	SINET	0400
RLPT1	0020	RLPT2	0022	IMPT1	0024	IMPT2	0026
SINPT	0028	CELNUM	002A	CELCT	002B	PAIRNM	002C
CELDIS	002D	DELTA	002E	SCLFCT	002F	COSA	0030
SINA	0031	TREAL	0032	TIMAG	0033	MSBY	0034
LSBY	0035	MPA	0036	INPD	0202	REAL	0204
IMAG	0206	SINE	0208	START	020A	CLEAR	020D
CLR1	0211	MOVE	0217	MOV1	0221	BITREV	0238
BRV1	023C	SWAP	0249	SWP1	0257	PASS1	025C
PA1	0264	FPASS	027A	NPASS	0286	NCELL	029B
NC1	02A2	NP1	031F	DONE	0330	SCALE	0333
SCL1	0337	SCL2	033A	SCL3	0345	SCL4	034D
SCL5	0355	SCL6	0358	MPY	036A	MPY1	037D
MPY2	0385	MPY3	0387	MPY4	039B		

TOTAL ERRORS 00000

Listing 2: The object code listing in hexadecimal format of the assembly language program given is listing 1. This listing can be used to manually enter the program or as a confirmation copy for the PAPERBYTE^{tm} bar code representation given in figure 2. The format used for this listing is a 2 byte address field, followed by up to 16 bytes of data, with a 1 byte check digit at the end of each line. Note that the data in hexadecimal locations 0400 to 04FF constitute the sine and cosine lookup table which must be loaded with the transform subroutine.

```
0200  20 08 08 00 05 00 06 00 04 00 7F 00 2F FE 02 06    F3
0210  5F 6F 00 08 5A 26 FA FE 02 02 DF 20 FE 02 04 DF    34
0220  22 DE 20 A6 00 08 DF 20 DE 22 A7 00 7C 00 23 26    39
0230  F0 FE 02 04 DF 20 DF 22 C6 08 96 21 46 79 00 23    5B
0240  5A 26 F9 96 23 91 21 25 0E DE 20 A6 00 DE 22 E6    A1
0250  00 A7 00 DE 20 E7 00 7C 00 21 26 DC BD 03 33 FE    1C
0260  02 04 DF 20 DE 20 A6 00 E6 01 36 1B A7 00 32 10    CA
0270  A7 01 7C 00 21 7C 00 21 26 EA 86 40 97 2A 97 2E    3E
0280  86 02 97 2C 97 2D BD 03 33 96 2A 97 2B FE 02 04    88
0290  DF 20 DF 22 FE 02 06 DF 24 DF 26 FE 02 08 DF 28    1D
02A0  D6 2C 96 21 9B 2D 97 23 97 27 37 DE 28 A6 00 97    73
02B0  30 A6 40 97 31 DE 22 A6 00 36 D6 30 BD 03 6A 97    81
02C0  32 32 D6 31 BD 03 6A 97 33 DE 26 A6 00 36 D6 31    46
02D0  BD 03 6A 9B 32 97 32 32 D6 30 BD 03 6A 90 33 97    7C
02E0  33 DE 20 A6 00 16 9B 32 A7 00 DE 22 D0 32 E7 00    4A
02F0  DE 24 A6 00 16 9B 33 A7 00 DE 26 D0 33 E7 00 96    B7
0300  29 9B 2E 97 29 7C 00 21 7C 00 25 33 5A 26 93 96    CC
0310  21 9B 2D 97 21 97 25 7A 00 2B 27 03 7E 02 9B 74    BB
0320  00 2A 27 0C 78 00 2C 78 00 2D 74 00 2E 7E 02 86    4E
0330  39 00 00 FE 02 04 5F 37 C6 02 A6 00 08 81 C0 22    AC
0340  04 81 40 24 08 5A 26 F2 33 5A 26 EB 39 33 7C 00    E9
0350  2F FE 02 04 5F 37 C6 02 A6 00 8B 80 44 80 40 A7    ED
0360  00 08 5A 26 F3 33 5A 26 EC 39 97 37 D7 39 4F 97    17
0370  36 97 38 97 34 97 35 5D 2C 03 73 00 38 7D 00 37    87
0380  2C 03 73 00 36 C6 0F 77 00 36 76 00 37 24 0C 96    CD
0390  39 9B 35 97 35 96 38 99 34 97 34 78 00 39 79 00    65
03A0  38 5A 26 E3 96 34 79 00 35 49 39                   95
```

SINE TABLE

```
0400  7F 7F 7F 7F 7F 7F 7E 7E 7D 7D 7C 7B 7A 79 78 77    C9
0410  76 75 73 72 71 6F 6D 6C 6A 68 66 65 63 61 5E 5C    A4
0420  5A 58 56 53 51 4E 4C 49 47 44 41 3F 3C 39 36 33    78
0430  31 2E 2B 28 25 22 1F 1C 19 16 12 0F 0C 09 06 03    A2
0440  00 FD FA F7 F4 F1 EE EA E7 E4 E1 DE DB D8 D5 D2    8F
0450  CF CD CA C7 C4 C1 BF BC B9 B7 B4 B2 AF AD AA A8    B1
0460  A6 A4 A2 9F 9D 9B 9A 98 96 94 93 91 8F 8E 8D 8B    78
0470  8A 89 88 87 86 85 84 83 83 82 82 81 81 81 81 81    40
0480  81 81 81 81 81 81 82 82 83 83 84 85 86 87 88 89    37
0490  8A 8B 8D 8E 8F 91 93 94 96 98 9A 9B 9D 9F A2 A4    5C
04A0  A6 A8 AA AD AF B2 B4 B7 B9 BC BF C1 C4 C7 CA CD    88
04B0  CF D2 D5 D8 DB DE E1 E4 E7 EA EE F1 F4 F7 FA FD    5E
04C0  00 03 06 09 0C 0F 12 16 19 1C 1F 22 25 28 2B 2E    71
04D0  31 33 36 39 3C 3F 41 44 47 49 4C 4E 51 53 56 58    4F
04E0  5A 5C 5E 61 63 65 66 68 6A 6C 6D 6F 71 72 73 75    88
04F0  76 77 78 79 7A 7B 7C 7D 7D 7E 7E 7F 7F 7F 7F 7F    C0
```

```
0 0 0 0 0 0 0 0 0 0 0 0 0 0 0 0 0 0 0 0 0 0 0 0 0 0 0 0 0 0 0 0 0 0 0 0 0 0 0 0
0 0 0 0 0 0 0 0 0 0 1 1 1 1 1 1 1 1 1 1 2 2 2 2 2 2 2 2 2 2 3 3 3 3 3 3 3 3 3 3
0 1 2 3 4 5 6 7 8 9 0 1 2 3 4 5 6 7 8 9 0 1 2 3 4 5 6 7 8 9 0 1 2 3 4 5 6 7 8 9
```

```
0 0 0 0 0 0 0 0 0 0 0 0 0 0 0 0 0 0 0 0 0 0 0 0 0
2 2 2 2 2 2 2 2 2 2 3 3 3 3 3 3 3 3 4 4 4 4 4 4 4 4 4 4 4 4
0 1 3 4 6 7 9 A C D F B B C 5 6 8 9 0 1 2 4 5 7 8 A B D E F
0 A 2 B 3 C 4 B 3 B 3 B 3 C 4 C 4 C 0 6 E 6 C 3 C 4 A B 2 A F
```

Figure 2: Paperbyte[TM] bar code version of listing 2.

```
0 0 0 0 0 0 0 0 0 0 0 0 0 0 0 0 0 0 0 0 0 0 0 0 0 0 0 0 0 0 0 0 0 0 0 0 0 0 0 0
0 0 0 0 0 0 0 0 0 0 1 1 1 1 1 1 1 1 1 1 2 2 2 2 2 2 2 2 2 2 3 3 3 3 3 3 3 3 3 3
0 1 2 3 4 5 6 7 8 9 0 1 2 3 4 5 6 7 8 9 0 1 2 3 4 5 6 7 8 9 0 1 2 3 4 5 6 7 8 9
```

Photo 1: The author's polyphonic music keyboard system, which allows more than one note to be played simultaneously. The scanning keyboard interface is just behind the 61 note manual in the foreground. The stand alone ASCII keyboard in front is dedicated to music related tasks, and allows two easily distinguished levels of system control.

Polyphony Made Easy

Steven K Roberts

It was not long after the successful implementation of a hardware chromatic tone and envelope generator for my system that I began to wish for a method of playing music that would be somewhat less cumbersome than tune encoding with the ASCII keyboard. The ability to store a melody by defining all the notes and then allowing the computer to perform it was worthwhile, but without some technique for spontaneous interaction the system could hardly be called an instrument. A music keyboard was clearly called for.

I obtained a 61 note (5 octave) organ manual from the Kimball Organ Company for about $75, and considered the interface task in depth. Among the primary performance specifications for the design were:

- Polyphonic capability (not limited to single notes)
- Undiscernible response delay
- Very low processor overhead

The last of these requirements precluded the

use of a software scan, which would have reduced hardware to its simplest form, and the need for polyphony called for either a bit map interface or a multiplexer with its own memory. To simplify the software as much as possible, the latter approach was selected.

A note should be inserted here about the touchy subject of software simplification. An argument frequently heard in the world of the microprocessor is that *everything* should be done with the program. If the processor in question is a dedicated controller, then by all means all the work that can be reasonably handled by the program should be so assigned. However if the processor is at a higher level of system abstraction, it may be more efficient to delegate certain repetitive tasks either to hardware or to another microcomputer. There is no convenient generalization defining the tradeoff, but in cases where software complexity gets out of hand due to the presence of a fairly mundane but demanding task, some parallelism is usually called for. In the specific

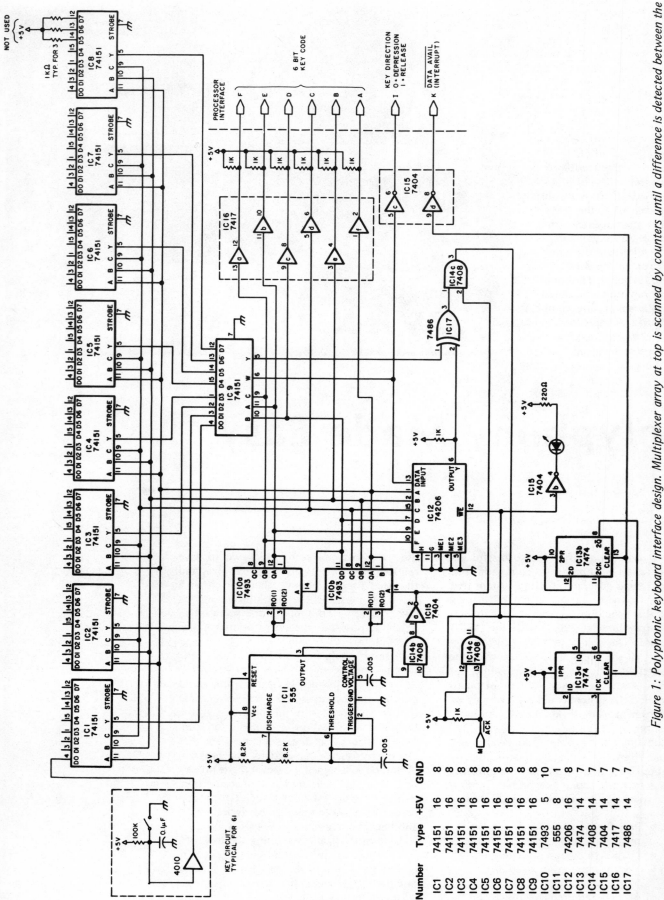

Figure 1: Polyphonic keyboard interface design. Multiplexer array at top is scanned by counters until a difference is detected between the addressed key and the corresponding bit in memory. The scan is stopped and the key address and direction are read by the processor, allowing the scan to continue.

Table 1.: Power wiring table for figure 1.

Number	Type	+5V	GND
IC1	74151	16	8
IC2	74151	16	8
IC3	74151	16	8
IC4	74151	16	8
IC5	74151	16	8
IC6	74151	16	8
IC7	74151	16	8
IC8	74151	16	8
IC9	74151	16	8
IC10	7493	5	10
IC11	555	8	1
IC12	74206	16	8
IC13	7474	14	7
IC14	7408	14	7
IC15	7404	14	7
IC16	7417	14	7
IC17	7486	14	7

case of the music system, keyboard scanning and envelope generation can impose such a burden that the ability to simultaneously do complex real time data manipulation is lost.

Thus, optimization of the keyboard interface design was undertaken with the system considerations given uppermost priority, and the result is shown in figure 1. The 61 key switches of the manual are scanned completely every 5 ms, and with each step of the scan the position of the presently addressed key is compared with its last known position, which is stored in a 256 by 1 memory segment. If there is no difference, the scan proceeds, but if the key has changed state, the processor is interrupted with the binary value of the key in question along with a direction bit, and the corresponding memory location is changed to reflect the new status of the keyboard. The scan is suspended until the information is accepted by the computer. In this fashion, any combination of simultaneous key depressions and releases, at any practical speed, will result in a series of asynchronous "change of state" notices to the processor, which remains ignorant of interface function at all other times. The software maintains a list of keys currently depressed, and deals with them appropriately.

Action of the scanning interface is synchronized with the host computer by means of a simple handshaking scheme: when a change of state is detected, the data available signal appears (this may be treated as an interrupt or polled periodically, depending upon available time). It is then the processor's job to read the input port upon which the 6 bit key code and the direction bit appear, whereupon the acknowledge signal is created by the port strobe, allowing the scan to continue. It is important to note that the scan stops whenever a change is encountered (awaiting processor intervention) because ultimate keyboard servicing time is then largely a function of the support software. In the unlikely event that a user of this system chooses to implement such real time functions in BASIC, it will be found that a forearm laid in jest upon the keyboard results in a sweep up the musical scale lasting on the order of a second. In a more realistic situation (assembler level coding) the delay is unnoticeable.

Construction, of course, should follow the usual procedures required of random logic interfacing. Cables between the board and the processor should be kept short, with intervening grounds between the handshake lines. The keyboard shown in photo 1 consists of simple normally-open contacts; their noise is filtered by the resistor-capacitor (RC) networks shown in the schematic. Any remaining bounce may be trimmed out by

Photo 2: Keyboard interface hardware. The circuit fits perfectly onto a Robinson-Nugent 30 socket wirewrap panel. It could just as easily be implemented on an S-100 card if there is no objection to the wire bundle. Any combination of simultaneous key depressions and releases on the musical keyboards, at any practical speed, will result in a series of asynchronous "change of state" notices to the processor, which remains ignorant of interface function at all other times. The software maintains a list of keys currently depressed and deals with them appropriately. A simple handshaking scheme makes the interface synchronous with the host computer.

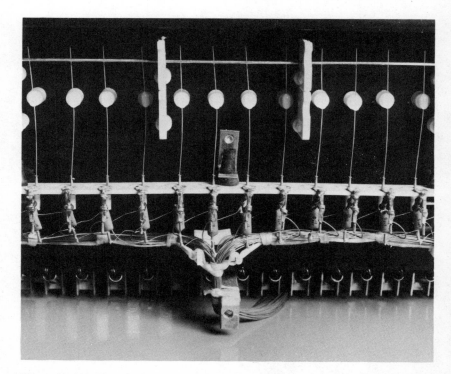

Photo 3: Underside of organ manual. The resistor-capacitor networks shown are used with each key for noise reduction. The wire bundle exiting at the bottom terminates in the interface's edge connector.

119

adjusting the clock rate, which is nominally 12.5 kHz. There is one light emitting diode (LED) on the board to provide a visual check of operation: "Key In Progress" is lit between the data available signal and the acknowledgment signal.

The circuit concept is directly expandable to accommodate many more inputs, with the memory and counter capable of addressing up to 256 points. This interface concept would be quite at home in many industrial control environments, as well as anywhere a large number of contact closures must be observed.

In the music system shown in photo 1, the keyboard interface has provided the much needed flexibility in the interactive utilization of the instrument. The "feel" is not unlike that of a standard electronic organ, and with the available processing horsepower taken into consideration, the unit is a composer's delight. From teaching applications (where the human must correctly repeat "by ear" a computer generated phrase) to the support of creative effort, an efficiently integrated polyphonic keyboard is an essential link between artist and computer. ■

Music from the Altair 8800 Computer

Loring C White

Those of you who would like to make music with computers can easily do so with an Altair 8800 (or other S-100 based system). The MITS 88-ACR audio cassette interface board may be used to send musical signals to an audio amplifier or speaker. The method described here employs a flip flop which is normally intended for use by the interrupt function of the 88-SIO B board.

The output of this device varies from +5 V to 0 V, providing a square wave which is under the control of software. The number of times per second this occurs determines the fundamental pitch of the output tone. The duration of the event determines the sustain time. Thus, by connecting an amplifier and speaker (or just a speaker) between the output and ground, the Altair 8800 becomes a musical instrument of sorts.

Hardware

These instructions assume that we are using the 88-SIO B board which has been set up for ports 5 and 6 as recommended by MITS. The device which is central to our plan is the input-output (IO) interrupt flip flop. This logical entity is actually composed of two sections of a 74L00 integrated circuit (a quad NAND gate) which is referred to as integrated circuit B. The output of each section is fed back to the other section as an input, forming a simple set-clear flip flop. These two sections (of the four on the device) are taken together and called *side a*.

The flip flop is adapted for our purposes by the following procedure (see figure 1):

- Connect a jumper wire between one output of the flip flop and pin 4 of integrated circuit U (an 8T97 device

which is used to buffer the serial data line). Output may come from pin 2 or pin 6 of the 74L00, as these pins are connected together.
- Connect one side of the speaker or amplifier input to pin 5 of integrated circuit U. The other amplifier connection should be made to the +5 V bus through a 0.1 to 0.5 μF capacitor (16 V or better).

The other half (side b) of integrated circuit B could be used for another control function in the same manner. Integrated circuit U has three other spare drivers that could be used for additional buffering. We ran the output connections to a pair of the unused pins on the IO connector at the back of the computer.

We decided to mount the capacitor inside the computer, so that if the +5 V supply was accidently shorted from outside, the capacitor would prevent the power supply from burning out. The capacitor thus blocks DC, but passes the audio frequencies quite readily because of its low reactance at these frequencies. The capacitor also has the effect of causing the plateau of the square wave to slope down somewhat.

It is at this point in the circuit that the square wave may be processed if you wish to change the tonal character of the music coming from the computer. For the sake of simplicity and elegance we elected not to do this.

Software

The software for producing music by this method is written in MITS (Microsoft) 8K BASIC, version 3.2. About 2.5 K bytes of memory are required beyond the space used for the BASIC interpreter. The program uses

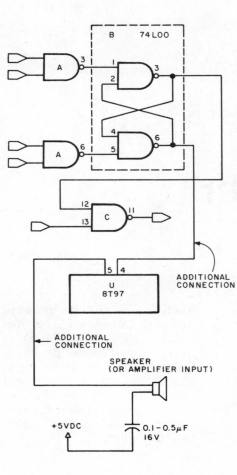

Figure 1: Detail of the schematic for the MITS 88-SIO B circuit board, showing the modifications necessary for producing music by the method described in the article text. Both sides of the output taken from the interrupt flip flop should float above electrical ground. The user should, however, be careful to avoid shock hazard.

a machine language routine stored above BASIC at decimal address 11601 (hexadecimal 2D51). The routine takes only about 30 bytes of memory, which are set aside during the initializing of BASIC.

During the procedure of loading BASIC, you should answer the question "Memory Size" with the number 11600. That is all that has to be done if you have BASIC version 3.2, that has the address of "userloc" (user defined function pointer location) at decimal addresses 73 and 74 (hexadecimal 49 and 4A).

If you have another version of MITS BASIC that has the user location pointer stored at an address other than that given, you should enter the new location in the first step of the BASIC program, in line 10.

The program writes the machine language routine into upper memory. This is called from the BASIC program by executing the user defined function in the statement X = USR (Y). The program also writes zeroes into all unused locations so that changes in the program may be made easily, without fear of gathering unwanted bugs.

The 8080 processor instructions which are loaded by the BASIC program lines 100 and 180 perform the actual setting and clearing of the interrupt flip flop. The machine code is used for greatest possible speed of execution. When I first developed the program, I attempted to do this in BASIC using the usual INP and OUT statements, but found that the audio frequencies obtained were much too low.

You will note that the delay loop timing between the ON (set) and OFF (clear) functions is controlled by "poking" the desired number (P) into the 8080 code routine at BASIC lines 610 and 620. This parameter controls the pitch of each note. The duration of time that the ON and OFF function is on (Y) is also controlled by a delay loop which is executed between the OFF and return (to BASIC) instructions.

Running The Music Program

When starting the program, you make a choice between a pseudo-random "tune" and a stored composition derived from the data given in the DATA statements, lines 650 on.

The random tune derives tone frequencies (pitch) and durations from the instructions at lines 570 and 580 which use the RND function to select numbers for poking pitch and duration into the instructions at lines 590 thru 620. If you allow the program to run in this mode long enough, I suppose that you will eventually hear Beethoven's Fifth Symphony. This is a musical application of the British Museum Algorithm (monkeys pounding typewriters randomly to eventually produce all the books in the museum). We assume that the computer will last that long.

In the stored composition mode, which is started by typing an "S" in response to the input question, the pitch, duration and also rests are derived from the BASIC DATA statements, lines 650 on. Each number and letter combination represents one note of the song. The number is the relative note duration, and the letter is the note pitch in the same sense that it is in regular music. A sharp is also the same symbol, #, as used in standard music notation. No flats were programmed because they were considered redundant.

So, the symbols "2C" and "4C" represent two notes, identical in pitch, but with the second note having twice the duration of the first. "2R" and "4R" would be two rests of different durations. An exclamation mark is placed at the end of the note specification symbol to transpose up one octave.

Although no effort was made to tune the frequency of A to 440 Hz, I am sure this could be done with some simple numerial manipulation. There was originally some interaction of the note timing and pitch. This was compensated for in the BASIC instructions at lines 559 through 561.

A musical composition may be entered into the program by simply reading the notes from any piece of sheet music, determining the proper symbols, and writing these into the DATA statements. I have provided a familiar melody in the DATA statements in listing 1, but you will have to run the program to find out what it is. I was thinking of renaming it the Altair POKEr (Polka). ∎

Listing 1: Program to produce computer music from the MITS 88-ACR audio cassette interface board, written in MITS (Microsoft) 8 K BASIC. The POKE statements from line 10 to line 320 set up the machine language subroutine which toggles the interrupt flip flop on the 88-SIO B board. The POKE statements at lines 590 thru 620, and at lines 690 thru 720, pass parameters to this subroutine.

```
10 POKE 73,81:POKE 74,45
20 FORN=11601TO12128
30 POKE N,0
40 NEXT
50 POKE 11605,17
60 POKE 11610,62
70 POKE 11611,1
80 POKE 11612,211
90 POKE 11613,6
100 POKE 11618,1
110 POKE 11621,13
120 POKE 11622,121
130 POKE 11623,167
140 POKE 11624,194
150 POKE 11625,101
160 POKE 11626,45
170 POKE 11700,62
180 POKE 11701,0
190 POKE 11702,211
200 POKE 11703,6
210 POKE 11704,27
220 POKE 11705,123
230 POKE 11706,167
240 POKE 11707,194
250 POKE 11708,89
260 POKE 11709,45
270 POKE 11710,122
280 POKE 11711,167
290 POKE 11712,194
300 POKE 11713,89
310 POKE 11714,45
320 POKE 11715,201
330 INPUT"TYPE 'R' FOR RANDOM MUSIC; 'S' FOR SONG";J$
340 IFJ$="R"THEN570
350 RESTORE
360 FORN=0TO200
370 READ D$
380 IF D$="$$"THEN330
390 Y$=LEFT$(D$,1)
395 R$=MID$(D$,2,3)
400 P$=RIGHT$(D$,1)
401 Q$=MID$(D$,2,2)
402 IFQ$="C#"THENP=36
403 IFQ$="D#"THENP=31
404 IFQ$="E#"THENP=27
405 IFQ$="G#"THENP=20
406 IFQ$="A#"THENP=16
407 IFQ$="B#"THENP=13
408 IFQ$="F#"THENP=24
410 IFP$="C"THENP=39
420 IFP$="D"THENP=34
430 IFP$="E"THENP=29
440 IFP$="F"THENP=27
450 IFP$="G"THENP=22
460 IFP$="A"THENP=18
470 IFP$="B"THENP=14
475 IFY$="1"THENY=1
480 IFY$="2"THENY=2
490 IFY$="3"THENY=3
500 IFY$="4"THENY=4
501 IFR$="D#!"THENP=INT(12/45*30)
502 IFR$="E#!"THENP=INT(12/45*27)
503 IFR$="G#!"THENP=INT(12/45*20)
504 IFR$="A#!"THENP=INT(12/45*16)
505 IF R$="B#!"THENP=INT(12/45*13)
510 IFY$="5"THENY=5
520 IFY$="6"THENY=6
530 IFY$="7"THENY=7
540 IFY$="8"THENY=8
550 IFQ$="C!"THENP=INT(12/39*39)
551 IFQ$="D!"THENP=INT(12/42*33)
```

```
552 IFQ$="E!"THENP=INT(12/43*28)
553 IFQ$="F!"THENP=INT(12/45*26)
554 IFQ$="G!"THENP=INT(12/45*22)
555 IFQ$="A!"THENP=INT(12/45*18)
556 IFQ$="B!"THENP=INT(12/45*14)
557 IFR$="C#!"THENP=INT(12/45*36)
558 IFR$="F#!"THENP=INT(12/45*24)
559 IFP$="B"THENY=2*Y
560 IFP$="!"THENY=2*Y
561 IFP$="A"THENY=INT(1.5*Y)
562 IFP$="R"THENY=Y:FORE=1T0Y*50:NEXT:G0T0370
569 G0T0690
570 Y=INT((8-2)*RND(1)+2)
580 P=INT((39-12)*RND(1)+12)
590 POKE 11606,Y
600 POKE 11607,Y
610 POKE 11619,P
620 POKE 11620,P
630 X=USR(Y)
640 G0T0570
650 DATA 3D,2C#,1E,3D
651 DATA 3B,3A,2G#,1A,4E,2R
652 DATA 3F#,2F,1F#,3B
653 DATA 3A,1F#,3E,3D#,5D,1R
654 DATA 3D,2C#,1E,3D
655 DATA 3B,3A,2G#,1A,4E,2R
656 DATA 3G,2F#,1G,3D!
657 DATA 3B,3A,1E,1F#,5G
670 DATA $$
680 END
690 POKE 11606,Y
700 POKE 11607,Y
710 POKE 11619,P
720 POKE 11620,P
730 X=USR(Y)
740 NEXT
750 G0T0330
```

Listing 2: The subroutine which toggles the interrupt flip flop, in assembler
format. The entry point is stored in decimal locations 73 and 74, (hexadecimal 49 and 4A). Much room is left in the form of NOPs for modification
by the user. The values which appear in the BASIC listing in decimal are here
translated into hexadecimal.

```
2D51   00   USR    NOP              ROUTINE TO TURN FLIP FLOP
2D52   00          NOP              ON AND OFF
2D53   00          NOP              CALLED BY USR(X)
2D54   00          NOP              FROM BASIC PROGRAM
2D55   11          LXI   D
2D56   00   Y      :00              BASIC PROGRAM POKES VALUE
2D57   00          :00              OF Y HERE
2D58   00          NOP
2D59   00   LOOP   NOP
2D5A   3E          MVI   A,:01      TURN FLIP FLOP ON
2D5B   01
2D5C   D3          OUT   :06
2D5D   06
2D5E   00          NOP              SPACE IS LEFT HERE FOR
2D5F   00          NOP              USER MODIFICATION
2D60   00          NOP
2D61   00          NOP
2D62   01          LXI   B
2D63   00   P      :00              BASIC PROGRAM POKES
2D64   00          :00              VALUE OF P HERE
2D65   0D   SOUND  DCR   C
2D66   79          MOV   A,C
2D67   A7          ANA   A          TEST FLAG Z
2D68   C2          JNZ   SOUND      BRANCH IF A=0
2D69   65
2D6A   2D
2D6B   00          NOP              LOTS OF ROOM LEFT
2D6C   00          NOP              HERE ALSO

            ORG   :2DB4
2DB4   3E          MVI   A,:00      TURN FLIP FLOP OFF
2DB5   00
2DB6   D3          OUT   :06
2DB7   06
2DB8   1B          DCX   D          (AND E)
2DB9   7B          MOV   A,E
2DBA   A7          ANA   A          TEST FLAG Z
2DBB   C2          JNZ   LOOP
2DBC   59
2DBD   2D
2DBE   7A          MOV   A,D
2DBF   A7          ANA   A          TEST
2DC0   C2          JNZ   LOOP
2DC1   59
2DC2   2D
2DC3   C9          RET              GO BACK TO BASIC PROGRAM
            END              IF ZERO
```

Teach KIM to Sing

Peter H Myers

Consider playing musical compositions on a KIM-1 MOS Technology microcomputer module. Although music is one of the most highly developed languages of man, it is possible within a few hours for your KIM-1 system to be educated to speak this language and to create computerized musical sounds. Furthermore, the total cost for enhancing your system to express music is minimal. It is likely that you have everything you need already.

Music essentially consists of a waveform expressed repetitively at some frequency and persisting for a particular time duration. The acoustical characteristics of an instrument greatly affect the ear's perception of the musical composition being played upon it. The basic waveform is modified by the instrument by means of phase shifting, and the production of various simple and complex harmonics which may vary greatly in amplitude.

Now consider a square wave form, an expression of only two amplitudes. The 18th century French mathematician, Joseph Fourier, discovered that the square wave is actually comprised of odd numbered harmonics of the fundamental frequency plus the fundamental frequency itself (all expressed as sine waves)

This is the same thing as saying that a square wave form is harmonically rich. This is fortunate from the point of view of this application, because it allows us to use a very simple program to have a microprocessor system generate just such a harmonically rich fundamental wave form to express any musical note. All that must be known is the note's pitch (or frequency) and duration.

Program Description

A program using this technique, written for the KIM-1 system (which uses the 6502 processor), is shown in listing 1. The duration of a note and its pitch are stored alternately in memory. This is all the main program needs to play a given piece of music. The duration, when read by the main program from memory, is always stored in the X register. The pitch is stored in the Y register.

When the program begins, the location of the first note's duration is in hexadecimal memory byte 0300. The next note's duration value is always the next *even*-numbered memory location (in the latter example, the next note's duration would be at 0302). The values for pitch are stored in the *odd*-numbered memory locations, beginning at hexadecimal byte 0301 (the next note's pitch value at 0303, and so on).

The main program starts by initializing the nonmaskable interrupt (NMI) and interrupt request (IRQ) vectors and the input and output ports, clearing the interrupt mask bit, and starting the interval timer. The note duration interrupt system is initialized (more about this later). After this preparation, the program proceeds into the note loop.

The note loop starts by reading the pitch value from memory and loading it into the Y register. The procedure then subtracts 1 from the Y register. After comparing for detection of a zero in the Y register, the loop jumps back on itself to subtract a 1 again. Thus, every seven machine cycles a 1 is subtracted from the Y register until it becomes equal to zero.

When the Y register is zero, the test

```
0200  A9 00      LDA      ;SAVE MACHINE            023C  4C 23 02   JMP      ;RESTART NOTE.
0202  8D FA 17   STA      ;ROUTINE LOC             023F  EE 20 02   INC      ;INCREMENT
0205  A9 1C      LDA      ;STORED IN NMI           0242  EE 20 02   INC      ;NEXT NOTE
0207  8D FB 17   STA      ;VECTOR.                 0245  EE 29 02   INC      ;PITCH, DURATION
020A  A9 FF      LDA      ;PADD BITS               0248  EE 29 02   INC      ;POINTERS.
020C  8D 01 17   STA      ;INST TO "WRITE".        024B  EA         NOP      ;SPACER.
020F  A9 7F      LDA      ;PBDD BIT 7              024C  A9 65      LDA      ;CHANGE
0211  8D 03 17   STA      ;INST INP IRQ.           024E  8D FE 17   STA      ;IRQ VECTOR
0214  A9 5F      LDA      ;INTERRUPT               0251  A9 02      LDA      ;TO NEW
0216  8D FE 17   STA      ;VECTOR, IRQ,            0253  8D FF 17   STA      ;SERVICE ROUTINE.
0219  A9 02      LDA      ;SERVICE ROUTINE         0256  A9 FF      LDA      ;START TIMER
021B  8D FF 17   STA      ;LOC.                    0258  8D 0E 17   STA      ;T / 64 / 256.
021E  58         CLI      ;ALLOW IRQ.              025B  58         CLI      ;ALLOW IRQ.
021F  AD 00 03   LDA      ;LOAD DURATION           025C  4C 5B 02   JMP      ;DO NOTHING LOOP.
0222  AA         TAX      ;IN X REGISTER.          025F  8D 07 17   STA      ;SHUT OFF IRQ.
0223  A9 FF      LDA      ;START TIMER             0262  4C 38 02   JMP      ;SERVICE ROUTINE LOC.
0225  8D 0E 17   STA      ;T / 64 / 256.           0265  8D 07 17   STA      ;SHUT OFF IRQ.
0228  AD 01 03   LDA      ;LOAD PITCH              0268  4C 14 02   JMP      ;RESTART PROG.
022B  A8         TAY      ;IN Y REGISTER.          026B  A9 00      LDA      ;START PROGRAM
022C  88         DEY      ;NOTE TIMER              026D  8D 20 02   STA      ;RUN HERE
022D  F0 03      BEQ      ;LOOP 7                  0270  A9 03      LDA      ;TO RESET
022F  4C 2C 02   JMP      ;MACHINE CYCLES.         0272  8D 21 02   STA      ;MEMORY READ
0232  EE 00 17   INC      ;TOGGLE OUTPUT.          0275  A9 01      LDA      ;LOCATIONS
0235  4C 28 02   JMP      ;RESTORE LOOP.           0277  8D 29 02   STA      ;BACK TO
0238  CA         DEX      ;COUNTDOWN               027A  A9 03      LDA      ;0300-0301
0239  F0 04      BEQ      ;DURATION.               027C  8D 2A 02   STA      ;AND BEGIN
023B  58         CLI      ;ALLOW IRQ.              027F  4C 00 02   JMP      ;MUSIC.
```

Listing 1. Music playing program for the MOS Technology KIM-1 system, which uses the 6502 processor. The program assumes that data for a particular musical composition has been stored in memory beginning at hexadecimal location 0300.

causes the program to jump out of the loop. Output port pin PA 0 is toggled to change the square wave amplitude of the tone. The program then jumps back to the beginning of the note loop, reloads the pitch value, and the process is repeated. This uninterrupted process produces a square waveform tone which emerges at PA 0. The pitch value can be calculated for a given frequency by the formula in table 1.

The initialization of the note duration interrupt system proceeded as follows. The duration value is read from memory and loaded into the X register. Also, the interval timer is started and asked to interrupt the main program after 16,384 machine cycles.

While the note loop is generating notes, the interval timer is counting down. When the counter reaches 0, the timer has timed out. This interrupts the main program by loading the program counter with the IRQ vector. The IRQ vector is initialized to direct the processor to the interrupt service routine.

The interrupt service routine shuts off the interrupt request flag (IRQ) and subtracts 1 from the duration value in the X register. The X register is compared for detection of a zero. If X is not equal to 0, the program resets the interrupt mask bit so that interrupts can occur again. Then the routine returns to main program execution, starting the interval timer and falling into the note loop.

Each interrupt is serviced in the same way until the X register becomes equal to 0. When this occurs, that interrupt will be recognized as the end of the note. Instead of jumping back to the main program after resetting the mask bit, the interrupt service routine program continues.

The routine proceeds to increment both the X register loading pointer and the Y register loading pointer by 2. This automatically gets the next pitch and duration value pair when the main program is run again.

A pause must be inserted at the end of each note to distinguish the duration. This is accomplished by changing the IRQ vector to a different location after an interrupt request.

After this change, the interval timer is started and the program falls into a "do nothing" loop. It will stay in this wait state until an interrupt directs it to a new program location. A special routine beginning at this location will service the interrupt by turning off the IRQ request and jumping back to the beginning of the main program. The main program will play the next note for the duration requested.

The main program can play a musical composition which is 128 notes in length or less, with the pitch and duration values stored in one relative memory page. Each note will be played in the same manner previously described. The program can be revised to read note specifications to the end of memory, thus giving the capability of playing compositions longer than 128 notes. This was not done in the original program because I wanted the program to loop back and play the composition over and over.

Preparing the Music

A musical score is converted for playing by the computer in a note-by-note process. It is begun by reading each note in a melody, observing the octave it is to be played in, and then finding the corresponding frequency in a table, as may be found in the appendix. The frequency is converted into a one byte pitch value by using the formula in table 1 and then calculating the hexadecimal equivalent.

The duration of the note is calculated as a function of time in seconds by the formula in table 2. Construct a table containing this information for each note in the melodic line. Using monitor commands, store the hexadecimal values for the duration and pitch in sequential memory locations, starting at hexadecimal location 0300. The specifications for the second note will start at 0302, the third at 0304, and so on.

Whenever an interval of silence is desired, whether at the end of the piece, or embedded within, store a pitch value of 01 hexadecimal. The duration value becomes the desired length of the silent period. The pitch value of 01 produces a note at a frequency of slightly over 24 kHz, which is perceived by the human ear as silence.

$$P_n = \frac{1}{0.000014\,(f_n)} - 2$$

f_n = frequency in Hz of note
P_n = pitch value of note

Table 1. Formula for calculating the pitch value for a desired note. The result should be rounded to the nearest whole number, and then must be converted from decimal notation to hexadecimal for entry into the computer. The pitch value is the first byte of the note specification pair.

$$D_n = \frac{t_n}{0.016384}$$

t_n = time in seconds of note
D_n = duration value of note

Table 2. Formula for calculating the time duration value of a note. The result must be rounded and converted to hexadecimal. The duration value is the second of the note specification byte pair.

Note	Frequency (Hz)	Pitch Value Decimal	Pitch Value Hexadecimal
G	392.7	180	B4
G♯, A♭	415.7	170	AA
A	441.4	160	A0
A♯, B♭	467.4	151	97
B	490.0	144	90
C	522.1	135	87
C♯, D♭	554.5	127	7F
D	586.3	120	78
D♯, E♭	622.1	113	71
E	662.3	106	6A
F	701.4	100	64
F♯, G♭	737.7	95	5F
G	786.3	89	59

Table 3. One octave table of prepared pitch values, which begin at G above middle C. The frequencies given for each note are not quite standard, but are close enough for noncritical applications. Also, the frequencies will vary within the clock tolerances for different processors. The user may transpose these pitches down one octave by changing the output port used from PA 0 to PA 1.

	Time (seconds)	Duration value (hexadecimal)
Whole note	2.18	85
Half note	1.09	43
Quarter note	0.545	20
Eighth note	0.2725	10
Sixteenth note	0.1362	07

Table 4. Set of suggested time duration values for preparing melodic data from standard musical notation. These yield a tempo with about 120 quarter notes per minute.

A short hexadecimal conversion table for one octave beginning at G above middle C appears in table 3. Table 4 contains a suggested set of duration values. The duration values given are appropriate for a tempo of about 120 quarter notes per minute, which usually works out to a moderately fast march tempo.

0300	10	87	10	87	20	87	20	B4
0308	10	6A	10	6A	20	6A	20	87
0310	10	87	10	6A	20	59	20	59
0318	10	64	10	6A	43	78	10	78
0320	10	6A	20	64	20	64	10	6A
0328	10	78	20	6A	20	87	10	87
0330	10	6A	20	78	20	B4	10	8F
0338	10	78	43	87	10	87	10	87
0340	20	87	20	B4	10	6A	10	6A
0348	20	6A	20	87	10	87	10	6A
0350	20	59	20	59	10	64	10	6A
0358	43	78	10	78	10	6A	20	64
0360	20	64	10	6A	10	78	20	6A
0368	20	87	10	87	10	6A	20	78
0370	20	B4	10	8F	10	78	43	87
0378	FF	01	FF	01	01	01	01	01

Listing 2. Melodic data for use by the music playing program. This was prepared from a musical score by the procedure given in the text. The tune is the American traditional song, My Darling Clementine. *The pairs of digits represent the contents of one byte of memory. The user should place this data in programmable memory by monitor commands. The first byte specifies the time duration of the first note; the second byte specifies the pitch of the first note. The third byte gives the duration of the second note; the fourth byte, the second pitch, and so on.*

The lowest pitch which may be obtained using the output port configuration described is the C sharp just above middle C. To obtain lower pitches, change the output port used from PA 0 to PA 1. This causes all notes to be transposed down one octave.

To prepare the hardware for music making, you should connect a jumper wire from the interval timer interrupt output to the interrupt request (IRQ) pin. Normal output is taken from PA 0 and referenced to ground. The interval timer is found at connector A pin 15, and IRQ at connector E pin 4. The output PA 0 comes from connector A pin 14. PA 1 may be found at connector A pin 4.

The audio signal present at the output port may be monitored using a number of methods. You can listen to it directly with high impedance earphones. One of the best ways is to connect the output into the auxiliary input jack of a tape recorder and use the tape monitor audio amplifier for output.

Also, since the output voltage is 1.4 V peak-to-peak, it is quite easy to use a stereo amplifier's high level input jack and play it through a stereo system.

Editor's note: When playing the output of the KIM-1 system through a high fidelity music system, the user should take care not to overtax the speaker systems by playing at high volume. The complex waveforms generated by the computer contain much more energy at high frequencies (above 10,000 Hz) than is contained by conventional music. As a consequence, the tweeter sections of speaker systems may burn out if they are made to reproduce these waveforms at high volumes . . . . RSS

It is interesting to note that the harmonics of the tones are so rich that an FM radio, when held close by the KIM-1 board, will play the tones as audio because it receives them as radio frequencies. This is, however, not the ideal system for monitoring the tones, mainly because non-musical harmonics often become louder than the desired musical notes.

For a demonstration piece I have selected an old time favorite tune. The note specifications of the melody are given as listing 2, and should be programmed into memory as listed.

Provided you have made the hardware changes needed, have a working audio monitor, and have entered listings 1 and 2 into memory properly, you are ready for the KIM to play its first musical piece. Start the execution of the program at hexadecimal memory location 026B. Reset the system by depressing the RS key, and then depressing GO.

The program will repeat the tune indefinitely, but may be stopped by depressing the ST key. Always start the program at location 026B. This will initialize the X and Y register pointers for starting at the beginning of the composition. After this subroutine has finished, control is transferred to the main program.

So it can be done. Music is being played on your KIM-1 system with a minimum of hardware. This system is now expressing a high level language that can be interpreted by all.

May you enjoy many hours of music lessons with KIM. ■

A Terrain Reader

Richard Gold

Introduction

The program described here was written for use in a piece of musical theater called "Fictional Travels in a Mythical Land", which was performed at the Center for Contemporary Music of Mills College, at Oakland CA in December 1977. While the sounds that the program generated did not sound like traditional music, they worked well within the production for two reasons: they provided an interesting sonic backdrop during a long scene where a mime performed, and secondly, the method by which the program generated the sounds was conceptually related to what was transpiring on stage. Before I talk about the program itself, which was written for the KIM-1 (a 6502 microprocessor based computer), I am going to discuss "new" or avante-garde music itself and talk about some of the issues that are involved in this art form.

A Brief History of New Music

In the early part of the 20th century, composers such as Shönberg, Webern and Berg began working with *serial* or *twelve-tone* music. Their compositions used the principle that no note could be played a second time before the other eleven notes of the scale were sounded. Once the original sequential order of the notes was given, that order would be maintained throughout the piece. This sequence came to be known as the *tone row*. The twelve-tone row is not a theme, per se, but rather a musical "idea" that permeates the composition. The music produced in this way sounded rather dry. However, the aspect relevant here was the introduction of a new way of thinking about music, a way that leads directly to much of the computer music produced today.

Twelve-tone composers began to think of sound in terms of numeric parameters. The serial techniques relied on reducing pitches to a series of numbers. It was not a great leap to the representation of durations, timbres and dynamics in the same manner.

Sound, which had been thought of as a unified harmonic structure, was broken down into a collection of component parts. Composers began to study textbooks on calculation and derivation instead of harmony and counterpoint.

It was this fascination with mathematical processes for composing pieces of music, instead of using themes, melodies and motives, that formed the seed of a second powerful idea: music could be a realization of a concept or idea, and that concept could be as important as the sounds produced. The interplay between the concept and the sonic reality provides the excitement and fun of such compositions.

Composer John Cage brought conceptual or new music to wide attention. He performed or realized pieces based on random throws of dice, choices from the *I Ching*, overlays of transparent sheets, and the sounds produced by phono cartridges scraping over everything but records. John Cage said that he "liberated sound", by which he meant that *any* sound could be used in a piece of music, not just sounds that came from traditional instruments and not just pretty sounds. The artistic criterion is that the sounds must be true to the composer's conception of the piece.

The parameterization of sound, "concept" music, and the liberation of sound were all involved in the development and use of the *analog modular voltage-controlled synthesizer*, a remarkable device in which these three ideas were combined. The synthesizer parameterized sound; the pitch was gener-

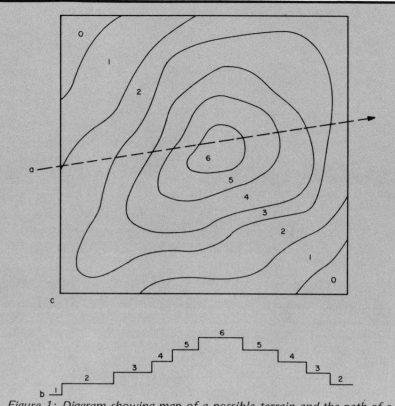

Figure 1: Diagram showing map of a possible terrain and the path of a traveler across it. The topography of the terrain is indicated in the map by contour lines. Below the map is a graph showing the changes in the altitude of the traveler as it moves in two dimensions across the surface.

ated by the oscillator, the dynamic volume was produced by the amplifier, and the timbre was formed by ring modulators and filters. Furthermore, each of these functions was controlled by an array of devices such as sequencers, random voltage generators, pulse generators, envelope generators, and touch pads. These control devices took the place of the mathematical charts of the serial composers.

Concept music was a natural application for the synthesizer, particularly for concepts involving the expanding subject of cybernetics. Positive and negative feedback, open and closed loops, control lines, propagation delay, stability, and response time became common words in the early electronic studios. With the synthesizer not only was it possible to produce music, but (since the synthesizer is an analog computer) it was now possible to model all sorts of things from the real world, from population booms to planetary motion, and to have the synthesizer directly respond to the environment, and vice versa.

The analog synthesizer created a new palette of aural colors to work with. While the early promises of being able to generate *any* sound turned out to be fallacious, users

of the synthesizer are still concocting sonic surprises, sounds and patterns that were never even dreamt of.

These new musical ideas and new instruments resulted in a music that is, in some ways, more estranged from mainstream Western music than Tibetan music is from bluegrass. Not only were the sounds liberated, but the entire structure was radically altered. A given composition might divide an octave into three steps or a thousand; it might be highly rhythmic or the notes might fall randomly; some of the sounds might be simpler than those produced by a flute, while others might be so complex that one would be hard pressed to say it had a pitch at all.

The analog synthesizer has been used for all varieties of music from rock and roll to Bach. Microprocessors, however, were not designed with any kind of musical usage in mind. That they can be used to produce music is, of course, much more than simply fortuitous.

Microprocessors are some of the most general purpose devices ever designed. It is quite conceivable that they can produce sounds never before heard or imagined. Certainly they will be able to realize concepts that even the synthesizer cannot touch.

Most of the literature available dealing with this subject shows the processors used in conservative ways. The computer is used to emulate such things as pianos, organs and even analog synthesizers. Very few authors deal with the ways that processors can be used to realize concepts. Even fewer deal with unusual sounds and structures. In an attempt to do both, I present the following program.

The Terrain Reader Conceptual Scheme

I began with one large conception and a number of smaller ones. My overall plan was to try to incorporate as many of the small conceptions as I could, while realizing the large one. I shall first explain the main idea and then go through the smaller ones before I proceed to explain the program itself.

The idea for the Terrain Reader came from a concept developed by my fellow composer Randy Cohen a number of years ago. The concept contains a three dimensional surface, or terrain, with coordinates given in an X, Y, Z axis system. For this application, the depth axis Z is treated as a function of X and Y. The value of Z varies in a topographical fashion as an observer travels across the terrain. Refer to figure 1 for a two dimensional representation or map of the terrain.

For the purposes of the program, we assume that a "traveler" is moving across the surface of the terrain. We describe its position on the map in terms of **X** and **Y** coordinates. As the traveler moves across the surface, the value of the **Z** or depth coordinate varies continuously according to the "lay of the land."

We employ a digital to analog converter to transform this change in **Z** to a change in an electrical voltage **V**. If the traveler is moving over the terrain at a sufficient rate, we can use the voltage to produce sound by having it drive a speaker. That is the basic idea of the Terrain Reader.

It should be clear that for audible sound to be produced in this manner, the traveler has to climb up a hill and move back down into a valley between a minimum of 20 times per second and a maximum of 20,000 times per second (refer to figure 2). Further, if the traveler is just taking a random walk, nothing is produced but white noise. The traveler's path must be fairly periodic. Given periodicity, certain interesting consequences result. The time it takes to make one circuit of the path determines the base frequency of the sound, while the hills and valleys of the land determine the timbre.

The secondary criteria for the program were as follows: first, I wanted to implement the program in the 1 K memory of my KIM-1, with nothing more than a digital to analog converter between the computer and the amplifier. Secondly, I wanted the sound output to be fairly rhythmic and to sound like music from a "fictional" culture, music that a group of people *could* have come up with, but didn't.

Also, the music had to be repetitious enough so I could play another instrument along with it, and yet varying enough to maintain interest. I wanted the changes to sound intelligent, and yet I wanted the process to be automatic enough so I wouldn't have to type in new numbers for every change.

Lastly, I wanted a wide range of timbres. No attempt was made to produce every possible timbre or every pitch from 20 to 20,000 Hertz. I was looking not for the perfect, general music program, but for the realization of the Terrain Traveler.

Program Description

The assembler format code of the program is shown in listing 1. Page three of computer memory contains the surface or land represented as a 16 by 16 matrix; the main program and variables are contained in page 0. The subroutines are in pages 0, 1 and 2. The GETKY subroutine is used to access the KIM-1 keyboard. That subroutine is contained in the KIM monitor at hexadecimal location 1F6A. The GETKY routine scans the keyboard and returns the value found there to the accumulator. If nothing is found, GETKY returns a hexadecimal value of 15.

The method used to move the traveler about the surface is conceptually similar to the method by which *Lissajous* figures are produced on oscilloscopes. Lissajous figures are seemingly three dimensional images created by interaction between two different input signals on an oscilloscope, one on the x-axis and one on the y-axis (see figure 3).

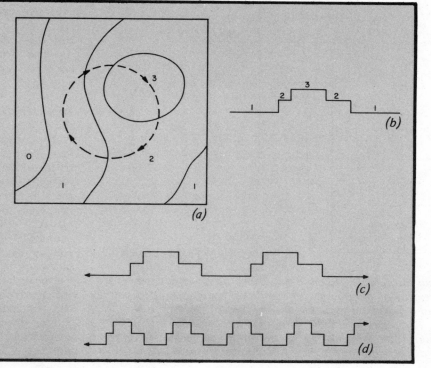

Figure 2: (a) Experimental section of the terrain showing a circular traveler path. (b) A graph of the traveler's altitude as it moves across the surface. Continuous motion in this circular path gives a regular waveform (c) whose frequency depends on the speed of the traveler. The frequency may be doubled (d) by making the traveler move faster. In this application, the traveler should move fast enough that the frequency generated is in the audio region.

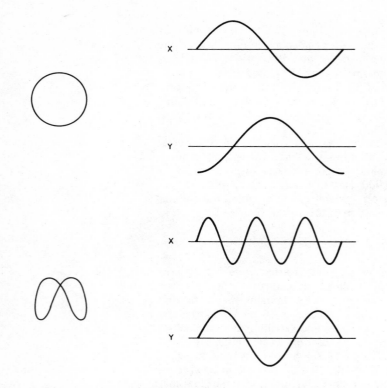

Figure 3: Circular Lissajou patterns are formed on the screen of an oscilloscope when two sine waves of equal frequency and amplitude, but 90 degrees out of phase, control the X and Y axes. Different patterns may be formed by varying amplitude, frequency, and relative phase of the input signals.

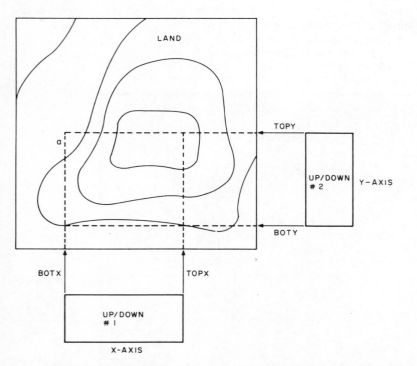

Figure 4: Diagram showing the region in which two up/down counters may control the movement of the traveler. The up/down counter counts from a minimum value to a maximum value in increments of 1. When it reaches this maximum value, it reverses and decrements by 1 until the lowest value is reached once more. In this way, the two up/down counters approximate Lissajou figure type paths for the traveler by acting as software oscillators.

In the program, there are two up/down counters, one for the x-axis and one for the y-axis, which act essentially as triangle wave oscillators, these are used as indices for addressing the matrix (observe figure 4). The maximum and minimum points of both counters are alterable. It is by changing these end points that different sounds are generated.

As seen in figure 5, if the range of both counters is the same (for instance counting up and down between 4 and 9), then a straight diagonal path across the terrain will be generated. If, however, the values counted are not in such a simple relationship, the resulting path is much more complicated. Several such patterns are shown in figure 6. It should be noted that it is the relationship in magnitude between the end points, and not the specific end points that determines the patterns.

The majority of the execution time of the program is spent in the first part of the program. The second part of the program executes in the interval between notes. The first part of the program generates the sound, and the second part alters the variables to produce different paths over the surface. It is during the second part of the program that the keyboard is scanned and new information entered into the program.

The output of the program is sent to a latched output port at hexadecimal address 1700 (direction register 1701 is set to hexadecimal FF), which is attached to a digital to analog converter as shown in figure 7. The digital to analog converter from Hal Chamberlain's *A Sampling of Techniques for Computer Performance of Music*, page 47, is inexpensive and works quite well for this application. I have not included a filter circuit. Users who wish greater filtering versatility than that provided by amplifier tone controls may wish to add appropriate circuitry.

Program Flow

The program begins by updating both up/down counters, checking to see if they have hit the top or the bottom of their count, and reversing their directions if they have. Using the values of the two counters, the program next loads the proper value from the terrain matrix. This is done by simply shifting the Y counter left four times, adding it to the X counter, and storing the result in the Y index register. An absolute Y indexed fetch is executed and the retrieved value is sent to the output port.

After returning from the OUTPUT subroutine, the program jumps to the CLOCK subroutine. There it updates a counter and compares the new value with the value of

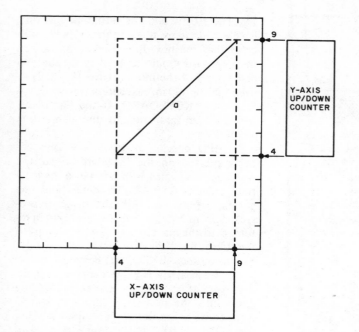

Figure 5: Straight line path produced by the two up/down counters operating over the same magnitude between minimum and maximum values (or limits).

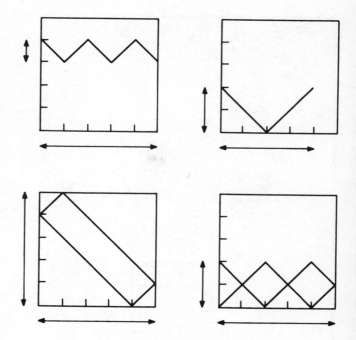

Figure 6: Various patterns obtained by varying the limits and phase of the up/down counters.

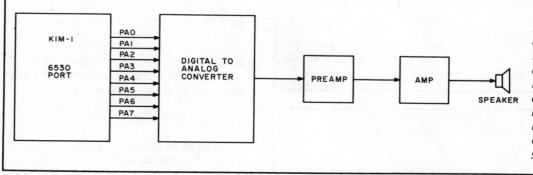

Figure 7: Connecting the KIM-1 output port and the digital to analog converter. If this scheme is applied to another system having no latched port, a digital to analog converter with a latched buffer must be used. The audio sections of the connections are straightforward.

DONE. If the counter does not equal DONE, the flow loops to the top of the program. If, however, the counter value does equal the value of DONE, flow drops through to the second part of the program. Here new values for the variables are computed and new information from the keyboard taken in.

Figure 8 shows the four up counters that determine the values for the end points of the two up/down counters. One of the up counters determines the value for each of the four end points. The MUSIC subroutine updates the four up counters and assigns their values to the four end points, which are labeled BOTX, TOPX, BOTY and TOPY.

The end points of BOTX's up counter are labeled X1 and X2, while TOPX's points are X3 and X4. The end points of BOTY and TOPY are labeled Y1, Y2, Y3 and Y4. When new values are typed in via the keyboard, or when the program is in its automatic mode, it is these eight values, X1 thru Y4 that are altered.

The program next checks to see which mode it is in, automatic or manual. If in manual mode, program execution proceeds to the next process. If the status check reveals the automatic mode, the program jumps into subroutine AUTO.

If the program changes one of the end point values every time AUTO is called, the music changes too rapidly and tends to sound random. So the AUTO subroutine first checks to see that a sufficient amount of time has elapsed. If it has not, COUNT is decremented and control is returned to the main routine. If, however, COUNT equals 0, the subroutine AUTO alters an end point of one of the up counters. The pointer INDX (which is subsequently incremented) determines which end point to alter. The value inserted into the list of endpoints is derived from the value being output at the time. Finally, AUTO resets COUNT and returns control to the main section of the program.

The program next checks to see if the

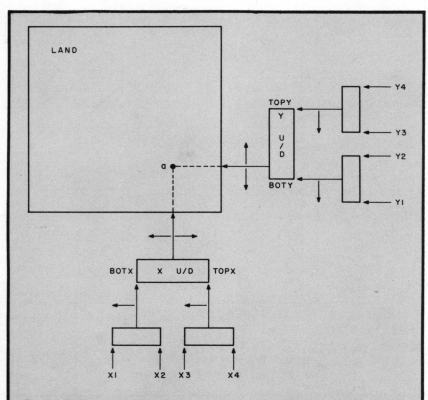

Figure 8: Changing the path of the traveler. The instantaneous values of the two up/down counters determine a single point a. The altitude value stored in the matrix determines the output voltage. The limits of the up/down counters are determined by four up counters. The counting limits of the up counters are determined either by keyboard input or by the AUTO subroutine.

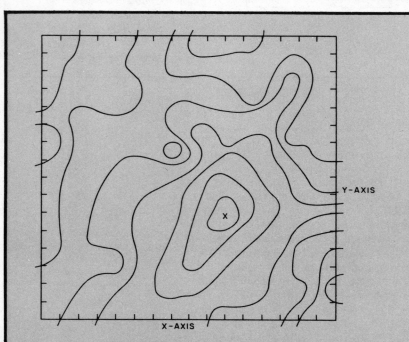

Figure 9: Contour map of the hypothetical land used in the program (for which the numeric values appear in listing 2). Each contour line represents a difference of hexadecimal 20. Both smooth plains and mountainous regions are found in this terrain.

TMCHK flag is set. The setting of this flag, which is done by pressing the *PC* key, indicates that the next numeric key pressed on the keyboard should be used to set the general tempo of the music. If the flag has not been set, program execution proceeds to subroutine KEYBOARD. If the flag is set, the program branches to the subroutine TEMPO.

TEMPO checks to see if any keys are being pressed on the keyboard. If so, the corresponding value is inserted into the location called RATE. RATE determines the general tempo at which the program progresses from note to note. Control is then returned to the main program, which jumps to the subroutine KEYBOARD.

Subroutine KEYBOARD begins by checking to see if a key is being depressed on the keyboard. If so, it inserts the corresponding value into the proper location. Thereafter it proceeds to set the proper flags, including the BOUNCE flag, which insures that a key is looked at only once and scanning for additional user input occurs.

The keyboard may be used to enter new values into the end points of the up counters. This is accomplished by a procedure similar to that used by the subroutine AUTO, except that the values inserted come from the keyboard and not the terrain matrix. The first number entered via the keyboard is inserted into the first end point (X1), the second into X2, and so on through Y4, then back to X1 with INDX keeping track.

Keyboard Operation

In addition to accepting values of the end points for the up counters, the keyboard serves a few other functions. One is the selection between two available voices, which are represented by separate lists of values. One voice is selected by pressing the **AD** key, the other by the **DA** key. In this way two different patterns can be stored and selected at the touch of a switch. These voices can have different tempi, and can be either automatic mode or manual.

To set a voice to automatic, the **plus** (+) key is pressed; the voice that is presently operative is thus set to automatic. To take that voice out of automatic, the corresponding voice key is hit. This procedure allows human controlled repetition of a pleasing pattern discovered by the computer operating in the automatic mode. The pattern will then repeat until the operator intervenes.

Observe that operating the **PC** key causes the TMCHK flag to be set, which in turn causes the next value depressed on the keyboard to be placed in the RATE variable. In this way, the general tempo of the program may be speeded up or slowed down.

Housekeeping and Details

Because of the time constraints of real time music, it is impossible for the program to be constantly scanning the keyboard. In fact, the keyboard may be scanned only between the notes. This makes it difficult to take care of such housecleaning activities as debouncing the keys, ie: checking to see that a single depressed key isn't looked at twice.

To handle these problems, the program uses the BOUNCE flag. This flag is set when the program first accepts input from the keyboard. The program will not accept another key input until BOUNCE is turned off once again. BOUNCE is reset whenever the subroutine KEYBOARD checks the keyboard and finds no key depressed. This method entails a few inconveniences: for a key input to be accepted, the key must be depressed while a note is changing to another note. Secondly, at least one note change must go by with no key depressed

before another key input can be entered.

The last subroutine the program executes before returning to the top of the program is SETTIME. This section of code sets the duration of the next note. As in the AUTO subroutine, this value is derived from the value it finds at the output port. Since there are 256 different durations possible, the resultant music is slightly less rhythmic than may be desired, though I personally like the slight shimmering quality this gives the music.

The program is almost entirely written in subroutines. This modularity makes it easy to alter and add new ideas and concepts. It is of course very easy to change the "land" and explore the sounds of other surfaces. One interesting program alteration I have been working with is a way to change the values of the surface as the program progresses. I have included the coding for one such method at the end. Interested readers can develop other methods. ∎

Listing 1: Machine code listing in hexadecimal of the Terrain Reader program, accompanied by a pseudo-assembly language mnemonic code. It is designed to run in a KIM-1 micro-computer in 1 K bytes of memory. It can be adapted to other 6502-based computers. To use this program on a different system, the KEYBOARD and TEMPO input subroutines have to be altered and the OUTPUT subroutine changed.

Address	Hex Code	Label	Op Code	Operand	Comments
1700	00	OUT			;OUTPUT REG
1701	FF	OUTD			;OUTPUT DIRECTION REG
1F6A		GETKY			;KIM KEYBOARD SCANNER ENTRY
0000		MAIN			;PROGRAM START
0300		LAND			;THIRD PAGE IS SURFACE

;LIST OF VARIABLES
;VOICE "DA"

Address	Hex Code	Label	Op Code	Operand	Comments
00AF	01	X1			;END POINTS FOR UP-COUNTERS
00B0	06	X2			
00B1	07	X3			
00B2	0B	X4			
00B3	02	Y1			
00B4	05	Y2			
00B5	09	Y3			
00B6	0E	Y4			
00B9	01	DIM			;X OSC POSITION
00BA	01	SLPD			;X OSC DIRECTION (01 0R FF)
00BB	01	BOTD			;X OSC BOTTOM
00BC	07	TOPD			;X OSC TOP
00BD	02	DIM			;Y OSC POSITION
00BE	01	SLPD			;Y OSC DIRECTION (01 0R FF)
00BF	02	BOTD			;Y OSC BOTTOM
00C0	09	TOPD			;Y OSC TOP
00C1	00	AUTOCHK			;AUTO FLAG (00 OFF, 01 ON)
00C2	00	TMCHK			;TEMPO JUMP FLAG (00 OFF, 01 ON)
00C3	0C	RATE			;SETS GENERAL TEMPO

;VOICE "AD"

Address	Hex Code	Label	Op Code	Operand	Comments
00C8	02	X1			;END POINTS FOR UP-COUNTERS
00C9	08	X2			
00CA	0A	X3			
00CB	0F	X4			
00CC	01	Y1			
00CD	0A	Y2			
00CE	0B	Y3			
00CF	0F	Y4			
00D2	02	DIM			;X OSC POSITION
00D3	01	SLPD			;X OSC DIRECTION
00D4	02	BOTD			;X OSC BOTTOM
00D5	0A	TOPD			;X OSC TOP
00D6	01	DIM			;Y OSC POSITION
00D7	01	SLPD			;Y OSC DIRECTION
00D8	01	BOTD			;Y OSC BOTTOM
00D9	0B	TOPD			;Y OSC TOP
00DA	00	AUTOCHK			;AUTO MODE FLAG
00DB	00	TMCHK			;TEMPO JUMP FLAG
00DC	06	RATE			;SETS GENERAL TEMPO

;PROGRAM VARIABLES

Address	Hex Code	Label	Op Code	Operand	Comments
00E2	AF	AORB			;VOICE FLAG (AF OR C8)
00E3	FF	CLK1			;CLOCK ONE
00E4	FF	CLK2			;CLOCK TWO
00E5	80	DONE			;SETS LENGTH OF NOTE
00E6	00	BOUNCE			;DEBOUNCER FLAG
00E7	00	TEMP			;TEMPORARY STORAGE
00E8	00	INDX			;POINTS TO PROPER VARIABLE
00E9	00	COUNT			;SLOWS DOWN MUSIC CHANGES

;MAIN PROGRAM

Address	Hex Code	Label	Op Code	Operand	Comments
0000	A90A	MAIN	LDA	#$0A	;SET FOR X OSC
0002	18		CLC		
0003	65E2		ADC	AORB	;SET PROPER VOICE
0005	AA		TAX		;SET X INDEX

```
0006    202300              JSR     OSC         ;UPDATE X AXIS
0009    A90E                LDA     #$0E        ;SET FOR Y OSC
000B    18                  CLC
000C    65E2                ADC     AORB        ;SET PROPER VOICE
000E    AA                  TAX                 ;SET X INDEX
000F    202300              JSR     OSC         ;UPDATE Y AXIS
0012    A6E2                LDX     AORB        ;SET X INDEX
0014    205500              JSR     OUTPUT      ;OUTPUT VALUE TO
                                                    D/A
0017    206C00              JSR     CLOCK       ;UPDATE CLOCK AND
                                                    NEW VALUES
001A    4C0000              JMP     #0000       ;LOOP TO TOP OF
                                                    PROGRAM


;SUBROUTINE OSC
;UPDATES THE UP DOWN COUNTERS
0023    B500        OSC     LDA     DIM,X       ;GET VALUE OF
                                                    COUNTER
0025    18                  CLC
0026    7501                ADC     SLPD,X      ;UPDATE COUNTER
0028    9500                STA     DIM,X       ;STORE NEW VALUE
                                                    OF COUNTER
002A    D502                CMP     BOTD,X      ;VALUE HIT BOTTOM?
002C    F00D                BEQ     UPD         ;YES. CHANGE TO
                                                    COUNT UP
002E    D503                CMP     TOPD,X      ;VALUE HIT TOP?
0030    F00E                BEQ     DWND        ;YES. CHANGE TO
                                                    COUNT DOWN
0032    C910                CMP     #$10        ;VALUE GONE OFF
                                                    TOP OF LAND?
0034    F00F                BEQ     ZERO        ;WRAP-AROUND
                                                    BOTTOM IF YES
0036    C9FF                CMP     #$FF        ;VALUE GONE OFF
                                                    BOTTOM OF LAND?
0038    F010                BEQ     ARND        ;YES. WRAP-AROUND
                                                    TOP OF LAND.
003A    60                  RTS                 ;EVERYTHING OK.
                                                    RETURN
003B    A901        UPD     LDA     #$01        ;01 COUNTS UP
003D    9501                STA     SLPD,X      ;PUT IT IN SLPD
003F    60                  RTS                 ;RETURN
0040    A9FF        DWND    LDA     #$FF        ;FF COUNTS DOWN
0042    9501                STA     SLPD,X      ;PUT IN SLPD
0044    60          RTS                         ;RETURN
0045    A9FF        ZERO    LDA     #$FF        ;FF IS BOTTOM OR
                                                    LEFT OF LAND
0047    9500                STA     DIM,X       ;PUT IN COUNTER
                                                    POSITION
0049    60                  RTS                 ;RETURN
004A    A910        ARND    LDA     #$10        ;10 IS TOP OR RIGHT
                                                    OF LAND
004C    9500                STA     DIM,X       ;PUT IN COUNTER
                                                    POSITION
004E    60                  RTS                 ;RETURN


;SUBROUTINE OUTPUT
;OUTPUTS VALUE TO OUTPUT PORT
0055    B50E        OUTPUT  LDA     DIM,X       ;GET Y AXIS COUNTER
0057    0A                  ASL                 ;SHIFT OVER 4 TIMES
0058    0A                  ASL                 ;THAT IS, MULTIPLY
                                                    BY 16
0059    0A                  ASL
005A    0A                  ASL
005B    18                  CLC
005C    750A                ADC     DIM,X       ;ADD X AXIS COUNTER
005E    A8                  TAY                 ;PUT SUM IN Y INDEX
005F    B90003              LDA     LAND,Y      ;GET VALUE FROM
                                                    LAND (PAGE 3 OF
                                                    MEMORY)
0062    8D0017              STA     $1700       ;SEND VALUE TO
                                                    OUTPUT PORT
0065    60                  RTS                 ;RETURN


;SUBROUTINE CLOCK
;CHECKS TO SEE IF CLOCK HAS RUN DOWN AND IF IT HAS,
;CLOCK SENDS PROGRAM FLOW TO SUBROUTINES TO UPDATE VARIABLES
006C    B514        CLOCK   LDA     RATE,X      ; GET RATE
006E    0A                  ASL                 ;MULTIPLY IT BY TWO
006F    18                  CLC                 ;CLEAR CARRY
0070    EA                          NOP
0071    65E3                ADC     CLK1        ;ADD TO CLOCK ONE
0073    85E3                STA     CLK1        ;AND RESTORE TO
                                                    CLOCK ONE
0075    A900                LDA     #00         ;CLEAR ACCUM.
0077    65E4                ADC     CLK2        ;ADD CARRY BIT TO
                                                    CLOCK TWO
0079    85E4                STA     CLK2        ;AND RESTORE TO
                                                    CLOCK TWO
```

007B	C5E5		CMP	DONE	;DOES CLOCK TWO EQUAL DONE?
007D	F001		BEQ	MSC	;YES, SET NEW VARI-ABLES
007F	60		RTS		;NO. RETURN TO SOUND MAKING
0080	200002	MSC	JSR	MUSIC	;CHANGE UP/DOWN END POINTS
0083	A900		LDA	#00	;CLEAR ACCUM.
0085	D512		CMP	AUTO-CHK,X	:AUTO MODE?
0087	F003		BEQ	TME	;NO. SKP AUTO SUB.
0089	200001		JSR	AUTO	;YES. AUTO UPDATE UP END POINTS
008C	A900	TME	LDA	#00	;CLEAR ACCUMU-LATOR.
008E	D513		CMP	TMCHK,X	;WAITING FOR TEMPO CHANGE?
0090	F003		BEQ	KEYB	;NO. SKIP TEMPO
0092	20D702		JSR	TEMPO	;YES. CHECK KEY-BOARD FOR NEW VALUE
0095	204702	KEYB	JSR	KEYBOARD	;CHECK KEYBOARD FOR NEW VALUES
0098	20C102		JSR	SETTIME	;SET TIME FOR NEXT NOTE
009B	60		RTS		;BACK TO MAIN FLOW

;SUBROUTINE MUSIC. CHANGES UP/DOWN COUNTER'S END POINTS

0200	B50C	MUSIC	LDA	BOTX,X	;GET BOTTOM OF U/D COUNTER (X)
0202	18		CLC		;CLEAR CARRY
0203	6901		ADC	#$01	;ADD ONE
0205	D501		CMP	X2,X	;EQUAL TOP OF BOTTOM UP COUNTER?
0207	1005		BPL	COR1	;YES. RESET UP COUNTER
0209	950C		STA	BOTX,X	;NO. STORE ANSWER IN BOTX
020B	4C1202		JMP	B	;JMP TO B AND CHECK TOP OF U/D COUNTER
020E	B500	COR1	LDA	X1,X	;GET BOTTOM OF UP COUNTER
0210	950C		STA	BOTX,X	;PUT VALUE IN BOTX
0212	B50D	B	LDA	TOPX,X	;GET TOP OF U/D COUNTER (X)
0214	18		CLC		;CLEAR CARRY
0215	6901		ADC	#$01	;ADD ONE
0217	D503		CMP	X4,X	;EQUAL TOP OF TOP UP-COUNTER?
0219	1005		BPL	COR2	;YES. RESET UP COUNTER
021B	950D		STA	TOPX,X	;NO. STORE NEW VALUE IN TOPX
021D	4C2402		JMP	C	;GO TO C AND CHECK BOT OF Y U/D COUNT.
0220	B502	COR2	LDA	X3,X	;GET BOTTOM OF UP COUNTER
0222	950D		STA	TOPX,X	;PUT IN TOPX
0224	B501	C	LDA	BOTY,X	;GET BOTTOM OF U/D COUNTER (Y)
0226	18		CLC		;CLEAR CARRY
0227	6901		ADC	#$01	;ADD ONE
0229	D505		CMP	Y2,X	;HIT TOP OF BOTTOM UP COUNTER?
022B	1005		BPL	COR3	;YES. RESET COUNTER
022D	9510		STA	BOTY,X	;NO. STORE ANSWER IN BOTY
022F	4C3602		JMP	D	;JMP D AND CHECK TOP OF Y U/D COUNTER
0232	B504	COR3	LDA	Y1,X	;GET BOTTOM OF UP COUNTER
0234	9510		STA	BOTY,X	;STORE IN BOTY
0236	B511	D	LDA	TOPY,X	;GET TOP OF U/D COUNTER (Y)
0238	18		CLC		;CLEAR CARRY
0239	6901		ADC	#$01	;ADD ONE
023B	D507		CMP	Y4,X	;HIT TOP OF TOP UP COUNTER?
023D	1003		BPL	COR4	;YES. RESET UP COUNTER

138

023F	9511		STA	TOPY,X	;NO. STORE NEW VALUE
0241	60		RTS		:RETURN
0242	B506	COR4	LDA	Y3,X	;GET BOTTOM OF TOP UP-COUNTER
0244	9511		STA	TOPY,X	;PUT IN TOPY
0246	60		RTS		;RETURN

;SUBROUTINE KEYBOARD.
;TAKES IN VALUES FROM THE KEYBOARD AND SETS SPECIAL FLAGS

0247	A5E6	KEYBOARD	LDA	BOUNC	;GET THE BOUNCE FLAG
0249	D023		BNE	FG	;SET? YES-GO TO FG. NO-DROP THRU
024B	206A1F		JSR	GETKY	;WHAT'S UP ON KEY-BOARD?
024E	A6E2		LDX	AORB	;RELOAD X INDEX WITH VOICE SETTING
0250	C913		CMP	#$13	;GO ON KEY PRESSED.
0252	F019		BEQ	RETURN	;YES- GO HOME. NO-DROP THRU
0254	C915		CMP	#$15	;NOTHING ON KEY-BOARD?
0256	F015		BEQ	RETURN	;YES. GO RETURN
0258	C912		CMP	#$12	;"PC" ON KEYBOARD?
025A	F01D		BEQ	AUTOO	;YES. GO AUTOO
025C	C914		CMP	#$14	;"+" ON KEYBOARD?
025E	F01E		BEQ	TIME	;YES. GO TIME
0260	C910		CMP	#$10	;"AD" ON KEYBOARD?
0262	F01F		BEQ	AVOICE	;YES. GO AVOICE
0264	C911		CMP	#$11	;"DA" ON KEYBOARD?
0266	F026		BEQ	BVOICE	;YES. GO BVOICE
0268	85E7		STA	TEMP	;MUST BE NUMBER. STORE IN TEMP
026A	209F02		JSR	STORE	;THEN GO STORE IT PROPER
026D	60		RTS		;RETURN
026E	206A1F	FG	JSR	GETKY	;BOUNCE IS SET. CHECK KEYBOARD
0271	C915		CMP	#$15	;IS NOTHING THERE?
0273	F001		BEQ	CORR	;YES. GO DEBOUNCE
0275	60		RTS		;RETURN
0276	C6E6	CORR	DEC	BOUNCE	;DEBOUNCE BOUNCE (SET TO ZERO)
0278	60		RTS		;RETURN
0279	F612	AUTOO	INC	AUTO-CHK,X	;RAISE THE AUTOCHK FLAG
027B	E6E6		INC	BOUNCE	;SET BOUNCE
027D	60		RTS		;RETURN
027E	F613	TIME	INC	TMCHK,X	;RAISE THE TMCHK FLAG
0280	E6E6		INC	BOUNCE	;SET BOUNCE
0282	60		RTS		;RETURN
0283	A9AF	AVOICE	LDA	#$AF	;BASE NUMBER FOR A VOICE
0285	85E2		STA	AORB	;PUT IN AORB
0287	E6E6		INC	BOUNCE	;SET BOUNCE
0289	A900		LDA	#$00	;CLEAR ACCUM
028B	9512		STA	AUTO-CHK,X	;BRING DOWN AUTO-CHK FLAG
028D	60		RTS		;RETURN
028E	A9C8	BVOICE	LDA	#$C8	;BASE NUMBER FOR B VOICE
0290	85E2		STA	AORB	;PUT IN AORB
0292	E6E6		INC	BOUNCE	;SET BOUNCE
0294	A900		LDA	#$00	;CLEAR ACCUM
0296	9512		STA	AUTO-CHK,X	;BRING DOWN AUTO-CHK FLAG
0298	60		RTS		;RETURN

;SUBROUTINE STORE. PUTS NEW VALUES INTO PROPER LOCATIONS

029F	8A	STORE	TXA		;PUT VOICE INFO INTO ACCUM
02A0	18		CLC		;CLEAR CARRY
02A1	65E8		ADC	INDX	;ADD INDX TO FIND EXACT LOCATION
02A3	A8		TAY		;PUT IN Y INDEX REG.
02A4	A5E7		LDA	TEMP	;GET KEYBOARD VALUE FROM TEMP
02A6	990000		STA	ENDS,Y	;PUT VALUE INTO CORRECT VARIABLE
02A9	E6E8		INC	INDX	;UPDATE INDX
02AB	A908		LDA	#$08	;EIGHT INTO ACCUM
02AD	C5E8		CMP	INDX	;DOES INDX EQUAL EIGHT?

```
02AF    F003        BEQ      CORRR     ; YES. GO TO CORRR TO
                                         RESET
02B1    E6E6        INC      BOUNCE    ;SET BOUNCE
02B3    60          RTS                ;RETURN
02B4    A900  CORRR LDA      #$00      ;CLEAR ACCUM
02B6    85E8        STA      INDX      ;RESET INDX
02B8    E6E6        INC      BOUNCE    ;SET BOUNCE
02BA    60          RTS                ;RETURN
```

;SUBROUTINE SETTIME. SETS DURATION OF NEXT NOTE AND RESETS
CLOCKS

```
02C1    AD0017  SETTIME  LDA   $1700     ; GET WHATEVER IS
                                           IN OUTPUT PORT
02C4    2A          ROL                  ;MIX IT UP . . .
02C5    2A          ROL
02C6    2A          ROL
02C7    2A          ROL
02C8    85E5        STA      DONE      ;PUT VALUE IN DONE
02CA    A900        LDA      #$00      ;CLEAR ACCUM
02CC    85E3        STA      CLK1      ;RESET CLK1
02CE    85E4        STA      CLK2      ;RESET CLK2
02DO    60          RTS                ;RETURN
```

;SUBROUTINE TEMPO. GETS NEW VALUE FROM KEYBOARD AND SETS TEMPO

```
02D7    A900  TEMPO LDA      #$00      ;CLEAR ACCUM
02D9    C5E6        CMP      BOUNCE    ;IS BOUNCE SET?
02DB    F001        BEQ      CONT      ;NO. GO TO CONT.
02DD    60          RTS                ;YES. RETURN
02DE    206A1F  CONT JSR      GETKY     ;GO SEE WHAT'S ON
                                         THE KEYBOARD
02E1    A6E2        LDX      AORB      ;PUT VOICE INFO
                                         INTO X REG
02E3    C915        CMP      #$15      ;WAS THERE NOTHING
                                         ON KEYBOARD?
02E5    F008        BEQ      RETURN    ;YES. RETURN
02E7    9514        STA      RATE,X    ;NO. PUT VALUE INTO
                                         RATE
02E9    E6E6        INC      BOUNCE    ;SET BOUNCE
02EB    A900        LDA      #$00      ;CLEAR ACCUM
02ED    9513        STA      TMCHK,X   ;RESET TMCHK
02EF    60          RTS                ;RETURN
```

;SUBROUTINE AUTO. SETS END POINTS AUTOMATICALLY

```
0100    A5E9  AUTO  LDA      COUNT     ;GET TIMER
0102    F003        BEQ      ATUO      ;IF EQUAL ZERO GO
                                         ATUA
0104    C6E9        DEC      COUNT     ;OTHERWISE, SUB-
                                         TRACT ONE
0106    60          RTS                ;AND RETURN
0107    8A    AUTO  TXA                ;PUT VOICE INFO IN
                                         ACCUM
0108    18          CLC                ;CLEAR CARRY
0109    65E8        ADC      INDX      ;ADD INDX TO GET
                                         PROPER VARIABLE
010B    A8          TAY                ;PUT IN Y REG
010C    AD0017      LDA      $1700     ;GET WHATEVER IS IN
                                         OUTPUT PORT
010F    290F        AND      #$OF      ;MASK IT
0111    990000      STA      X1,Y      ;AND STORE REMAIN-
                                         DER IN VARIABLE
0114    E6E8        INC      INDX      ;INCREMENT INDX
0116    A908        LDA      08        ;SET ACCUM TO 08
0118    C5E8        CMP      INDX      ;DOES INDX EQUAL
                                         EIGHT?
011A    F005        BEQ      CORRRR    ;YES. GO TO CORRRR
011C    E6E6        INC      BOUNCE    ;NO. INC BOUNCE
011E    4C2701      JMP      CONNT     ;AND GO TO CONNT
0121    A900  CORRRR LDA     #$00      ;CLEAR ACCUM.
0123    85E8        STA      INDX      ;CLEAR INDX
0125    E6E6        INC BOUNCE         ;SET BOUNCE
0127    AD0017  CONNT LDA     $1700     ;GET WHATEVER IS IN
                                         OUTPUT PORT
012A    29FF        AND      $FO       ;MASK IT
012C    EA          NOP                ;IF A FASTER CHANG-
                                         ING  PROGRAM  IS
012D    EA          NOP                ;DESIRED, CHANGE
                                         NOP TO LSR
012E    EA          NOP
012F    EA          NOP
0130    85E9        STA      COUNT     ;PUT IN COUNT
0132    60          RTS                ;RETURN
```

;ONE WAY TO CHANGE LAND DURING PROGRAM IS THE FOLLOWING:

```
0062    8D0017              STA     $1700       ;OUTPUT NUMBER
0065    65BA                ADC     SLPD        ;ADD   01   OR   FF
                                                  DEPENDING
0067    990003              STA     LAND,Y      ;PUT  NEW  VALUE  IN
                                                  LAND
006A    60                  RTS                 ;RETURN
;ALL OTHER CODING REMAINS THE SAME
```

Listing 2: *Hexadecimal representation for a typical terrain. This data is stored in page three of programmable memory. The leftmost item in a row is the starting address for the loading of the values in that row.*

Hexadecimal
Address

0300	47	62	78	81	86	80	95	94	83	79	70	6B	6A	4F	2D	3E
0310	40	52	75	86	91	90	9F	A1	A5	96	89	8A	7F	70	51	11
0320	41	54	67	73	82	9F	AE	A0	B4	B7	A8	99	8E	7B	52	26
0330	33	58	6C	57	78	99	BD	B2	C3	D8	C7	A8	94	5C	43	35
0340	39	5B	69	76	80	98	9C	B9	BA	E9	E4	C6	95	5D	47	44
0350	3A	4E	54	75	84	98	8B	9A	B2	E2	F5	E7	A2	91	7E	78
0360	30	4F	55	62	73	87	6C	8D	A1	D0	E6	C4	A3	A0	9C	9D
0370	20	37	46	61	66	65	66	7D	AE	CE	C3	A2	99	88	9F	55
0380	19	38	54	43	52	67	3D	6E	9F	A9	A1	9A	87	78	6A	59
0390	0A	3C	5C	4B	51	58	4B	91	90	7F	8C	8D	45	66	5B	3C
03A0	39	5E	3D	3E	4F	54	83	80	7A	4E	78	84	40	3F	3E	3D
03B0	3E	3C	2B	29	30	45	79	7C	4B	49	68	63	41	42	27	2E
03C0	0F	3D	3A	26	36	47	7A	5B	47	38	45	35	64	58	49	30
03D0	10	22	31	36	49	58	55	5C	45	47	3C	3D	46	67	45	31
03E0	02	11	20	3F	3E	4D	59	3C	3B	36	2F	3E	33	4C	4B	3A
03F0	04	13	27	26	35	43	54	3A	04	0A	10	11	32	2D	2E	23

APPENDIX

Frequencies in Hertz for an Evenly Tempered Scale

This table gives frequencies for the 12 note scale for nine octaves. It is based on the standard pitch of A4=440 Hz. Middle C is the note at 261.626 Hz. These are valid for any electronic or computer music application. Normally tuned pianos, however, may use a slightly different tempering.

	0	1	2	3	4	5	6	7	8	
C	16.3516	32.7032	65.4064	130.813	261.626	523.251	1046.50	2093.00	4186.01	8372.02
C#	17.3239	34.6478	69.2957	138.591	277.183	554.365	1108.73	2217.46	4434.92	
D	18.3540	36.7081	73.4162	146.832	293.665	587.330	1174.66	2349.32	4698.64	
D#	19.4454	38.8909	77.7817	155.563	311.127	622.254	1244.51	2489.02	4978.03	
E	20.6017	41.2034	82.4069	164.814	329.628	659.255	1318.51	2637.02	5274.04	
F	21.8268	43.6536	87.3071	174.614	349.228	698.456	1396.91	2793.83	5587.65	
F#	23.1247	46.2493	92.4986	184.997	369.994	739.989	1479.98	2959.96	5919.91	
G	24.4997	48.9994	97.9989	195.998	391.995	783.991	1567.98	3135.96	6271.93	
G#	25.9565	51.9131	103.826	207.652	415.305	830.609	1661.22	3322.44	6644.88	
A	27.5000	55.0000	110.000	220.000	440.000	880.000	1760.00	3520.00	7040.00	
A#	29.1352	58.2705	116.541	233.082	466.164	932.328	1864.66	3729.31	7458.62	
B	30.8671	61.7354	123.471	246.942	493.883	987.767	1975.53	3951.07	7902.13	

AUTHORS

Hal Chamberlin
29 Mead St
Manchester NH 03104

Richard Gold
6024 College Av
Oakland CA 94618

Robert Grappel
148 Wood St
Lexington MA 02173

Carl Helmers
BYTE Publications Inc
70 Main St
Peterborough NH 03458

Benjamin Jacoby PhD
Information Conversion Devices Co
88 W Frankfort St
Columbus OH 43206

Jeffrey H Lederer
Tom Dwyer
Margot Critchfield
Project Solo
University of Pittsburgh
Pittsburgh PA 15260

Richard Lord
Bennett Rd
Durham NH 03824

Chris Morgan
BYTE Publications Inc
70 Main St
Peterborough NH 03458

Peter H Myers
1612 Tiffany Way
San Jose CA 95125

Jef Raskin
Apple Computer Co
10260 Bandley Dr
Cupertino CA 95014

Steven K Roberts
129 North Galt Av
Louisville KY 40206

Thomas G Schneider
706 Amherst SE
Albuquerque NM 87106

Ted B Sierad
146 Sunset Rd
Mamaroneck NY 10543

William D Stanley
Steven J Peterson
Electrical Engineering Dept
Old Dominion University
Norfolk VA 23508

Bill Struve
800 Madison Av
Memphis TN 38163

Hal Taylor
3480 Sawtelle Blvd #2
Los Angeles CA 90066

Loring C White
26 Boswell Rd
Reading MA 01867

BYTE Publications, Inc.
Production Credits

Christopher P. Morgan - Technical Editor
Blaise W. Liffick - Assistant Technical Editor
Richard Shuford - Assistant Technical Editor
Edmond Kelly, Jr. - Publisher
Patricia Curran - Production Editor
William Hurlin - Production Editor
Risa Swanson - Production Artist
E.S. Associates - Production Art
George Banta Company - Printing
Robert Tinney - Cover Art
Dawson Advertising Company - Cover Design